FROM CROESUS TO CONSTANTINE

JEROME LECTURES

Tenth Series

FROM CROESUS TO CONSTANTINE

*The Cities of Western Asia Minor
and Their Arts in Greek and Roman Times*

GEORGE M. A. HANFMANN

THE UNIVERSITY OF MICHIGAN PRESS

Ann Arbor

In memory of
Axel Boëthius
and
Gisela M. A. Richter

Preface

The privilege to present the Thomas Spencer Jerome Lectures gives me a welcome opportunity to place in a wider framework researches which I have pursued for the past twenty-five years at Sardis and elsewhere in Asia Minor. These lectures were delivered in winter, 1971, at the University of Michigan in Ann Arbor and in spring, 1972, at the American Academy in Rome. The infectious enthusiasm of Gerald F. Else, Secretary of the Jerome Committee and a friend of many years, and the kindness of John Griffiths Pedley and other colleagues made the stay in Ann Arbor a memorable experience. We are deeply indebted to the Jerome Lectures Committee and to its Chairman, Dean Donald F. Stokes for their generous hospitality.

The American Academy in Rome is a wonderful haven for scholars. It was a great pleasure to renew contacts with the devotees of Rome, young and old, and to learn from the Roman colleagues of their new, exciting discoveries. To the Director of the Academy, Bartlett Hayes, to Inez Langobardi of the Academy Library, and to Janet Martin and Margaret Dubois I owe special debts of gratitude in connection with the lectures.

The first draft and the final work were done at Harvard University, where Glen Bowersock and Ernst Kitzinger supplied much relevant information. On visits to Dumbarton Oaks I had the opportunity of receiving valuable advice from Cyril Mango. At the intermediate stage of the project during a sabbatical leave, I enjoyed the admirable facilities of the Institute for Advanced Study in Princeton. I should like to thank Carl Kaysen, Director, and Homer A. Thompson of the School of Historical Studies for their help in all respects. It was providential for my Jerome Lectures subject to have as fellow members at the Institute T. R. S.

Broughton, C. P. Jones, R. P. Duncan-Jones, and A. G. Woodhead who patiently answered assorted queries.

It was my ambition, very nearly fulfilled, to visit all major sites discussed in these lectures. I am keenly appreciative of the kindness of the excavation leaders and their staffs who took time out to show me their work and discuss their results. They, as well as colleagues in many countries, have obliged me by sending photographs, slides, and information. For these favors I extend my thanks to: E. Akurgal, A. Alföldi, E. Rosenbaum-Alföldi, W. Alzinger, A. Bammer, M. Baran, C. A. Blessing, J. Boardman, J. Borchhardt, E. Çakir, P. Devambez, N. Dolunay, J. Fagerlie, F. Fasolo, N. Firatli, A. Giuliano, E. Gombosi, C. H. Greenewalt, Jr., H. Gürçay, D. E. L. Haynes, K. Jeppesen, S. Karwiese, J. C. Kern, G. Kleiner, T. K. Kempf, K. Kaval, L. J. Majewski, T. Marasović, S. McNally, M. J. Mellink, R. Meriç, H. Metzger, H. Möbius, R. Naumann, R. V. Nicholls, M. Önder, W. Peschlow, A. Ramage, N. H. Ramage, W. Reusch, K. Schefold, H. Stronach, H. Sürmelioğlu, R. Temizer, H. Vetters, J. B. Ward-Perkins, D. H. Wright, F. K. Yeğül, M. Yenim, and G. Yüğrüm.

Deborah E. S. Shastok assisted in preparing the first draft. My valued collaborator in recent years, Jane C. Waldbaum, had a major share in transforming the lectures into a form suitable for publication. I should like to thank Ilse Hanfmann and K. Patricia Erhart for help with the index.

By my dedication I should like to pay tribute to the memory of two illustrious Jerome Lecturers who in their later years became close associates of the American Academy in Rome—the two neighborly dwellers along the *Mura Gianicolensi*—Axel Boethius and Gisela M. A. Richter. Their inspiration has led me to the two major themes of my lectures—urbanism and sculpture. Boethius's splendid *Golden House of Nero* has pioneered the modern approach to Roman urbanism. His warm-hearted friendship is unforgettable for all who were privileged to share in it. Gisela Richter has organized for us the entire field of Greek sculpture. Her *Ancient Italy* represented an attempt to apply this knowledge and much more to the problem of defining the development of arts in an originally unGreek region, a problem analogous to that posed in my lectures. She was the first American archaeologist I met upon my arrival in the United States in 1934, and she was still able to come to the first of the Jerome Lectures at the Academy in 1972. Her unwavering dedication to scholarly life, her love of classical art, and her unfailing openness to young scholars were an inspiration for nearly a century of our studies.

George M. A. Hanfmann

Contents

Abbreviations

PERIODICALS AND STANDARD WORKS

AA—Archäologischer Anzeiger.

Acta A—Acta Archaeologica.

AJA—American Journal of Archeology.

AMIran—Archäologische Mitteilungen aus Iran.

AnatSt—Anatolian Studies.

AnatSt Ramsay—Buckler, W. H., and W. M. Calder, eds. *Anatolian Studies Presented to Sir William Mitchell Ramsay.*

AnnIst—Istanbul Arkeoloji Müzeleri Yilliği.

AntCl—L'Antiquité classique.

AnzWien—Anzeiger der Akademie der Wissenschaften, Wien, Phil-Hist. Klasse.

ArchEph—Archaiologike Ephemeris.

Art Bull—Art Bulletin.

Art Treasures—Smithsonian Institution. *Art Treasures of Turkey.*

ASAtene—Annuario della R. Scuola Archeologica di Atene.

AthMitt—Mitteilungen des deutschen archäologischen Instituts, Athenische Abteilung.

BASOR—Bulletin of the American Schools of Oriental Research.

BCH—Bulletin de correspondance hellénique.

BSA—British School at Athens, Annual.

BZ—Byzantinische Zeitschrift.

CAH—Cambridge Ancient History.

CahArch—Cahiers archéologiques.

CMH—Cambridge Medieval History.

CP—Classical Philology.

CRAI—Comptes rendus de l'Academie des inscriptions et belles lettres.

CSEL—Corpus Scriptorum Ecclesiasicorum Latinorum.

Dergi—Türk Arkeoloji Dergisi.

DOPapers—Dumbarton Oaks Papers.

ERA—Boethius, A., and J. B. Ward-Perkins. *Etruscan and Roman Architecture.*

G.C.S.—Kg. Preussische Akademie der Wissenschaften. Kirchenväter-Commission. *Griechische christliche Schriftsteller der ersten drei Jahrhunderte.*

HSCP—Harvard Studies in Classical Philology.

IGRR—Inscriptiones Graecae ad Res Romanas Pertinents.

ILN—Illustrated London News.

IstFo—Istanbuler Forschungen.
IstMitt—Mitteilungen des deutschen archäologischen Instituts, Abteilung Istanbul.
JASAH—Journal of the American Society of Architectural Historians.
JdI—Jahrbuch des deutschen archäologischen Instituts.
JHS—Journal of Hellenic Studies.
JOAI—Jahreshefte des österreichischen archäologischen Instituts.
JOBG—Jahrbuch der österreichischen byzantinischen Gesellschaft.
JRS—Journal of Roman Studies.
Masterbronzes—Mitten, D. G., and S. F. Doeringer. *Master Bronzes from the Classical World.*
MonAnt—Monumenti Antichi.
Patria—(Pseudo-Codinus), *Patria Konstantinopoleos.*
PIR²—Prosopographia Imperii Romani.
RA—Revue archéologique.
RE—Pauly-Wissowa, Real-Encyclopädie der klassischen Altertumswissenschaft.
REG—Revue des études grecques.
Rev Phil—Revue de philologie, de littérature et d'histoire anciennes.
RömMitt—Mitteilungen des deutschen archäologischen Instituts, Römische Abteilung.
Studies Hanfmann—Mitten, D. G., J. G. Pedley, and J. A. Scott, eds. *Studies Presented to George M. A. Hanfmann.*

BOOKS AND ARTICLES

Akurgal, *Art*—Akurgal, E. *The Art of Greece: Its Origins in the Mediterranean and Near East.*
Akurgal, *Civilizations*—Akurgal, E. *Ancient Civilizations and Ruins of Turkey.*
Akurgal, *KunstAnat*—Akurgal, E. *Die Kunst Anatoliens von Homer bis Alexander.*
Alzinger, *Stadt*—Alzinger, W. *Die Stadt des siebenten Weltwunders: die Wiederentdeckung von Ephesos.*
Aziz, *Guide*—Aziz, A. *Guide du Musée de Smyrne.*
Berve-Gruben—Berve, H., G. Gruben, and M. Hirmer. *Greek Temples, Theaters and Shrines.*
Bieber, *ScHell*—Bieber, M. *The Sculpture of the Hellenistic Age.*
Böhlau and Schefold, *Larisa* I—Böhlau, J., and K. Schefold. *Larisa am Hermus* I *Die Bauten.*
Bowersock, *Augustus*—Bowersock, G. W. *Augustus and the Greek World.*
Bowersock, *Sophists*—Bowersock, G. W. *Greek Sophists in the Roman Empire.*
Brinkerhoff, *Collection*—Brinkerhoff, D. M. *A Collection of Sculpture in Classical and Early Christian Antioch.*
Buckler, *Sardis* VI.2—Buckler, W. H. *Sardis* VI.2 *Lydian Inscriptions.*
Buckler and Robinson, *Sardis* VII.1—Buckler, W. H., and D. M. Robinson. *Sardis* VII.1 *Greek and Latin Inscriptions.*
Cadoux, *Smyrna*—Cadoux, C. J. *Ancient Smyrna: A History of the City from the Earliest Times to 324* A. D.
Claude—Claude, D. *Die byzantinische Stadt im 6. Jahrhundert.*

Cook, *Greeks*—Cook, J. M. *The Greeks in Ionia and the East.*

Coupel and Demargne, *Xanthos 3*—Coupel, P., and P. Demargne. *Fouilles de Xanthos 3 Le monument des Néreides. L'architecture.*

Dörner—Dörner, F. K. *Inschriften und Denkmäler aus Bithynien.*

Eichler, *FoEph V:1*—Eichler, F. *Forschungen in Ephesos V:1 Die Bibliothek.*

Fasolo, *L'architettura a Efeso*—Fasolo, F. *L'architettura romana a Efeso* in *Bolletino del centro di studi per la storia dell'architettura.*

Ferrari, *Commercio*—Ferrari, G. *Il Commercio dei sarcofagi asiatici.*

Festschrift Eichler—Österreichisches Archäologisches Instituts, *Festschrift für Fritz Eichler zu dessen achtzigstem Geburtstag am 12. Oktober 1967.*

Firatli, *Izmit*—Firatli, N. *Izmit Şehri ve Eski Eserleri Rehberi.*

Firatli, *Iznik*—Firatli, N. *Iznik (Nicée). Son histoire, ses monuments.*

Firatli, *Stèles de Byzance*—Firatli, N. *Les stèles funéraires de Byzance gréco-romaine.*

von Gerkan, *Theater*—Gerkan, A. von. *Das Theater von Priene.*

Giuliano, *Ritrattistica*—Giuliano, A. "La ritrattistica dell'Asia Minore dall' 89 A.C. al 211 D.C.," *Rivista dell'Instituto Nazionale d'Archeologia e Storia dell'Arte* N.S. 7.

Grabar, *Sculptures byzantines*—Grabar, A. *Sculptures byzantines de Constantinople (IVe-X siècles).*

Gusmani, *LW*—Gusmani, R. *Lydisches Wörterbuch.*

Hanfmann, *Rayonnement*—Hanfmann, G. M. A. "Greece and Lydia: The Impact of Hellenic Culture," *Le Rayonnement des Civilizations Grecque et Romaine sur les Cultures Péripheriques.*

Hanfmann, "Sardis und Lydien"—Hanfmann, G. M. A. "Sardis und Lydien," *Akademie der Wissenschaften und der Literatur Mainz, Geistes-und sozialwissenschaftliche Klasse, Abhandlungen 1960, Nr. 6.*

Hanfmann and Waldbaum, "New Exc"—Hanfmann, G. M. A., and J. C. Waldbaum. "New Excavations at Sardis and Some Problems of Western Anatolian Archaeology," in J. A. Sanders, ed. *Near Eastern Archaeology in the Twentieth Century, Essays in Honor of Nelson Glueck.*

Hansen, *Attalids*—Hansen, E. V. *The Attalids of Pergamon.*

Helbig and Speier—Helbig, W., and H. Speier. *Führer durch die öffentlichen Sammlungen klassischer Altertümer in Rom.*

Inan-Rosenbaum—Inan, J. and E. Rosenbaum. *Roman and Early Byzantine Portrait Sculpture in Asia Minor.*

Janin (1964)—Janin, R. *Constantinople Byzantine: Developpement urbain et répertoire topographique.*

Janin (1953)—Janin, R. *La géographie écclesiastique de l'empire byzantin 3, Les églises et les monastères.*

Jones, *Greek City*—Jones, A. H. M. *The Greek City from Alexander to Justinian.*

Jones, *Plutarch and Rome*—Jones, C. P. *Plutarch and Rome.*

Keil, *Führer*—Keil, J. *Führer durch Ephesos.*

Kleiner, *Ruinen*—Kleiner, G. *Die Ruinen von Milet.*

Krautheimer, *ECBA*—Krautheimer, R. *Early Christian and Byzantine Architecture.*

Krischen, *Griechische Stadt*—Krischen, F. *Die griechische Stadt.*

Krischen, *Weltwunder*—Krischen, F. *Weltwunder der Baukunst in Babylonien und Ionien.*

Lippold, *Plastik*—Lippold, G. *Die griechische Plastik.*

MacMullen, *Enemies of the Roman Order*—MacMullen, R. *Enemies of the Roman Order: Treason, Unrest, and Alienation in the Empire.*

MacMullen, *Soldier and Civilian*—MacMullen, R. *Soldier and Civilian in the Later Roman Empire.*

Magie, *Roman Rule*—Magie, D. *Roman Rule in Asia Minor to the End of the Third Century After Christ.*

Mamboury (1951)—Mamboury, E. *Istanbul Touristique.*

Mango, *Art*—Mango, C. *The Art of the Byzantine Empire, Sources and Documents.*

Mango, *Brazen House*—Mango, C. *The Brazen House: A Study of the Vestibule of the Imperial Palace of Constantinople.*

Marcadé, *Recueil*—Marcadé, J. *Recueil des signatures de sculpteurs grecs.*

Martin, *Urbanisme*—Martin, R. *L'Urbanisme dans la Grèce antique.*

Meriç, *Ephesus Guide*—Meriç, R. *Ephesus Archaeological Guide.*

Metzger, *Xanthos* 4—Metzger, H. *Fouilles de Xanthos* 4 *Les céramiques archaiques et classiques et l'acropole lycienne.*

Miltner, *Ephesos*—Miltner, F. *Ephesos, Stadt der Artemis und des Johannes.*

Morey, *ECA*—Morey, C. R. *Early Christian Art.*

Morey, *Sardis V*—Morey, C. R. *Sardis V:1 Roman and Christian Sculpture. The Sarcophagus of Claudia Antonia Sabina.*

Nylander, *Ionians*—Nylander, C. *Ionians in Pasargadae.*

Öztüre—Öztüre, A. *Nicomedia-Izmit Tarihi.*

Pedley, *Sardis*—Pedley, J. G. *Sardis in the Age of Croesus.*

Pedley, *Sources*—Pedley, J. G. *Sardis Monograph 2 Ancient Literary Sources on Sardis.*

Picard, *Manuel*—Picard, C. *Manuel d'archéologie grecque: La sculpture.*

Pliny—Pliny the Younger. *Letters.*

Pryce, *BMC*—Pryce, F. N. *Catalogue of Sculpture, British Museum I:1 Prehellenic and Early Greek. I:2 Cypriote and Etruscan.*

Ramage, *Studies*—Ramage, A. *Studies in Lydian Domestic and Commercial Architecture at Sardis.*

Ramsay, *Asianic*—Ramsay, W. M. *Asianic Elements in Greek Civilization.*

Richter, *Portraits*—Richter, G. M. A. *The Portraits of the Greeks.*

Robert, *NIS*—Robert, L. *Nouvelles inscriptions de Sardes.*

Rodenwaldt, *SSBerlin*—Rodenwaldt, G. "Griechische Reliefs in Lykien."

Schede, *Ruinen*—Schede, M. *Die Ruinen von Priene.*

Schefold, *Propyläeen*—Schefold, K. *Die Griechen und ihre Nachbarn, Propyläen Kunstgeschichte.*

Schneider (1943)—Schneider, A. M. *Die römischen und byzantinischen Denkmäler von Iznik-Nicaea.*

Schneider and Karnapp—Schneider, A. M., and W. Karnapp. *Die Stadtmauer von Iznik (Nicaea).*

Sherrard—Sherrard, P. *Constantinople: Iconography of a Sacred City.*

Smith, *BMC*—Smith, A. H. British Museum, *A Catalogue of Sculpture in the Department of Greek and Roman Antiquities.*

Squarciapino, *Scuola*—Squarciapino, M. *La scuola di Afrodisia.*

Vermeule, *ImpArt*—Vermeule, C. C. *Roman Imperial Art in Greece and Asia Minor.*

Wheeler, *RAA*—Wheeler, Sir M. *Roman Art and Architecture.*

Wiegartz, *Säulensarkophage*—Wiegartz, H. *Kleinasiatische Säulensarkophage: Untersuchungen zum Sarkophagtypus und zu den figürlichen Darstellungen.*

Winter, *Greek Fort*—Winter, F. E. *Greek Fortifications.*

Zosimus, *Hist.*—Zosimus. *Historia Nova.*

I: Sardis, Croesus, and the Persians

"Some element or aspect of history, institutions, or civilization . . . of the peoples embraced in the ancient Roman Republic or Empire" was postulated by Thomas Spencer Jerome as one of the permissible themes of the Jerome Lectures. Taking courage from this generous definition I propose to investigate the zone of the peninsula of Asia Minor which represents most immediately the interplay and interpenetration of the Mediterranean and Anatolian—and also that of Near Eastern cultures.

Geographically, this is the zone which reaches from the coast to the highlands of the interior. It includes, approximately, the ancient countries of Bithynia, Mysia, Lydia, Caria, and Lycia. My overall purpose is to trace the changing *Fig. 1* character of the cities in that zone and of the arts which these cities had created, especially that of sculpture. It will be my special purpose to show how the Romans affected and influenced these cities and their arts, and how the Roman-Asiatic or eastern Roman art in turn was transformed into the art of Byzantium.[1]

Many years ago Sir William Ramsay pointed out the importance of what he

[1]See David Magie's splendid historical account *Roman Rule in Asia Minor to the End of the Third Century After Christ* and C. C. Vermeule's *Roman Imperial Art in Greece and Asia Minor* which takes "Imperial" in the rather strict sense of "official Roman." Accounts of particular relevance to the first part of this book are E. Akurgal, *Die Kunst Anatoliens von Homer bis Alexander,* and by the same author, *Ancient Civilizations and Ruins of Turkey* and *The Art of Greece: Its Origins in the Mediterranean and Near East;* J. M. Cook, *The*

Greeks in Ionia and the East. M. J. Mellink's "Archaeology in Asia Minor," annual reports in *American Journal of Archaeology,* have been of greatest service. Over the past three decades I have commented on several aspects of archaic Anatolia: "Horsemen from Sardis," *AJA* 49 (1945): 570–81; "Archaeology in Homeric Asia Minor," *AJA* 52 (1948): 135–55; "Ionia, Leader or Follower," *HSCP* 61 (1953): 1–37; *Sardis und Lydien;* "Archaeology and the Origins of Greek Culture: Notes on Recent Work in Asia

called "Asianic" and what is now generally designated as "Anatolian" elements in the population of classic Asia Minor, that is, peoples who preceded the Greeks, and who in some cases still maintained their linguistic and religious identity into the Roman era.[2] The court and kingdom of Croesus in Lydia were their most impressive attainments as independent peoples. With the transfer of the court of Constantine to Asia Minor, there began a new splendid chapter in the history of the region in which the Anatolian element was submerged. Thus I have selected the title *From Croesus to Constantine* to characterize as a unit the nine centuries between these two rulers which witness a fascinating interplay of Anatolian, Persian, Greek, and Roman elements. The material which we shall consider is the architectural and artistic counterpart of that "Loom of History" which Herbert J. Muller has so eloquently described.[3]

When we examine western Asia Minor during the time of Croesus in the sixth century B.C. and consider the character of the cities, we must first look at the settlement pattern of the countryside in which these cities arose. Along the east-west highway which runs through the Hermus valley, the heartland of ancient Lydia, *Figs. 2, 3* small groups of ancient burial mounds are seen every couple of miles. These mound cemeteries are burial grounds of noble families who owned sizeable estates including one or more villages. It is a striking testimony to the continuity of rural settlements that modern villages are still to be found in the immediate vicinity of these mound groups. In Caria, *pyrgoi* (towers, castles, *Burgen*), mentioned by ancient writers and in the inscriptions of the mid-first millennium B.C. were some sort of fortified demesnes.[4] The countryside of western Anatolia was then

Minor," *Antioch Review* (Spring, 1965): 41–59; and with J. C. Waldbaum, "New Excavations at Sardis and Some Problems in Western Anatolian Archaeology," in J. A. Sanders, ed. *Near Eastern Archaeology in the Twentieth Century, Studies in Honor of Nelson Glueck*, pp: 299–326.

[2]The tenet that "the Anatolian mind is what was in the beginning" (*Asianic* viii) is not systematically carried out in the book with the suggestive title *Asianic Elements in Greek Civilization*. The twenty-one essays treat of a variety of subjects, some religious, others social and economic. While Ramsay makes in passing a number of generalizations, he never gives an overall characterization of "the Anatolian mind." He was predisposed to consider pre-Hittite, pre-Lydian peoples as truly Anatolian in origin. For other writings of W. R. Ramsay see *AnatSt Ramsay*, pp. xiii–xxxviii. For survival of Phrygian see G. Neumann, *Untersuchungen zum Weiterleben hethitischen und luwischen Sprachgutes in hellenistischer und römischer Zeit*, pp. 14–15,

and A. Heubeck in B. Spuler, ed. *Handbuch der Orientalistik* vol. 2. 1 "Altkleinasiatische Sprachen," (Leiden: E. J. Brill, 1969) and cf. n. 7, below.

[3]H. J. Muller, *The Loom of History*. Fundamental for Hellenistic and Roman periods are the books by A. H. M. Jones on *The Cities of the Eastern Roman Provinces* and *The Greek City from Alexander to Justinian*. For the later third century and the early Byzantine era see his *The Later Roman Empire 284–602*.

[4]A. and N. H. Ramage, "The Siting of Lydian Burial Mounds," *Studies Hanfmann*, pp. 143–60; F. Winter, *Greek Fort*, pp. 101–2, 106–9; D. W. S. Hunt, "Feudal Survivals in Ionia," *JHS* 67 (1947): 68–76 discusses *pyrgos, tyrsis, pergama, baris,* all Anatolian words for towers or castles. W. Radt, "Siedlung und Bauten auf der Halbinsel von Halikarnassos," *Ist Mitt* Beiheft 3, p. 13, "feudal upper stratum of Leleges living in castles or fortified towns with citadels."

divided into holdings of a feudal type with most of its population living in agricultural villages large and small.

The social-architectural organization of western Anatolian villages would deserve a study of its own. Their vernacular, almost timeless architecture, shows remarkably skillful adaptation to local materials and climate.[5] In the plains, mud brick, wattle-and-daub, and thatch shelters are most prevalent; on the mountain, the walls are often found to be made of flat stones. In many villages there is a tendency to crowd together so that occasionally roofs instead of streets are used for access. Space for animals may take as much as thirty percent of the built-up area.

Fig. 4

Fig. 6

A typical village plan, like that of the village of Lower Çeltikci shows fifty-two family units heaped compactly along three major intersecting streets providing housing for a population of 600. A small central space has the mosque and the fountain. Of the two houses seen in the plan, one is a small, almost nuclear unit attached to a courtyard; only a third of the space is human dwelling. The other house is a large enclosed complex with a two-storied broadside dwelling which opens on a porch. Animal and storage spaces are grouped around the dwelling unit.[6]

Fig. 5

Fig. 6

Our illustration shows a mountain village house from a Tmolus mountain village south of Sardis made of stone, mud, and thatch, with stable on the left, porch and dwelling in center, and storage space on the right. A house from the swampy country between Miletos and the Lake of Herakleia, the Bossekis site made of wattle and daub, is even more basic and venerable.

Fig. 4

These traditional, modest dwellings of Anatolian farmers have never been more charmingly described than in the Philemon-Baucis legend: "An oak and a linden tree surrounded by a low wall . . . a marsh the haunt of divers and coots . . . one home . . . humble, indeed, thatched with straw and reeds from the marsh . . . the lowly door . . . the bench covered with rough coverlet . . . the fire with the little copper kettle . . . the blackened beam . . . the bed of willow frame and grass; and the three-legged table, the leg of which had to be propped up by a sherd" (Ovid *Metamorphoses* 8.618–723)—all of these can still be found today.

Although this Anatolian countryside absorbed waves of invaders, it followed

---

[5]Axel Boëthius has remarked on the similar timelessness phenomenon in the Italian countryside and reproduced a wonderful picture of prehistoric looking twig and thatch-roofed huts of swineherds in Calabria: *Golden House of Nero* (Ann Arbor: The University of Michigan Press, 1960), p. 6 fig. 3.

[6]These illustrations are from a series of graphic analyses

made by F. K. Yeğül for his excellent, so far unpublished study of this village. For modern comprehensive studies of a central Anatolian village see *Yassıhüyük: A Village Study* (Ankara: Middle East Technical University, 1965) and W. A. Mitchell, "Turkish Villages in Interior Anatolia," *Middle East Journal* 25 (1971): 355–69.

its own folkways, with its worship of uncanny natural powers and strange gods and godlings who might have wandered on the earth: did not Zeus and Hermes appear to Philemon and Baucis in the hills of Phrygia? And were not the people of Lykaonia ready to take Barnabas and St. Paul for Zeus and Hermes in disguise? (*Acts* 14.11–12).[7]

But how far were these regions urbanized? From the third millennium B.C. on, if not earlier, there were agglomerations in western Anatolia which by their size and function must be considered urban; and when in 401 B.C. Xenophon marched through this inland part of the country he unhesitatingly described a number of settlements as "towns" (*poleis*) distinguishing some as being large and populous—Kolossai, Kelainai, Keramon Agora, versus Peltai, Kaystrou Pedion, Thymbrion (*Anabasis* 1.2. 5–13).

For the Anatolian Bronze Age and Early Iron Age, Hittite archives and excavations at Troy and Beyce Sultan indicate that the fortified palace, the adjacent residential town area in the plain, and the sacred area or areas with temples were the important components of a typical urban configuration. Hittite archives imply royal or princely palaces at Apasas (Ephesus?) and Milawatas (Miletus).[8] Eighth *Fig. 7* century Gordion in Phrygia seemed to continue the pattern.[9] It is very probable that sacred precincts, "monasteries" (rather than large temple structures) often lay near but outside such towns—sometimes in the marshes such as the sanc- *Fig. 8* tuaries of Artemis of Ephesus or of Hera of Samos.

On the basis of material from historical times, W. M. Ramsay formulated a theory that these Anatolian temple monasteries had large land holdings, exerted economic influence, and functioned as primitive banks. Indeed, Denis van Berchem has spoken of Ephesus as a "theocratic state."[10] It is certain that they had

[7]On the actual location of Philemon and Bacis (Baucis) story see L. Robert, *Noms indigènes dans l'Asie Mineure gréco-romaine,* p. 238. On Barnabas and St. Paul: the people of Lystra "lifted up their voices saying *in the speech of Lycaonia*: 'the gods are come down to us in the likeness of men.' "

[8]Troy: R. Naumann, *Architektur Kleinasiens,* 2nd ed., pp. 341–45; Beycesultan: S. Lloyd, *Beycesultan* I (Ankara, 1962); II (1965); Apasas, Milawatas: G. M. A. Hanfmann, "A Hittite Priest from Ephesus," *AJA* 66 (1962): 1–4; O. R. Gurney, *The Hittites* (Harmondsworth: Penguin Books, 1961), pp. 46–58; J. Garstang and O. R. Gurney, *Geography of Hittite Asia Minor* (Ankara: British Institute of Archaeology, 1959), pp. 75, 80–81, 83–84, 96, 101–7, 104, 111, 112, 115. In general: Naumann, pp. 236–478. On urbanism of

the Bronze Age in Anatolia and North Syria, Naumann, pp. 389–432; on palaces and houses in Thermi, Troy, Kusura, esp. 389–94, fig. 314, analysis of Troy II d as Bronze Age palace; pp. 433–73 on sanctuaries, pointing out that Megaron A at Troy might have been a shrine and the prehistoric forerunner of the Greek temple at Larisa, fig. 578.

[9]Gordion: R. S. Young, "The Gordion Campaign of 1967," *AJA* 72 (1968): 237–39; "The 1963 Campaign at Gordion," *AJA* 68 (1964): 285–88; "Doodling at Gordion," *Archaeology* 22 (1969): 270–72; Akurgal, *Civilizations,* pp. 279–83.

[10]W. M. Ramsay, *The Cities and Bishoprics of Phrygia* I (Oxford: Clarendon Press, 1895), p. 131; II (Oxford, 1897), p. 354 et passim; M. I. Rostovtzeff, in *AnatSt Ramsay,* pp.

enormous spiritual and emotional power—"Great is the Diana of the Ephesians" was a cry that resounded even more powerfully in the time of Croesus than in the time of Saint Paul. Whether palace or temple counted for more in Anatolian urbanism of the sixth century B.C. is a question we shall need to ponder in looking at the capital of Croesus.

"Golden Sardis" had a reputation for luxury ever since King Gyges came to the Lydian throne in the seventh century. Its urban composition and its actual appearance can be pieced together from the literary sources and the excavations.[11] The plans indicate conjecturally the area possibly covered by the Lydian city, *Fig. 9* perhaps some 250 acres. It was a populous city, and where inhabited, it was densely built up. The economic historian Carl Roebuck has calculated the population of Miletus, the greatest of Ionian city states, as 64,000 in 494 B.C.[12] On that scale, a population between 20,000 and 50,000 might be possible for Croesan Sardis. The palace, the temple or temples, the town, the cities of the dead, even the royal mound cemetery were traditional components. Heralds of a new age were the commercial agora—considered by Karl Polanyi as the first free market in the world's history[13]—and the industrial area, especially the gold refineries which we have discovered. These commercial and industrial complexes owed their emer- *Fig. 10* gence to the same impetus: the mining of gold and its use in the first monetary economy by early Lydian kings. Subsequently, Croesus refined into gold and silver currencies the invention of state guaranteed coinage which concentrated *Fig. 12* enormous power in the palace as compared with the temple. The mint and special

369–71, 384–90; *Social and Economic History of the Hellenistic World* I, pp. 493–96, 503–7, 1440–41, 648–49, 1477–78; *Social and Economic History of the Roman Empire* (Oxford, 1926), p. 541 n. 45 on survival of large and influential temples as banking concerns. T. R. S. Broughton, "New Evidence on Temple Estates in Asia Minor," in P. R. Coleman-Norton, ed. *Studies in Roman Economic and Social History in Honor of Allen Chester Johnson*, pp. 236–50, after reviewing the evidence concludes (p. 247) that the sacred land was originally much smaller in extent than was previously assumed. E. van Berchem, "Trois cas d'asylie archaïque, I Ephèse," *Museum Helveticum* 17 (1960): 24–26, discusses a silver plaque of ca. 550 B.C. (D. G. Hogarth, *The Archaic Artemision* [1908], p. 120) which enumerates tribute to the temple *"ek ton doron"*: from salt tax *"ek tou halos"*; from sale? of wood *"ek tou doratos"*; from merchandise imported *"ek tou nautikou"*; on objects manufactured in the city *"ek tou poleos"* and interprets it as reflecting the complex financial administration of a theocratic state. For the

theories of "temple economies" in the ancient Near East cf. most recently the critical assessment by I. J. Gelb "On the Alleged Temple and State Economies in Ancient Mesopotamia," *Studi in Onore di Edoardo Volterra* 6 (1969): 137.

[11] An excellent description and analysis of Lydian urbanism as far as it can be reconstructed from the archaeological remains is given by A. Ramage, "Studies in Lydian Domestic and Commercial Architecture at Sardis (Ph.D. diss., Harvard University, 1969), summary in *HSCP* 75 (1971): 214–15. As the plans in Fig. 9 show, the archaeological data leave a certain latitude. For a good summary of historical and archaeological data on Sardis through 1967 cf. J. G. Pedley, *Sardis*.

[12] C. Roebuck, "The Economic Development of Ionia," *CP* 48 (1953): 12.

[13] K. Polanyi et al. eds. *Trade and Market in the Early Empires*, p. 67.

treasuries for gold were probably appended to the palace. On the other hand, at Sardis the gold refineries and some jewelers' workshops were apparently located not in the royal palace under the direct control of the king, but next to the common civic and commercial agora. Perhaps not all of the luxury arts and crafts were a royal monopoly.

Fig. 10   The gold refineries were small factories to purify gold and separate it from silver. On the eastern bank of the Pactolus, in the sector called "Pactolus North," we have excavated completely one workshop and there are indications of at least

Fig. 13   one, possibly two more to the north. The precinct surrounded by walls measured about 25 by 20 meters, with one or two structures containing small furnaces for "cementation" (the parting of silver and gold), and open spaces for "cupels" (small cup-like hollows for removing the base metals from the ore by melting it with lead). Refuse from rock crystals, a rock crystal lion, and small jewelry seem to indicate that the jewelers' shops were nearby.

A. Ramage, who excavated the precinct, believes that the gold refineries were in operation from 600–550 B.C. An altar to the goddess Cybele, adorned with four

Fig. 10   lions at the corners, was found in the center of the area flanked by two oblong structures, perhaps for priests. It was built after the refineries were abandoned, according to Ramage; I believe, however, that some religious protection of the workshop area by the great mountain goddess Cybele was an essential part of the gold refining procedures from the beginning of the operation.[14] Two gold trinkets

Fig. 11   and several dozen bits of gold foil, and droplets of gold are as close as we are likely to come to the vanished treasure of Croesus.

In its general aspect Sardis is a typical Anatolian acropolis town. The citadel was located on a spur of the mountain range which accompanies the river valley, an urban location repeated at Magnesia ad Sipylum, Pergamon, and frequently in other Anatolian river valleys. The town extends along the great east-west valley

Fig. 9   and into the north-south valley of the Pactolus torrent. Our excavations along the Pactolus, probably south of the civic agora, and along the old royal road, probably east of the agora, indicate only very general orientation and a heaped-up, continuous dense urban settlement of local simple materials. They do bear out to some extent Herodotus's surprising description of the richest city of the ancient world as it was in 499 B.C. when the Ionian Greeks attacked it. "The greater part of

[14]A. Ramage, *BASOR* 199 (1970): 18–25; G. M. A. Hanfmann, *Dergi* 18 (1969): 61; D. G. Mitten, *Dergi* 17 (1968): 111; Hanfmann and Waldbaum, "New Exc," pp. 310–15; M. J. Mellink, *AJA* 73 (1969): 222. J. H. Jongkees, "Maulis-terion eine lydische Glosse," *Acta Orientalia* 16 (1937): 150 had suggested that metals were considered sacred to the mountain goddess.

houses in Sardis were of reeds, and those which were of mud brick had roofs of reeds . . . when one of these was set afire [by Ionian attackers] the flames spread over the whole city . . .'' (Herodotus 5.101). In actual fact, we found that the houses were built on rather slight foundations of river stones with a kind of mud pisé, or less frequently, large mud bricks; some certainly had roofs of reeds, though the only sure traces date from an earlier destruction by the Kimmerians.[15]

Apart from the two major axial roads, little attention seems to have been paid to streets. The city seems to have been divided into precincts or wards enclosed by tall walls. Systematic placing of public wells and some type of water supply and drainage system for the industrial area indicate an incipient interest in hygiene. But no terracotta baths have yet been found as were found in contemporary Smyrna.[16]

A major road, perhaps a sacred road, led to the great temple of Artemis, which was certainly on the periphery but may have been outside the city area. An archaic altar to Artemis has been discovered but the location of the archaic temple is still not known.[17]   *Fig. 16*

Nothing is known about a city wall of the archaic lower city; and in no reliable literary source is there any indication that there was a wall until the Hellenistic age.[18] On the other hand, the Greek maritime cities—Old Smyrna,[19] Larisa, and Miletus (Kalabaktepe)[20]—were all strongly fortified. At Gordion, a fort either con-   *Fig. 18* structed or tenanted by Lydian troops of Croesus, had a most formidable defensive bastion.[21] R. Koldewey thought that the Lydians had fortified the old town at Neandria in the Troad.[22]

[15]G. M. A. Hanfmann, *BASOR* 162 (1961): 12–13; 170 (1963): 6; 177 (1965): 13; 186 (1967): 32–33.

[16]J. M. Cook, ''Old Smyrna, 1948–1951,'' *BSA* 53–54 (1958–59): 16 and pl. 6 c.

[17]No clear evidence for an archaic temple has come from new soundings in 1972. Cf. *BASOR* 154 (1959): 8–13; 166 (1962): 34.

[18]A passage in Polyaenus, *Strategemata* (7.6.2–3) (Pedley, *Sources* no. 119, p. 39) says that in 547 B.C. Cyrus ''setting ladders against the unguarded walls took Sardis'' before he took the citadel; but the anecdotal story does not seem to represent a trustworthy tradition.

[19]Cook, *BSA* 53–54 (1958–59): 14–34, fig. 3 (imaginative reconstruction); R. V. Nicholls, ''Old Smyrna, The Iron Age Fortifications and Associated Remains,'' *ibid.* pp. 37–137, fig. 7; also J. M. Cook, *Greeks* pp. 72–74, fig. 20.

[20]Larisa: J. Böhlau and K. Schefold, *Larisa am Hermus I Die Bauten*, p. 44, pls. 2–6; K. Schefold, *Propylaeen*, p. 245,

pl. 262b ''votive column and fortress wall.'' Miletus: G. Kleiner, *Ruinen*, pp. 23–25. For expert discussion of Eastern Greek defenses cf. F. E. Winter, *Greek Fort*, pp. 15–18, 106, 126–31; figs. 7–9, 130 (Ephesus, Larisa, Smyrna, Miletus).

[21]''Lydian Fort'' at Gordion: R. S. Young, ''Making History at Gordion,'' *Archaeology* 6 (1953): 164–65, *AJA* 61 (1957): 324, pl. 89:14; ''Lydian Building'' *AJA* 60 (1956): 264, ''destroyed in conflict between Cyrus and Croesus, 547 B.C.'' It is of interest for relations with the Near East that F. E. Winter, *Greek Fort*, p. 129, n. 17 credits ''the Phrygian kings and their Lydian successors with transmission to the Aegean world of some of basic concepts of Near Eastern siegecraft and military architecture,'' and underlines the part played by ''the Lydian threat'' in making eastern Greek cities develop their fortifications.

[22]Neandria: R. Koldewey, ''Neandria,'' *51 Programm zum Winkelmannsfeste der Archäologischen Gesellschaft zu Berlin*

Herodotus (1.84) stated that the citadel of Sardis itself had a magically impregnable wall around which King Meles (late eighth century B.C.?) had carried a lion (symbol of a goddess like Cybele or Ishtar). King Meles had supposedly visited Babylon; and we are reminded of Mesopotamian belief in the magic sacredness of walls, as of the Imgur Bel—the Wall of Babylon. Anatolian comparisons of the breaching of divine or sacred walls appear in legends about the walls of Troy. The wall built by Apollo and Poseidon did not breach, but the section of wall built by human heroes, Aiakos or others, collapsed.[23]

Fig. 17   There may have been two palaces in Sardis; one on the citadel, and another somewhat lower down. The beautifully fashioned, large-masonry wall discovered in 1960 on the northern top of the citadel supported a staircase and then went on with bichrome effect into a green sandstone ashlar wall. Another terrace of similar fine masonry with drafted edges was found in 1971, slightly higher up.[24] Apparently, an archaic palace rose in many steps up the northern slope. This may well be the upper part of the palace of Croesus. There may have been a lower part of the palace at the foot of the citadel, for a tunnel starting high up on the northern slope went spiralling downward toward a flat-topped hill —later transformed into a Byzantine fort. This eminence commands a splendid view of the lower city.[25]

We have no cogent idea about the appearance and plan of the major palace structure. The suggestion has been made by Carl Nylander that a palace unit with a broad house plan, with a gabled pediment and towered facade at Aeolic Larisa may reflect the palace of Croesus.[26] However, the traditional structure in western

Fig. 7   Anatolia was the oblong megaron. It appears at Gordion and Larisa,[27] and the oblong form is known in Sardis in shops and possibly in priestly house dwellings or sacral structures.[28] Vitruvius's source implies that major walls in the palace of

---

(1891): 10–11, fig. 9 and plan at back. The old town was approximately 157 acres and as Koldewey suggested, might have been fortified by the Lydians against the Greek inhabitants after they took the Troad in the sixth century. For evidence of Lydians in the Troad, C. H. Greenewalt, Jr. cites Strabo 12.4.6; 13.1.22 (the whole Troad under the rule of Gyges).

[23]Pindar *Olympiad* 8.31, scholiast; cf. R. Graves, *Greek Myths* I (Harmondsworth: Penguin Books, 1955), p. 214.

[24]A. Ramage, *BASOR* 206 (1972): 16, fig. 6.

[25]As C. H. Greenewalt, Jr. convinces me, Arrian *Anabasis* I.17.6 is not conclusive for the location of the palace. A Hellenistic author used by Vitruvius (2.8.10) says that the Sardians turned over the palace as a meeting

place to the Council of Elders, the *Gerousia*. This sounds as if it were somewhere within or near the city area rather than on the steep citadel. In 1973, a Lydian fortress wall was found on the southern slope of the citadel.

[26]Nylander, *Ionians*, p. 117.

[27]Gordion: R. S. Young, *AJA* 72 (1968): 237–38, pls. 72:9, 73:11; 68 (1964): 285–88, pls. 85:15, 86:16; Akurgal, *Civilizations*, p. 280, fig. 117a, plan of town with palace area. The megaron house type is attested both by actual structures and "doodles" showing such megara with gable roof already in the eighth century B.C., R. S. Young, *Archaeology* 22 (1969): 270–72, fig. Larisa: Böhlau and Schefold, *Larisa* I, pl. 38a, pp. 86–88, fig. 15.

[28]A. Ramage, *Studies*, fig. 18.

Croesus were of mud brick and still stood plumb in Hellenistic times. The palace exterior may have been decorated with terracotta friezes such as that of a splendid Pegasus found on the citadel.[29]

Fig. 14

The existence of these terracottas supports the assumption of gabled megaron structures, as a tentative reconstruction by Å Åkerström shows[30]; for such gaily painted friezes came from both horizontal and from raking simas. The strong black-white-red ornamentation at the top of possibly whitewashed buildings against the blue sky must have made a striking effect in the appearance of such cities as Croesan Sardis.

Fig. 15

Being colonies, most of the Greek cities were situated along the coast frequently on promontories over jewel-like bays. Palaces existed only in the few cities where kings survived (Kyme) or tyrants emerged (Larisa? Samos, Miletus?). It was the port and the town, the agora and the temple, which were the distinctive traits of Greek cities.

Fig. 18

Enough has been excavated of old Smyrna-Bayrakli[31] to present at least conjectural restorations of the strongly fortified city with four or five hundred houses which is reminiscent in its site and appearance of Homer's city of the Phaeaceans in the *Odyssey* (7.43–45): "Harbors on each side . . . the trim, curved ships line the road . . . there is an agora and long walls with battlements." Some have hypothesized that by the late seventh century B.C. when Smyrna was destroyed by Alyattes, the father of Croesus, the town had streets laid out on a north-south axis, and houses built on a rectangular plan. "With the incorporation of the courtyard and the oblong plot, and the linking of plots in continuous street frontages, we seem to come up against regular townhouses for the first time in the history of Greek architecture," observes John M. Cook, one of the excavators of the site.[32]

Fig. 18

The temple, now known to belong to Athena, is located in a curiously eccentric position—just inside the city wall; it had a podium of two colors, very precisely joined masonry, and a great array of Oriental imports as well as an almost life-size Cypriot terracotta votive.[33]

As crown prince, Croesus spent some time at Adramyttium in the Troad.[34]

---

[29]*BASOR* 170 (1963): 32, fig. 22.

[30]Å. Åkerström *Die architektonischen Terrakotten Kleinasiens*, pp. 70–72, fig. 22 (reconstruction); p. 86, list of simas; p. 95, fig. 29, Pegasus and Lydian man.

[31]Cook, *BSA* 53–54 (1958–59): 1–34; Nicholls, *ibid.*, pp. 35–137.

[32]Cook, *Greeks*, p. 72.

[33]Cook, *Greeks*, p. 74; Akurgal, *KunstAnat*, pp. 182–84, figs. 131–33; *Civilizations*, p. 119.

[34]Nicolaus of Damascus, *FrGrHist* 90 F 65 = Pedley, *Sources*, no. 64. "Croesus was the oldest of Alyattes sons . . . who had been designated as ruler of Adramyttion and the plain of Thebe. . . ." Cf. Weissbach, s.v. "Kroisos," *RE* suppl. 5 (1931): 457–58.

Assos, a breath-takingly beautiful site on the coast of the gulf of Adramyttium, may have belonged to him. Not much is known about the exact layout of the archaic city of Assos; but might not the planning and beautification of the top of the *Fig. 19* site, where the monumental precinct and temple of Athena was to rise, be a legacy of the time when Croesus was crown prince? Croesus may have been at Assos at any time prior to 561, say 570–561 B.C. In my view, the temple with its lively "Middle Corinthian" Klitias-like metopes and friezes may have been finished by 550; plans for the precinct and temple might well date back to Croesus's residence; and even the beginning of construction might have taken place under his auspices.

Assos is otherwise a traditional "Acropolis" type of urban settlement; the temple is the dominant structure, as on the Acropolis of Athens. In the terracing of that geometric grid plan which came later to be connected with Hippodamus of has termed "Pergamene" type of terraced urban composition.[35]

Ephesus, on the other hand, may have been one of the pioneering examples of that geometric grid plan which came later to be connected with Hippodamus of *Fig. 8* Miletus. This revolutionary design would have been devised for the new "Croesus city" associated with the huge temple for which Croesus gave many columns. An attractive hypothesis has been developed by A. Bammer, architect of the Austrian expedition, from the following evidence.[36] About the year 560 Croesus captured Ephesus (Herodotus 1.26) and, according to one ancient tradition, "they settled around the present temple until the time of Alexander." The city was then moved (Strabo 14.c 640). As seen in the lower right corner of Figure 8 Bammer discerns in later periods the existence of a grid, possibly with blocks of 280 by 140 feet, conforming to the orientation of the archaic temple of Artemis, which he believes belong to archaic Ephesus, also known in later times as the suburb Smyrna. Excavators of Miletus suggest that there too, a rectangular street system was at least partly in use in the early city.[37]

Ionian cities are striking in their preconceived application of geometry to urban planning. Recent scholarship has rightly pointed to possible connection with the milieu of pre-Socratic philosophers. Thales, the founder of Greek geometry, was a friend of Croesus and with his technological skill helped the

[35]Assos: I. H. Bacon, *Investigations at Assos* (Archaeological Institute of America, 1902); Akurgal, *Civilizations*, pp. 64–69; R. Martin, *Urbanisme*, ch. 3; and cf. *infra*, ch. 2, p. 27, n. 22.

[36]A. Bammer, "Zur Topographie und städtebaulicher

Entwicklung von Ephesus," *JOAI* 46 (1961–3): 146–47.

[37]G. Kleiner, *Ruinen*, p. 25. "It would be natural for a city that founded so many colonies to use the same planning and measuring system in its own more recent parts."

Lydian army ford the Halys River (Herodotus 1.75). One may well speculate that Thales or some other archaic scientist with geometric-urban interests created at Ephesus an example of that abstract geometric grid plan that Hippodamus was to expand and elaborate into a social-geometric-urban theory in the replanning of classical Miletus.[38]

It is at Ephesus, rather than at Sardis, that we come closer to discovering Croesus as a builder; for it is at Ephesus that the fragments from the roundels at the top of column base(s) with the Greek inscription *BA(sileus) KRoisos AN-eTHEK-EN,* "King Kroisos dedicated," and from yet another "straight moulding of a drum," the less well-preserved Lydian: . . . *LIS INL,* "son of Alyattes?[39] gave" were found.[40] This bilingual quality—Anatolian and Greek—is symbolic of the character of the arts at the court of King Croesus.

Figs. 21, 22

On the walls of the quarries of Belevi, whence came the marble for the Artemision of Ephesus, were engraved archaic doodles of human figures, goddesses, warriors, and bearded men, and also inscriptions in a strange script midway between Lydian and Carian. Wolfgang Dressler, who published the inscriptions, concludes that some of the letters were strikingly reminiscent of those of the Croesus dedication on the columns and asks: "Did perhaps the same Anatolian stone masons cut the 'Carian-like' (*Karoid*) inscriptions in the quarry and the dedication of Croesus in the Artemision?"[41]

There were Lydian priestesses at the temple of Artemis in Ephesus (Aristophanes, *Clouds* 598–600); and there may have been Anatolian traits involved not only in the survival of the peculiar form of the inner shrine of the temple but also in the development of figurative relief at the bottoms of columns, comparable in principle to the "Late Hittite" type of palace decoration in such Phrygian strongholds as Ankara. Otherwise, the Greek architects, Chersiphron and Metagenes,

---

[38]Thales supposedly dug a semicircular trench dividing the Halys in two so that each arm was smaller and could be forded (before the battle at Pteria). On Hippodamus, see most recently, J. R. McCredie, *Studies Hanfmann,* pp. 95–100; G. Metraux, "Western Greek Land Use and City Planning in the Archaic Period," (Ph.D. diss., Harvard University, 1972); and F. Castagnoli, *Orthogonal Town Planning in Antiquity* (Cambridge, Mass.: M.I.T. Press, 1971) with important survey of recent finds and literature. Citing Urartian acropolis at Zernaki Tepe (p. 135) he suggests that "the Hippodamian plan . . . may be a gradual evolution of an archaic Anatolian tradition, possibly by way of the Ionian World."

[39]Because of the damage we do not know the Lydian form of the name of Croesus.

[40]F. N. Pryce, *BMC* I:1, figs. 31, 69; G. Lippold, *Die griechische Plastik* (Munich: C. H. Beck, 1950), pp. 60–61 who dates the column reliefs from ca. 550 to early fifth century.

[41]W. Alzinger, "Ritzzeichnungen in den Marmorbrüchen von Ephesos," *JOAI* 48 (1966–67): 61–72; W. Dressler, "Karoide Inschriften im Steinbruch von Belevi," *ibid.,* pp. 73–76, figs. 31–43. I have visited the quarries and copied the graffiti and inscriptions on Sept. 6, 1966.

and the famous architect, sculptor, and engineer, Theodoros of Samos, presented the colossal Greek temple of Artemis (closely akin to the somewhat earlier Heraion of Samos) as the first really developed example of the Ionic Greek order.[42]

Figs. 23–26

At Sardis in 1963, we found evidence of a more experimental, a more Anatolian, and perhaps a more Near Eastern structure with a number of very extraordinary traits. Probably dedicated around 550 B.C., this small scale marble model of a temple or shrine of the goddess Cybele, or, if one wants to be more cautious, of a goddess who had power over snakes and lions, is about two feet high as preserved.[43] The model possibly contracts the number of columns on the sides, but taken literally, the plan was square and included a central column in back. Unknown until now in archaic Ionic architecture were the three-quarter Ionic columns on simple torus bases at the corners and engaged half-columns at the centers of the walls.[44] There were painted reliefs rising the full height of the wall in three zones of panels. The panels are separated by horizontal bands with ornamental maeanders. One can read them (like Etruscan paintings) as friezes interrupted by columns, or as tall, metope-like, oblong panels without an architectural frame of their own. Figurative representations on the full height of the wall are found in Mesopotamia, as for instance in the nearly contemporary Ishtar Gate in Babylon,[45] and on part height of the wall in superposed Assyrian reliefs, but these lack the precise architectural compartmentalization. Within Greek architecture this figurative representation on the full height of the wall is unique.

Fig. 25

At the back of the temple are six mythological scenes including probably Herakles and the Nemean Lion, and the Lydian Pelops on his chariot. On the

Fig. 26

sides, priestesses, dancers, and sileni move in a procession toward the front, toward the image of the goddess waiting to receive them. It is the same theme and the same compositional device which was to have such splendid development in the Panathenaic procession on the north and south sides of the Parthenon.

The idea of a procession coming to offer gifts to the god or goddess must have

[42]G. Gruben in *Berve-Gruben,* pp. 456–62. E. Akurgal, *Art,* pp. 221–22, the reliefs of *"columnae caelatae . . .* constitute a very successful translation of Hittite orthostats into the Ionic idiom." Cf. his fig. 40 (p. 88) an Assyrian relief after Perrot and Chipiez II, p. 143, fig. 42; better in R. D. Barnett, *Assyrian Palace Reliefs* (London: Batchworth Press, n.d.), pls. 133–34. Priestesses: Akurgal, *Art,* p. 212, pl. 66, suggests that the so-called "Spinner" is a Lydian priestess, though the ivory was made by an Ionian.

[43]S63.51:5677. H. preserved: 0.62 m.; "in the shattered, fallen? masonry of a pier, apparently pier 4 counting from

west, E 73.5/N 17.20–17.70." D. G. Mitten, *BASOR* 174 (1964): 39–43, figs. 25–26; G. M. A. Hanfmann, *Rayonnement,* pp. 494–95, pls. 124.3, 125.3; K. Schefold, *Propylaeen,* p. 284, pl. 333; G. M. A. Richter, *Korai* (London and New York: Phaidon, 1968), no. 164, figs. 524–27; Hanfmann and Waldbaum, *Archaeology* 22 (1969): 268.

[44]B. Wesenberg, *Kapitelle und Bassen,* pp. 109–10 considers this a separate column type with base shape derived from the Near East (Syria?).

[45]Akurgal, *Art,* p. 51, pl. 20: Nebucchadnezer II, 604–562 B.C.

strongly appealed to the superstitiously pious Croesus. It recurs in the sculptures which he gave to the temple at Ephesus. It may well be that the thirty-six sculptured drums of the Croesan Artemision presented a processional vision of the court of King Croesus which was as much a projection of his ideology as the frieze of the Parthenon is of the Periclean democracy.[46]

These column friezes may have included divine or mythological ancestors of Croesus: A hero wearing a feline skin may be Herakles, who was related to the Lydian royal house through his service to the Lydian Queen Omphale, and was considered the originator of the royal dynasty of Herakleidai who preceded the House of Croesus—the Mermnadai.[47] There were priestesses bringing offerings on trays decorated with golden bulls' heads[48] (Croesus had given "golden bulls" to the temple [Herodotus I.92]). Anticipating the Ara Pacis, children were included, and allusions to Croesus's military might in armed men and horses were also seen in these friezes. One remembers the story of how Croesus left shipbuilding to the Greeks as long as the cavalry remained with the Lydians (Herodotus I.27).

Figs. 20, 28

Fig. 29

Fig. 27

Endowed with the right of refuge by Croesus, the Ephesian sanctuary had a "Mixo-Lydian" character. The fabulous hoard deposit in the pre-Croesan Artemision of Ephesus[49] strongly suggests that before and during the time of Croesus the goldsmiths (as the silversmiths in the time of Saint Paul), ivory workers, and other luxury craft workers tended to serve primarily the temple, and therefore, may well have settled around it. Lydian ivory working is already mentioned by Homer (*Iliad* 4.141). It is possible that at least part of the famous Ephesian archaic ivories was made by Lydian craftsmen working at Ephesus.[50]

Richness of attire can still be surmised from the painted patterns, but unfortunately less than one percent of the sculptures of the Artemision remains and these are mostly in small fragments. Fortunately we can recapture the full color of Lydian courtiers during the time of Croesus in two terracottas found at Sardis.

[46]A. H. Smith, *BMC* I (1892): 26–30, pl. I; F. N. Pryce, *BMC* I.1 (1928): 47–63, figs. 39–69. Herodotus 1.92: Croesus gave most of the columns of the temple at Ephesus. Cf. n. 56, below.

[47]The Lydian equivalent of Dionysos, the winegod Baki, is less likely; he would probably be shown bearded as on the contemporary Caeretan hydriae. Cf. M. Santangelo, "Les nouvelles hydries de Caeré au Musée de la Villa Giulia," *MonPiot* 44 (1950), pl. III center.

[48]Golden bull's head pendant from Western Asia Minor in the Boston Museum of Fine Arts, dated ca. 400 B.C., cf. H. Palmer and C. Vermeule, *Archaeology* 12 (1959): 2, and

cover (color); H. Hoffmann and P. Davidson, *Greek Gold* (Mainz: Philipp von Zabern, 1965), pp. 237–38; M. F. A. Boston, *Greek, Etruscan and Roman Art*, p. 172, fig. 180.

[49]P. Jacobsthal, "The Date of the Ephesian Foundation Deposit," *JHS* 71 (1951): 85–95, pls. 31–36; E. S. G. Robinson, "Coins from the Ephesian Artemision Reconsidered," *ibid.*, pp. 156–67, pl. 38.

[50]An argument for a Lydian school of ivorists was made by R. D. Barnett, "Early Greek and Oriental Ivories," *JHS* 68 (1948): 1–25, esp. 18. Evidence from Sardis remains scanty; the ivory head of a priest? of the moon god may be an import, Akurgal, *KunstAnat*, p. 100, pl. VIIa, b (color).

Fig. 30   One was part of a frieze—perhaps again a procession—the other a strange vase which was shaped perhaps as a Lydian clad in Persian costume.[51] This vase is almost as much a painting as it is a sculpture.

Fig. 32   In the reconstruction of an altar found in the gold refinery area of Sardis[52] we have placed four lions at the corners because we had found two and one half of *Fig. 31*   them still in place. Precisely the same arrangement of two lions in profile, with two more presumably concealed, appears in an Etruscan tomb painting of the Tomba dei Tori, Tarquinia (known since 1892).[53] The subject of the painting is Achilles, behind an altar-like fountain, lying in ambush for an equestrian Troilus *Fig. 33*   approaching from the right. The style is Eastern Greek-Ionian, about 540 B.C. With extraordinary perspicacity, G. W. Elderkin had utilized the Etruscan picture to reconstruct one of Croesus's fabulous presents to Apollo in Delphi—the golden lion on a pedestal built from four bricks of pure gold and one hundred thirteen *Fig. 34*   bricks of silver-gold.[54] The explanation for the extraordinary resemblance of the arrangement in places as far apart as Sardis and Tarquinia is that after the fall of Croesus in 547, many of his court artists fled, some apparently as far as Tuscany where wealthy patrons abounded. (In fact, there are some indications that the Etruscans may have considered themselves relatives of the Sardians.)[55]

Perhaps we should end the survey of Croesan arts with the famous picture of *Fig. 35*   Croesus on the pyre, a picture painted some fifty years after his death.[56] It is really noncommittal, but generally, it is thought to represent that version of the Croesus legend in which he was taken from the pyre by Apollo and brought to the Islands of the Blest (Bacchylides 3).

Such were the arts in the time of Croesus. Then "came the Mede," but strangely there are closer ties in architecture between Sardis, capital of the defeated Croesus, and Pasargadae, capital of the victorious Cyrus, than between

[51]G. M. A. Hanfmann, *BASOR* 174 (1964): 11, figs. 3, 4; C. H. Greenewalt, Jr., *Studies Hanfmann*, pp. 29–46.

[52]A. Ramage, *BASOR* 191 (1968): 11–12, figs. 9–11, lions *in situ*.

[53]L. Bonfante-Warren, "Etruscan Dress as Source: Some Problems and Examples," *AJA* 75 (1971): 280, pl. 67:12 with bibl. n. 14; G. Q. Giglioli, *L'arte etrusca* (Milan: Fratelli Treves, 1935) 22, pl. 107, with earlier lit. Color after water color: G. Koerte in Antike Denkmäler 2 (1908), pl. 41; M. Palotino *ML* 36 (1937): 302, fig. 70; *Etruscan Painting* (Geneva, Skira, 1952) color pl. 31; L. Banti, *Il mondo degli Etruschi,* 2nd ed. (Rome, 1969), pl. 62 below; A. Rumpf, *Malerei und Zeichnung der Klassischen Antike* (Munich: C. H. Beck, 1953), p. 55, pl. 15:2. It should not be dated later

than 540 B.C. and the riding youth is Lydo-Ionian, not Chalcidian in style as Rumpf opined. Cf. also M. Robertson, "Ibycus: Polycrates, Troilus, Polyxena," *Bulletin,* University of London Institute of Classical Studies, 17 (1970): 11–15.

[54]G. W. Elderkin, "The Golden Lion of Croesus," *Archaeological Papers* II.2 (1941), 8 pp., figs. 1, 2 (Tori).

[55]There is some curious but late evidence to this effect: "Sardians for sale" exclaimed triumphant Romans in selling Etruscan prisoners from Veii, Plutarch *Quaestiones Romanae* 53 (277D) = Pedley, *Sources,* no. 25, p. 12.

[56]Louvre G 197. P. E. Arias and M. Hirmer, *A History of 1000 Years of Greek Vase Painting* (New York: Harry N. Abrams, 1962), pl. 131. A second representation on red-

Pasargadae and the neighboring capital of Babylon. As we look at these two
stepped constructions, one at Sardis, the so-called Pyramid Tomb, the other a
staircase in the palace of Cyrus, 1,500 miles away, it is hardly doubtful that Lydian
architects went to Iran and worked there. The resemblance between the reliefs at
Pasargadae and Ephesus shows that sculptors as well as masons were involved in
the construction—probably Ionian Greeks as well as Lydians.[57]

The current did not run in quite the same fashion the other way. A number of
years ago I set myself the task to track down traces of Persians and their arts in the
western provinces of the Persian Empire. I arrived at the conclusion that they
lived in "Little Persias" similar to the Americans living in "Little Americas" after
World War II. It seemed as if only articles of personal attire, arms bestowed as
signs of honor by the king, jewelry, gold, silver, luxury glass vessels, and rich
textiles, in short, only arts immediately pertaining to the personal adornment of
members of satrapal courts were distinctively Persian.[58]

One should, however, credit the Persians with being the first regional planners, at least in a general administrative and military sense. It is they who first
rationalized the concept of overland roads, especially the famous royal road, as
the communications axis of the empire and organized the first efficient system of
horse-ridden relays with post stops from Susa to Sardis. The very system of
satrapies was regional planning and the choice of satrapal capitals was an exercise

Fig. 36

Figs. 37, 38

---

figure hydria fragments by the Leningrad Painter, ca.
480–450 B.C. showed Croesus being rescued by Cyrus(?).
D. L. Page, "An Early Tragedy on the Fall of Croesus?,"
Proceedings of the Cambridge Philological Society 188 (1962):
47–49. J. D. Beazley, "Hydria-Fragments in Corinth," *Hesperia* 24 (1955): 319, pl. 85, and *Attic Red-Figure Vase-
Painters*² (Oxford: Clarendon Press, 1963), vol. 1, p. 571,
no. 74.

On the pyre, Croesus supposedly uttered an incantation
in the magic "Ephesian Letters"; the same saying was allegedly written on the garment of the image of Artemis in
Ephesus. This peculiar tradition is cited by lexicographers
of the second century A.D. W. Helck, *Betrachtungen zur
Grossen Göttin und den ihr verbundenen Gottheiten* (Munich:
Oldenbourg, 1971) p. 264, n. 13, boldly attempts to read
the saying as an invocation in Hittite of certain Hittite gods
of oath. In any event, the story emphasizes the connection
of Croesus with Artemis of Ephesus. Cf. Eusthatius, *Com-
mentaria ad Odysseam*, Bk 19, 247, citing the lexicographers
Pausanias and Aelius Dionysius. I owe all of the material
in this note to the learning of C. H. Greenwalt, Jr.

[57]For the Pyramid tomb and the Tomb of Cyrus at

Pasargadae cf. Hanfmann and Waldbaum, "New Exc.," p.
316, pls. 38, 39. S. Kasper has reinvestigated the Pyramid
tomb and has reconstructed it as a twelve-step pyramid.
Cf. C. Nylander, *Ionians*, pp. 93, 97; D. Stronach, "A Circular Symbol on the Tomb of Cyrus", *Iran* 9 (1971): 155–58.
For Ephesus see H. Luschey, "Iran und der Westen von
Kyros bis Khosrow," *AMIran* N.F. I (1968): 17.

[58]Aristophanes *Acharnians* 74: "out of their glass and
gold cups (at the Persian court) we had to drink pure wine.
. . ." A. Oliver, "A Gold-Glass Fragment in the Metropoli-
tan Museum of Art," *JGS* 12 (1970): 9–16, esp. no. 1, fig. 3,
phiale from Ephesus, ca. 400–350 B.C. in fill from new
Artemis Temple; "Persian export glass." For seals with
Persian motifs made at Sardis cf. J. Boardman, "Pyramidal
Stamp Seals in the Persian Empire," *Iran* 8 (1970): 37.
Jewelry: C. D. Curtis, *Sardis* 13 (Rome, 1925), pp. 11–15,
pl. I a–f; H. Th. Bossert, *Altanatolien* (Berlin: Verlag Ernst
Wasmuth, 1942), figs. 168–79; G. M. A. Hanfmann *Sardis
und Lydien*, p. 30 and n. 2; Akurgal, *KunstAnat*, fig. 118; H.
J. Kantor, "Achaemenid Jewelry in the Oriental Institute,"
JNES 16 (1957): 4–7; P. Amandry, "Orfèvrerie
Achémenide," *Antike Kunst* I (1958): 9.

in urbanism on a high level. Sardis had been a capital before, but the choices of Kelainai and Daskylion were less obvious. Other passages in the works of ancient authors imply that the Persians planned "chains" of fortified places.[59]

In the urban sphere proper, it is probable that the Persians did considerable work and introduced improvements in military fortifications of places where they maintained garrisons. According to Xenophon, at Kelainai, a fortress, palaces, and a park were planned anew.[60] There were two palaces, one of the Great King, "strongly fortified and situated at the foot of the Acropolis, over the sources of the Marsyas river," and the other a palace of the Younger Cyrus. "Apparently adjacent to the paradeisos, the park full of wild animals, which he used to hunt on horseback . . . through the middle of this park flows the Maeander river; its sources are beneath the palace, and it flows through the city of Kelainai . . . the Marsyas also flows through the city and empties into the Maeander . . ." (*Anabasis* 1.2.7–9).

Daskylion is described by Xenophon as the "place where the palace (*ta basileia*) of Pharnabazus was situated, and round about were many large villages, stored with provisions, and animals, some fenced in parks (*perieirgmenois paradeisois*) and others in open space. There was also a river, flowing by the palace full of all kinds of fish. And besides, there was winged game in abundance for those who knew how to go fowling" (*Hellenica* 4.1.15–16).

Communications (Sardis, Kelainai, Daskylion are all nodal points on highways) and defensibility were the first Persian requirements in selecting sites of "state capitals," i.e., of satrapal residences. The Persians also demonstrated that they were among the first landscape planners and ecological planners. Clearly, water was the great attraction—the wonderful springs and two rivers at Kelainai-Dinar, the river and great lake of Daskylion, with green verdant plains and teeming "paradises" of wild life, a game preserve at Kelainai, and an incredible "bird paradise," which is still to be seen at the Daskylion Lake. Those who recall the loveliness of the gorge and river waters at Bishapur and the wonderful effect of the pool at Tak-i-Bostan will be willing to credit the choices of sites with

---

[59]Xenophon *Anabasis* 1.2.1, "Xenias is to leave only as many mercenaries as were necessary to guard the acropoleis."

[60]Kelainai: *RE* 11 (1921): 133–34; L. Robert, "Philologie et Géographie," *Anatolia* 4 (1959): 5–7, on the road from Kelainai-Dinar to Kolossai with much literature. L. Robert, "Inscription of the Sepulchral Stele from Sardis," *AJA* 64

(1960): 53–56, discusses the name and relation to later name of Apamea Kibotos. Cf. also L. Robert, *Hellenica* 2 (1946): 75–76; W. M. Ramsay, *Cities and Bishoprics of Phrygia* II, pp. 396–480, inscriptions nos. 281–351; Muller, *Loom of History* has an eloquent description of Dinar-Kelainai, pp. 1–31.

lovely waters to Iranian taste. The waters, the sites, even the towns were already there; the Persian contribution was the planning of palaces and preserves as additions to the existing towns.[61]

Consequently, because the Persians followed Assyrian and Babylonian precedents for "paradeisoi" and because the edict of Darius to Gadatas[62] concerning the sacred precinct of Artemis Leukophyrene at Magnesia on the Maeander seems to imply interest in actual landscaping, it is likely that landscape gardening and possibly use of waters, as well as overall planning of game preserves were part of Persian practices. Indeed, the Younger Cyrus is credited by Xenophon with planning the royal park at Sardis.[63]

Kelainai still has not been excavated. Nothing has been found at Sardis which would permit identification with satrapal residence; presumably they continued to use the palace of Croesus. Nor have we succeeded in locating that belvedere or castle of white stone which, according to Strabo (13.4, 5.625) the Persians built on the Tmolus south of Sardis, or the shrines of Artemis Anahita said to have existed at Sardis and Hypaepa in the Cayster Valley.[64]

Excavations have taken place at the satrapal residence of Pharnabazus at Daskylion, which was identified with complete assurance by the finding of clay imprints from satrapal archives. The general location at Kalehisar on the southeast bank over the Manyas Lake (near Ergili) has been ascertained, but the actual architectural layout remains unknown, although impressive parts have been found built into other buildings.[65] The superlatively cut masonry and architectural details in Ionic order[66] show that the building was not built in Persian style, and Akurgal believes the architects and masons were Greeks.

A Persian porch and hall with towers, but with pediments and columns in Greek style, has been reconstructed for the residence of some small potentate, *Fig. 39*

[61]E. Akurgal, "Recherches faites à Cyzique et à Erghili," *Anatolia* 1 (1956): 22, n. 33. For Daskylion Akurgal draws the interesting parallel with the selection of palace sites on lakes by the Selçuk Begs, who may have been influenced by an Iranian tradition of later times. For possible Lydian regal hunting ground at Zeleia cf. Strabo 13.1.17.

[62]A. R. Burn, *Persia and the Greeks, c. 546–478 B.C.* (London: Edward Arnold, 1962), pp. 113–14.

[63]Xenophon. *Oeconomicus* 4. 20–24. On his visit to Cyrus, the Spartan admiral Lysander praised the equal spacing and the straightness of the rows of trees. Cyrus replies: "I have measured and designed all of this, and I did some of the planting myself," presumably shortly after 407 B.C. Apparently the lay-out was quite geometric.

[64]J. Keil, "Die Kulte Lydiens," *AnatSt Ramsay*, p. 250; W. H. Buckler and D. M. Robinson, "Greek Inscriptions from Sardis III," *AJA* 17 (1913): 369–70; *RE* s.v. "Anaitis," vol. I.2 (1894): 2030–31. Pausanias 5.27, 5. R. Fleischer, "Artemis Anaitis von Hypaipa," *Artemis von Ephesos* (Leiden: E. J. Brill, 1973), pp. 185–87, pls. 75–76.

[65]E. Akurgal, *KunstAnat*, "Persische Kunst," pp. 167–74, esp. 171, fig. 115 (re-used parts), p. 321 n. 9–10; E. Akurgal, *Anatolia* 1 (1956): 20–24, pls. 7–12; K. Balkan, "Inscribed Bullae from Daskylion-Erghili," *Anatolia* 4 (1959): 123–28.

[66]Akurgal, *Anatolia* 1 (1956): 24, pls. 8–9; *KunstAnat*, pp. 170–71, 115.

presumably tributary to the Persians, at Larisa-Burunçuk in the Hermus estuary.[67] It resembles the palace constructed by the Persians at Babylon.[68] The excavator, Karl Schefold, has dated the structure to ca. 550 B.C.—the Croesus era—but his earlier dating of ca. 530 B.C. is more plausible as it allows time for the influence of Persian palaces to reach Asia Minor after they had been constructed by Lydians and Ionians in the 550–530s at Pasargadae and Susa.[69] The same type of palace may have been envisaged in the famous siege scene of the Lycian princely funerary precinct of Gjölbasi-Trysa, shortly after 400 B.C.; only here the wings project more markedly than in Larisa.[70]

If the evidence for the Persian palace, fortress, and city is still evasive, the evidence for Persianizing funerary art in Anatolia has been considerably enriched. Three funerary stelai, from Daskylion itself (one of them inscribed in Aramaic), *Fig. 40* reveal in a very curious style the funerary cart of Persian form and also the funerary meal with husband reclining and his veiled and crowned lady sitting by *Fig. 41* his side.[71] The style is certainly not Achaemenian court style but neither is it the style of Greek sculptors of the Aegean; it appears to be an Anatolian provincial version of a Western Aramaic-Mesopotamian funerary tradition. It is striking how much more Ionian the same subject of funerary meals presents itself as shown in a

[67]Larisa: Schefold, *Propylaeen*, p. 245, pl. 263 (new reconstruction) after *JOAI* 31 (1938–39): 42–45, and Böhlau and Schefold, *Larisa I*, pp. 153–56, pl. 30.

[68]R. Koldewey, *Die Königsburgen von Babylon* Teil 1 *Die Südburg* = *WVDOG* 54, pp. 120–25, pl. 28 (tentative reconstruction), pls. 26–27 (actual plan and elevation as found).

[69]Pasargadae: Nylander, *Ionians*, pp. 47, 69–70, 88–91, 102–21, fig. 38b, palace of Croesus as possible model of Larisa and Pasargadae. Milesians were deported to the region of Susa in 494 B.C., Herodotus 6.18–22, H. Luschey in Schefold, *Propylaeen*, pl. 350a. A similar synthesis of Greek and Persian elements might have occurred at the palace of Daskylion where, according to Akurgal, the town was never inhabited by Anatolians but was a Greek foundation. The name, however, is Lydian, and permission for Greeks to settle was given by Gyges so the Lydians might have had some share in the beginning.

[70]F. Eichler, *Die Reliefs de Heroons von Gjölbaschi-Trysa* (Wien: Franz Deuticke, 1950), pp. 23–26, 61–62, pl. 18:A 7–8, B 10, fig. 8.

[71]J.-M. Dentzer, "Reliefs au 'banquet' dans l'Asie Mineure du Ve siecle av. J.-C.," *RA* (1969), fasc. 2, pp. 200–5, fig. 2; E. Akurgal, "Griechisch-Persische Reliefs aus Daskyleion," *Iranica Antiqua* 6 (1966): 147–56; A. Dupont-Sommer, "Une Inscription Araméenne Inédite d'Epoque Perse Trouvée à Daskyléon (Turquie)," *CRAI* (1966):

44–57, pls. 1–6; N. Dolunay, *Istanbul Arkeoloji Müzeleri Yilliği* 13–14 (1966): 97–117, pls. 1–7; F. M. Cross and G. M. A. Hanfmann, "An Aramaic Inscription from Daskyleion," and "The New Stelae from Daskyleion," *BASOR* 184 (1966): 7–13. It should be noted that the purely epigraphic date proposed by Cross would have been 450 B.C., *loc.cit.*, p. 8, n. 14. H. Möbius by letter on Oct. 10, 1967, and independently P. Bernard, have suggested that the stelae were earlier, Aramaic inscriptions having been added later. (The thought expressed by Bernard that they are re-used Greek stelae is not tenable). See also, M. J. Mellink, *AJA* 69 (1965): 148; *Art Treasures*, p. 90, no. 128 ill. P. Bernard, "Les bas-reliefs gréco-perses de Dascylion à la lumière de nouvelles découvertes," *RA* (1969), fasc. 1, 17–28; J. Teixidor, "Bulletin d'épigraphie Sémitique," *Syria* 45 (1968): 375–77; R. S. Hanson, "Aramaic Funerary and Boundary Inscriptions from Asia Minor," *BASOR* 192 (1968): 3–11; J. Borchhardt, "Epichorische, gräko-persisch beinflusste Reliefs in Kilikien," *IstMitt* 18 (1968): 192–99, pls. 40–42, 44, 45.2, 46, 47.2, 48, 50 with complete bibl. to 1968; H. Möbius, "Zu den Stelen von Daskyleion," *AA* (1971): 442–55; G. M. A. Hanfmann, "A Pediment of the Persian Era from Sardis," *Mélanges Mansel* (Ankara, 1974), pp. 295–99. I see no cogent objections to dating all of the stelae to the first half of the fifth century, a dating made advisable by the early forms of palmette-lotus finials.

pediment from a small maussoleum, very likely of a noble Persian or a high-placed   *Fig. 42*
Lydian of the Persian era.[72] The piece was discovered at Sardis in 1968 and formed
about half of the pediment or temple-like structure, rather like the Nereid monument at Xanthos.[73] Although the relief having been discovered about 2 meters
under the present bed of the Pactolus, is very much washed out, its soft well-
rounded style resembles the opulent reliefs of the "Satrap Sarcophagus"[74] executed by Greek sculptors rather than the awkward linearism of the Daskylion
reliefs.

A number of very careful investigations of the "banquetting scene" have been
made by several scholars, notably by J. M. Dentzer.[75] The inscription and representation of the bearded gentleman on the Daskylion stele seem to establish
"Elnap son of SY," who invokes the Babylonian gods Bel and Nabu, and his
associates portrayed on the stelae as "Aramaic speakers," as Semites. The Semites
were carriers of that Irano-Semitic officialdom which effectively constituted the
administrative apparatus of the Persian Empire in the West. The iconographic
resemblances all point in the direction of the Syro-Aramaic area, and beyond it to
Mesopotamia, as in the famous relief of Asur-Banipal and his wife.[76] As A. Alföldi
has shown, the banquet scene carried with it the connotation of high regal life of
the east and luxury, of which the Persian kings were considered the most eminent
examples.[77]

We have then in figurative arts various kinds of Persian impact. The greatest
amount of Iranian subject matter and style is found in the luxury arts of the
satrapal courts, yet even here closer study reveals admixture of Anatolian and
Greek elements. Thus, John Boardman has just recently conclusively attributed to
Sardis some two hundred pyramidal seals of chalcedony, agate, and rock crystal.
Their motifs are usually Persian (as the horned griffin or the crowned bearded
sphinx), but their inscriptions are Lydian—and only one owner's name is Iranian   *Figs. 43, 44*
(*Mitratas*), the others all Lydian. The inscription shown in figure 43 reads *maneli*.[78]   *Fig. 43*

[72]S69.14:8047. Cf. *BASOR* 199 (1970): 38–39, fig. 29; *Archaeology* 23 (1970): 252, fig: Mellink, *AJA* 74 (1970): 173; Hanfmann, *Mélanges Mansel* (Ankara, 1974), pp. 289–301, pls. 99–102a.

[73]Nereid monument: P. Coupel and P. Demargne, *Xanthos* 3 (1969); G. Niemann and E. Reisch, *Das Nereiden-Monument in Xanthos* (Wien: E. Hölzel, 1921); Picard, *Manuel* 2:2 (1939): 864; A. H. Smith, *BMC* 2 (1900): 4–5, 38 no. 924, fig. 1; W. R. Lethaby, *JHS* 35 (1915): 214.

[74]Satrap Sarcophagus: I. Kleemann, *Der Satrapensarkophag aus Sidon, IstFo* 20 (1958).

[75]Dentzer, *RA* (1969), fasc. 2, 195–224; *RA* (1971), fasc. 2, 215–58; E. Akurgal, *Iranica Antiqua* 6 (1966): 152–54; R. N. Thönges-Stringaris, "Das griechische Totenmahl," *AthMitt* 80 (1965): 1–99; I. Kleemann, *IstFo* 20 (1958): 112.

[76]Dentzer, *RA* (1971), fasc. 2, 221, fig. 1, p. 218.

[77]A. Alföldi, "Zur Geschichte des Throntabernakels," *La nouvelle Clio* 2 (1950): 537–66.

[78]J. Boardman, *Iran* 8 (1970): 39, nos. 4, 5, pl. I, pp. 20–21 for Lydian inscriptions. Cf. also R. Gusmani, "Onomastica Iranica nei Testi Epicorici Lidi," in *Umanità e Storia, Scritti in Onore di Adelchi Attisani* (Naples, 1971), pp. 1–8.

In sculpture, more markedly Aramaic-Anatolian are such linear somewhat provincial reliefs as those of Daskylion and Hypaepa; the most sophisticated level is also the most heavily Hellenized—as in the new pediment from Sardis and the sarcophagus found at Sidon. The Iranian element is found in subject matter and externals of costume but hardly influences the style.

The Persian penetration remained limited in geographical extent and in depth. At Sardis, for instance, the Persians or their Lydian helpers seem to have provided better water supply, and possibly public fountains, but the native architecture remained basically unchanged, as did the popular crafts of pottery and, indeed, the general "material culture." Expressions of art such as sculpture and painting remained disparate and dissociated into different styles and different social strata. Theoretically, a synthesis would have been possible of native Anatolian customs, of Persian military and personal elevation of rulers by luxury and figurative propaganda, and of the aesthetic anthropomorphism of archaic and then classical Greek art, but this does not seem to have happened at the satrapal courts.

It was the local rulers of a fairly independent mountain country, the "Wolfsland," Lycia, who strove to emulate the satraps and who seemed to have achieved something of a "synthesis" in architecture, sculpture, and as very recent discoveries have taught us, in painting. This synthesis for Lycian architecture and sculpture of the Persian era has been pointed out by E. Akurgal, G. Rodenwaldt, and more recently by French scholars working at Xanthos.[79] Now discoveries of archaic and Persian period paintings found in chamber tombs of Kizilbel, two miles south of Elmali, have greatly enriched the scope of our materials[80]; sea-faring, warriors' departures, and local mythology in Greek guise attest a style which, while drawing on Eastern Greek experience is yet markedly original. I agree with the discoverer, M. J. Mellink, that these paintings should be considered Anatolian or Lycian achievements. A later painting shows more clearly (as do the sculptures of Xanthos) the introduction of Achaemenian elements glorifying the life of rulers—among them the winged disk and the banquet scene.

Fig. 45

[79]P. Demargne, H. Metzger et al., *Fouilles de Xanthos* I (1958), II (1963), III (1969), IV (1972); K. Schefold, "Xanthos und Südanatolien," *Antike Kunst* 13 (1970): 79–84; Akurgal, *KunstAnat*, pp. 122–49, figs. 77–101 and for recent bibl. *Civilizations*, p. 364. Relations to Persians: G. Rodenwaldt, "Griechische Reliefs in Lykien," *SSBerlin* (1933): 1030, 1041–43. For Limyra cf. chapter 2 below and J. Borchhardt, "Limyra: Sitz des lykischen Dynasten Perikles," *IstMitt* 17 (1967): 151–67.

[80]M. J. Mellink, "The Painted Tomb Near Elmali," *AJA* 74 (1970): 251–52, pls. 59–61; "Excavations at Elmali, 1971," *AJA* 76 (1972): 263–68, pls. 58–60; "Excavations at Elmali, 1972," *AJA* 77 (1973): 297–303, pls. 43–46; "Notes on Anatolian Wall Painting," *Mélanges Mansel* (Ankara, 1974), pp. 543–46, pls. 163–70. See also G. Neumann, "Neue Funde und Forschungen in Lykien," *Jahrbuch des Akademie der Wissenschaften in Göttingen* (1971): 34–49 for excavations in other Lycian graves.

With the Nereid monument of Xanthos,[81] the Lycian art attained at once a more sophisticated and more markedly Hellenized level (presumably prompted by migrant Greek masters), a true forerunner of the great Carian art program carried on by the dynasty of Hekatomnidae of Caria and culminating in the Maussoleum of Helicarnassus.

We shall next examine the purely or primarily Greek developments in western Anatolian cities. It is well to remember, however, that in late archaic times and during much of the Persian era we deal with surprisingly great contrasts: thus at the same time that a presumably Anatolian craftsman was creating the strange and awkward semi-Anatolian, semi-Oriental monuments for Elnap and other *Figs. 40, 41* "Aramaeans" at Daskylion, a Phidias, a Polykleitos, and a Kresilas, the greatest sculptors in the history of the world, were engaged in producing in purest Hellenic and in the most classical style, the famous statues of Amazons for the Artemision at Ephesus.[82]   *Figs. 46–48*

[81]Cf. n. 73, *above.*
[82]Cf. ch. 2, n. 1.

II. Hellenization Takes Command

Figs. 46–48 What an extraordinary sight it must have been to see this array of four or even five bronze Amazons, all wounded, and all on display before the great archaic Croesan temple of Artemis in Ephesus with the greatest sculptors in history competing for the attention of the judges.[1]

The time was about 435 B.C. and this visit of Phidias, Polykleitos, and Kresilas was a high point of high classical influence. But this high classical style was conveyed by visiting artists and statuary imported from the Greek mainland and islands—not by native Ionian sculptors of Asia Minor.

A visit to eastern Greece, to Ionia, soon became almost *de rigeur* for ambitious young mainland sculptors in the fourth century B.C., somewhat, perhaps, like visits to America in the late nineteenth and early twentieth centuries for enterprising European musicians and opera stars. Thus, Praxiteles went to Asia Minor, as did the four famous sculptors active at the Maussoleum—Timotheos, already elderly, Scopas, Leochares, and Bryaxis.[2]

There were historical, economic, and cultural reasons for the change we perceive in eastern Greece during the classical period. All through the fifth century, until the end of the war between Athens and Sparta (404 B.C.), and indeed, until the so-called King's Peace of 386 B.C., there had been much violent fighting

---

[1]"They made Amazons to be dedicated in the Temple of Artemis," wrote Pliny *N.H.*34.53. It is not clear whether the alleged competition was organized by the people of Ephesus or by the temple authorities. Cf. G. M. A. Richter, *Sculpture and Sculptors of the Greeks,* 4th ed. (New Haven: Yale University Press, 1970), pp. 174–75, figs. 662–64, 671, 700; Richter, "Pliny's Five Amazons," *Ar-* chaeology 12 (1959): 111–15; D. von Bothmer, *Amazons in Greek Art,* pp. 216–22, pl. 89; B. S. Ridgway, "A Story of Five Amazons," *AJA* 78 (1974): 1–18.

[2]Pliny *N.H.*36.30. For Praxiteles cf. Picard, *Manuel* 3:1 (1948), pp. 556–57; B. Ashmole, "Demeter of Cnidus," *JHS* 71 (1951): 13–25 (on Leochares); J. H. Jongkees, "New Statues by Bryaxis," *JHS* 68 (1948): 29–39.

and devastation in western Anatolia and especially along the west coast. Recovery and prosperity seem to have come with the weakening of Persian rule during the fourth century.[3]

Amazons were closely allied with the history of the sanctuary in Ephesus. According to the Hellenistic poet Kallimachos, they were the first servants of the goddess (*Hymn. Artem.* 237-247). At Ephesus, on local altars they had obtained "pardons" from Herakles and from Theseus. Perhaps because of this they were represented on the fourth century altar of Artemis.[4]

Fig. 57

Culturally, it is ascertainable from inscriptions that the Greek language was gaining ground against the Anatolian tongues in Lydia, Caria, and Mysia. Around 340 B.C., a Lydian thought it necessary to make his dedication to Artemis in Lydian and Greek.[5]

The eastward progress of the Hellenization of Anatolia was vigorous, though not always at an even rate. Sardis, the Lydian capital, became a Greek city during the third century B.C. Its complete repeopling—*synoikismos*—by Antiochus III put the seal on the transition. The colossal temple of Artemis, the fourth largest Ionic temple known, had a huge marble image of Zeus—perhaps assimilated to look like the ruler-pretender Achaeus (king, 220–213 B.C.).[6]

The mixed Greek-Iranian arts seen in western Anatolia in the sixth and fifth centuries receded toward the periphery to the regions of Cappadocia and Pontus where Iranian princes still ruled,[7] or to southeastern Anatolia and Syria, to Commagene, where they survived into the first century B.C.[8]

---

[3]M. I. Rostovtzeff, *The Social and Economic History of the Hellenistic World* 1 (Oxford, 1941), p. 81.

[4]G. W. Elderkin, "Theseus and the Metropolitan Amazon," *Art in America* 23 (1935): 129–34, has rightly observed that it is peculiar that the motive prescribed for the competition was not that of a sacrificing Amazon, or an Amazon at ease—which would have befitted their traditional role in the sanctuary, but the pathetic motif of the wounded—perhaps still defiant—but defeated Amazon. This could only be interpreted as defeat of the East by the Greeks, but the conception of the heroic, barbaric opponent is in a way the forerunner of the defiant, heroic Gauls. A. Bammer wrote (May 3, 1971) that the Amazon relief was found in 1900 near the theater with pieces of altar architecture. According to Bammer, it belongs to the inner corner of the fourth century B.C. altar, *AA* (1968): 400–23, fig. 28. If a Roman copy, it would have been a repair. For possible archaic Amazons, cf. F. N. Pryce, *BMC*

1:1 (1928): 66, 86, figs. 132, B 215–16, fragment of fine Scythian cap with laurel wreath (hence not in fight but in ritual, perhaps as supplicants) suggests presence of Amazons, possibly in combat with Greeks. The essential information is in Picard, *Manuel* 2:1 (1939), p. 300, n. 3.

[5]The famous inscription of Nannas Dionysokleos = *Nannas Bakivalis:* R. Gusmani, *LW* (1964), no. 20; W. H. Buckler, *Sardis* 6.2 (1924), no. 20, p. 38, pl. 8.

[6]G. M. A. Hanfmann, *BASOR* 166 (1962): 34, fig. 27, colossal head of Achaeus; *idem, Sardis und Lydien* (1960), p. 528; D. Magie, *Roman Rule* I, 9–11 (Achaeus); L. Robert, *NIS* (1963): 9–21 (on Antiochus III).

[7]H. von Gall, *AA* (1967): 585–87.

[8]Commagene-Nemrud Daǧ-Arsameia: F. Dörner, T. Goell, *Arsameia am Nymphaios, IstFo* 23 (1963); D. Schlumberger, *L'orient hellenisé*, pp. 41–56; Akurgal, *Civilizations*, pp. 346–51, bibl. 361, 364.

Historically, it is customary to take the Persian occupation from the fall of Croesus in 547 B.C. to the arrival of Alexander the Great in 334 B.C. as one historic period. Culturally and artistically, however, something may be gained by viewing, as a unit, the period from the Persian defeat at Mykale (479) through the early and high Hellenistic ages until the Romans appeared on the scene and inherited the Kingdom of Pergamon in 133 B.C.

I am making this statement in the light of our experience at Sardis where the urban pattern, domestic architecture, and material culture of daily life showed only gradual change under Alexander and his immediate successors, but were radically changed after the destruction in 213 B.C.

Asia Minor has been viewed as a kind of pilot plant of history, experimenting during the classical age with things which were to become popular in the Hellenistic world. This is certainly true of urbanism, for it was eastern Greece which pioneered the kind of city planning that was to be carried to Egypt and Africa and
Fig. 49   through Asia to India by Alexander the Great and his successors.

Figs. 50, 51   Miletus is a vast, nearly level site, quite difficult to comprehend. The only real eminence, that of the theater, also indicates approximately the position of the ancient waterfront with the Lion Harbor to the north and the Theater Harbor to the south. The fine domed mosque, erected by Prince Elyas of Mentese in 1404, now marks to some extent the position of the major north-south artery which passed by the place now occupied by the mosque, and issued from a southern city gate as the Sacred Road leading to the sanctuary of Apollo at Didyma, about 12 miles to the south.[9]

The reconstruction of Miletus, begun around 470 B.C., was an early example of a rationalized city plan; it was also the largest urban planning project hitherto attempted by the Greeks. Like some latter day urban planners, Hippodamus of Miletus seems to have been vocal, explicit, good with his pen, and something of a showman. He was perhaps the first socially conscious city planner, the first to associate Greek speculation on the ideal city-state which was a favorite subject of the classical age with actual experience in city planning. He got credit not only for

[9]Miletus and Hippodamus: Aristotle *Politics* II.5.1267b; A. von Gerkan, *Griech. Städte* (1924), pl. 6; Martin, *Urbanisme*, pp. 97–106, 124–25, figs. 6, 15; G. Kleiner, *Ruinen*, p. 25 notes the possibility that parts of pre-Hippodamian Miletus may have had rectagonal (grid) layout. Cf. Charles Blessing, "The Form of Cities in Perspective," Center for Coordination of Ancient and Modern Studies, the University of Michigan (Ann Arbor, 1973), pp. 16–18. J. R. McCredie, "Hippodamos of Miletos," *Studies Hanfmann*, pp. 95–100. The attribution of the plan of Miletus is a modern conjecture not based on ancient references.

this sufficiently important achievement and for his advanced city plans of Miletus and Piraeus, but also for inventing the grid plan, which had actually been used long before at Ephesus, Olbia, and in much earlier, non-Greek places.

We have seen that in the Croesus era, the focal points in terms of concentration of power and attraction for the arts in the Anatolian inland cities were the palaces and the temples, with the temples far more significant in artistic terms. In archaic coastal Greek cities it was the temple, and agora, and then the port—again with the temple far outweighing all else in terms of monumentality of architecture and wealth of artistic expression. Hippodamus acknowledged the importance of sacred tradition when he reserved one third of the land for sacred purposes in his ideal state. Another third he reserved for support of the warrior class; and one third for farmers. "His system" wrote Aristotle, "was for a city with a population of ten thousand, divided into three classes, artisans, farmers, and warriors" (*Politics* II.5–1267b).

It has been suggested that since farmers did not live in the city, the city would have been divided into a sacred area, and a residential area owned by the warriors but inhabited also by the nonlandowning artisans.[10]

From the example of Miletus one would surmise that Hippodamus included most public buildings in his "sacred" area. For the classical planners, public areas of the city were still hallowed by divine presence and protection. Thus, when the city of Colophon was vastly enlarged and replanned, the refounding began with a procession and prayers offered at all the altars of gods, goddesses, and heroes by priests, priestesses, the supreme magistrate (*prytanis*), and the Urban Renewal Committee of Ten.[11] It is noteworthy that Hippodamus did not envisage the ideal city as having a population larger than seven thousand, if three thousand lived outside the city itself. Miletus itself, however, was laid out on a remarkably large scale, in an area of about two hundred fifty acres, certainly for a population much larger than ten thousand.[12] And the very striking trend during the fourth century is for remarkably long defensive walls and large city areas (although the city areas were clearly not completely built up).

[10]G. P. R. Metraux, *Western Greek Land Use and City Planning in the Archaic Period* (Ph.D. diss., Harvard University, 1972).

[11]Colophon: Martin, *Urbanisme*, p. 55, citing the famous inscription concerning extension and refounding of the city. A transcription of this exemplary information is given by B. D. Meritt, "Inscriptions of Colophon," *AJP* 56 (1935): 361–72: (1) prayers by priests, priestesses, city officials, city planning committee at all altars of gods, goddesses, heroes; (2) appointment of architect; (3) layout of streets, assignment and sale of lots; (4) reservation by the committee of agora, shops, all public spaces; (5) fund raising for city walls. L. Robert, "Décrits de Kolophon," *RevPhil* ser. 3, vol 10 (1936): 158–70.

[12]Cf. W. Bendt, *Topographische Karte von Milet Milet* II.4 (Berlin, 1968).

Figs. 50, 51

As to the emphasis and position of the arts, the typical "Milesian" type layout defined the "sacred public" area or areas by subtraction of a certain number of blocks. Thus in Miletus itself, a kind of hinge was created owing to the existence of two major harbors. This public zone included three open Pi-shaped agorai (north, south, and west). The hallowing shrines, that of Athena (going back possibly to the Bronze Age) and that of Apollo Delphinios held emphatic, though peripheral positions. "The two sanctuaries were the starting points for the planned renewal of the city," says G. Kleiner.[13] Clearly, respect for sacred traditions was a strong consideration. Placed on both sides of the Theater Bay, in new monumental forms for the traditional athletic functions, the theater and the stadium were apparently also planned in the fourth century B.C.

The city government was probably placed close to the center of the oldest market, the North Market, in the so-called "Prytaneion."[14] Built only in the second century B.C., the council house placed between the North and South Markets monumentalized the traditional, deliberative body, symbolic of democratic government.

Fig. 50

Miletus, with its enormous trade, incorporated in her markets the most substantial examples of commercial buildings. The market took the form of a stoa, a colonnade accompanied by single or double row of shops. The South Market, said to be the largest of all Greek markets, covered over eight acres (33,000 square meters). Its east hall was known in ancient inscriptions as "Stadium Stoa" because it was a stade long (196.45 meters). Built under Antiochus I (280–261 B.C.) the seventy-eight triple-chambered stores provided income to support the huge sanctuary of Apollo at Didyma.[15]

The Milesian planners have been rightly praised for assembling previously dispersed elements of the Greek agora into "an organic unity," for creating by skillful use of colonnades "un édifice unifie . . . susceptible aux multiples fonctions qu'il devait assumer."[16]

Developed from a wedding of geometrical theory, rationalization of social life, and simplicity of layout, the Milesian city plan became a great success. It was notably assisted by the curious phenomenon of *cités errantes*, "wandering cities." In the late fourth and early third centuries B.C. Colophon, Priene, Smyrna, and

[13]Kleiner, *Ruinen*, pp. 25–26, Delphinion at the entrance to the North Agora and Main Street, Athena over the West Agora. As the sites of the sanctuaries predated the plan, it must have been developed with respect for the sacred traditions.

[14]Kleiner, *Ruinen*, fig. 29.
[15]Kleiner, *Ruinen*, pp. 61–62, fig. 37.
[16]Martin, *Urbanisme*, p. 275.

Ephesus changed locations and adopted modernized grid plans. So probably, did Sardis, though somewhat later.[17] The reasons were not always the same but an important factor affected the coast: undoubtedly the land had sunk while rivers were piling up alluvial plains and silting up earlier harbors. This had affected Priene and Miletus; and the site of archaic Smyrna (Bayrakli) too, became landlocked.[18]

Priene is our best preserved example of a small Hellenistic grid town. The city's houses consisted of the old palace unit, the megaron[19] on a small scale combined with the old rustic court plan of the Anatolian village house, but rationalized and built of permanent materials, at times even of regular masonry. Rooms built for comfort were raised to imposing heights of 5.5 to 6 meters. The ungainly materials such as stone rubble or mud brick were now concealed behind painted stucco which imitated marble walls. Such walls were conceived as structured along the lines of public buildings and did, at times, include loggia-like pilaster supports in their upper parts.[20]

Fig. 52

Figs. 53, 6

In archaic Sardis we noted the contrast between the splendor of temple and palace and the rustic modesty of habitations. Archaic Smyrna was only different in the degree of contrast. However, the social downward levelling brought features of both the temple and the palace into the houses of the citizens. Painting joined architecture in enhancing the attractiveness of the dwellings. Made of materials hitherto essentially limited to palace and temple, marble tables, marble stands, and bronze and ivory beds, were among the furnishings through which private houses began to claim palatial aesthetic values.[21]

At the same time, the old Anatolian acropolis-palace came back in a grandiose and monumental form. As Roland Martin has acutely recognized there arose in

[17]Priene: T. Wiegand and H. Schrader, *Priene,* p. 35; M. Schede, *Ruinen,* pp. 2–3. Smyrna: Cadoux, pp. 94–97 (Alexander's dream, Pausanias 7.5.1), p. 100 (actual foundation by Lysimachos); Akurgal, *Civilizations,* p. 121. Ephesus: J. Keil, *Führer,* pp. 20–21; Akurgal, *Civilizations,* p. 143; F. Miltner, *Ephesos,* pp. 13–14, stated that the wall of Lysimachos is 9 km. (ca. 5 miles) long and the area is 4 sq. km. or on the order of 4000 acres. He assumes that the center of civic life was the precinct and altar of Hestia Boulaia, p. 15, fig. 9. Sardis: Apparently the city was shifted eastward away from the Pactolus by the planners for Zeuxis, Vice-Regent for Antiochus III (213 B.C.), *BASOR* 182 (1966): 25; J. G. Pedley, *Sardis,* p. 12.

[18]Kleiner, *Ruinen,* pp. 2–5, figs. 4, 5; Schede, *Ruinen,* pp. 1–3, figs. 2, 3.

[19]Schede, *Ruinen,* figs. 118, 120 (House XXXIII); C. M. Havelock, *Hellenistic Art* (New York Graphic Society, 1971), pp. 76–77, fig. 52 (House XXXIII), pp. 73–74, figs. 43, 44 (plan and model of Priene). The design for the new town was, of course, late classical, drawn up around 350 B.C. but most of the buildings were Hellenistic.

[20]Schede, *Ruinen,* ch. 12, pp. 96–97, figs. 112–13, incised and plastic ashlar; fig. 115, window frame of terracotta.

[21]Schede, *Ruinen,* p. 98, fig. 121, marble table (round support); statuettes of marble and clay, figs. 122, 123. G. M. A. Richter, *Ancient Furniture* (Oxford: Clarendon Press, 1926), p. 79 (ivory table legs).

Asia Minor a new school of urban planning.[22] Working with three-dimensional units which emphasized vertical as well as horizontal composition, the new designs strove for a more dynamic and monumental environment than the linear Milesian grid based on two-dimensional geometry could provide. The new approach also paid much greater heed to the configuration of the landscape and utilized the site to create dramatic views.[23]

Figs. 54, 55

This development may have been pioneered during the late classical age by the Hekatomnid dynasty, the dynasty of Maussolus, known to some extent by the buildings at Labranda and the rebuilding of Halicarnassus in Southwest Asia Minor.[24] The magnificent site of Halicarnassus rises like an open-air theater around the wooded bay. Although inaccurate in detail, Fritz Krischen's sketch evokes the general impression of Hekatomnid Halicarnassus from the major approach to the city, that is, the approach from the sea.[25] From the fifteenth century of our era until the present day, the city has been dominated by the magnificent Castle of Saint Peter (built between 1404 and 1480); but the ancient city was dominated not by the palace but by the tomb—the famous Maussoleum: *Aere nec vacuo pendentia Mausolea* (Martial *De Spectaculis* I.5). Seemingly suspended in the air, its pyramid formed the visual center of the waterfront, symbolizing the immortalization of the ruler after death, not his activities on earth.

Excavations by Kristian Jeppesen have shown that the Maussoleum stood in a vast rectangular precinct (marked by arrow in figure 54) some 242.5 meters long—running parallel to the shore—which was never finished.[26]

Until recently we knew nothing about the palace of Maussolus except what the Roman writer Vitruvius—following a Hellenistic source—wrote: "everything was revetted with marble from Prokonnesos and the walls had stucco so polished that it gleamed like glass" (Vitruvius 2.8.10). Now Jeppesen surmises that the palace was under the Castle of Saint Peter, where, as Jeppesen writes in a letter

[22]Martin, "Pergame et l'urbanisme monumentale," *Urbanisme*, pp. 127–51.

[23]P. Lehmann, "The Setting of Hellenistic Temples," *Journal of the Society of Architectural Historians* 13 (1954): 15–20.

[24]Labranda: *Labraunda Swedish Excavations and Researches* K. Jeppesen, I:1, *The Propylaia* (Lund: Gleerup, 1955); A. Westbohn, I:2 *The Architecture of the Hieron* (Lund, 1963); P. Hellstrom, II:1 *Pottery of Classical and Later Date* (Lund, 1965); J. Crampa, *Greek Inscriptions* I (Lund, 1969).

[25]F. Krischen, *Weltwunder*, p. 72, pl. 25; Krischen saw in the Maussoleum "a tower rising over the city, comparable

to the Tower of Babel . . ." and thought that Maussolus wanted to compete with the tomb of Persian King Cyrus at Pasargadae. The former idea may have some merit, though the Pyramids of Egypt, already proverbial for Herodotus, must be considered as models. The scale and character of the tomb of Cyrus are so totally different that any idea of connection with the Maussoleum is ludicrous. Cf. chapter 1 above and figs. 37, 38.

[26]K. Jeppesen, "Excavations at Halicarnassus," *ActaA* 38 (1967): 29–58. "The Site of the Maussoleum at Halicarnassus Reexcavated," *AJA* 77 (1973), pp. 336–38, pls. 63–64.

(April 13, 1971), "there exist remains of walls and foundations technically comparable to those of the Maussoleum."

The building program undertaken by Kings Attalos I and Eumenes II of Pergamon during the late third and early second century B.C. presents the most striking example of this new, dramatic urbanism. The architects of Pergamon *Fig. 56* monumentalized and exaggerated the existing natural theater of the site, which in principle was like Sardis—an offshoot from a mountain range dominating a river valley. A mountain city is usually densely cramped but the Pergamene composition opened its units magnificently toward the landscape.[27] Enjoying the vast panoramas from Pergamon's windswept heights, we can experience an integration of landscape and architecture which is one of the great accomplishments of dynamic Hellenistic art.[28]

But was Pergamon really comparable to Versailles, as M. Collignon had suggested?[29] True, it was powerful King Eumenes II, who as Strabo observed (13.624), "built up the city [*polin*], planted a grove in the Nikephorion, and gave votives and libraries and raised the Pergamene urban area [*katoikian*] to the beauty which she shows to this day. . . ." On the one hand, the royal palaces and arsenals were at the top of the height, and the gods, Athena and Zeus, had their stations—the Athena Precinct, the Altar of Zeus—lower than the kings. On the *Fig. 56* other hand, the palaces did not unite into a vast monumental complex in the Oriental and Persian tradition. They remained a series of enlarged peristyle court houses of the same type as those of classical residential urban dwellings.[30]

Architecturally, these kings did not claim to dwarf humanity. Neither did they do so in other arts. To represent their battles with the Gauls as parallel to gods and giants, and to Greeks and Persians, was only to assert the customary classical heroization through mythical precedents. The truly novel ideological element of the propaganda by the Pergamenes was their insistence on their role as *Kulturtraeger* of the heritage of Hellas. They created a Greek library, second only to Alexandria, and assembled the first Royal Art Museum brought together for the sake of aesthetic values, that is, for the sake of possessing famous "classical" art.

[27]Plan of Pergamon: Martin, *Urbanisme*, pp. 131–43, fig. 17, pls. VII.1, IX.1; Havelock, *Hellenistic Art*, figs. 74–78.

[28]G. M. A. Hanfmann, "Hellenistic Art," *DOPapers* 17 (1963): 83, 88; Berve-Gruben, pls. 171, 175.

[29]M. Collignon and E. Pontremoli, *Pergame* (Paris: L. Henry May, 1898), p. 229; Martin, *Urbanisme*, p. 127.

[30]Martin, *Urbanisme*, pp. 235–36, fig. 47; p. 144, pl. IX; A. W. Lawrence, *Greek Architecture*, pp. 277–78, fig. 163. G. Kawerau and T. Wiegand, *Die Palaeste der Hochburg* (*Altertümer von Pergamon* V.1) (on Pergamon palaces); Akurgal, *Civilizations*, p. 81.

It is unfortunate that so little is known about this museum.[31] We can see the change in the function of sculpture, however, and in the change of Athena from the protecting divinity of an entire polis in the Parthenon, to a protectress of professors in the Library of Pergamon.[32]

I would like to examine now the changing role of sculpture in the life of the cities. First, some general observations on the social *loci* of sculpture. The temple and the temple precinct remained important as receptacles of sculpture. The highest honors for the *kaueis* (*kaves*), the Lydian-titled priestess of Sardis, for the *stephanophoros,* priest of Zeus in Priene, and for the highest priests, priestesses, and officials in general were statues placed in the major sanctuary of the city. But the attitude toward sculptured decoration of the temple in Ionia was ambivalent. Pytheos, the herald of Ionian Renaissance in architecture in the late classical era

Figs. 72, 73, 74 (ca. 350 B.C.) permitted sculptures galore on the Maussoleum, but kept his exemplary temple of Athena in Priene chastely devoid of a figured frieze.[33]

Where ancient colossal temples were renovated, as the Artemision of
Fig. 20 Ephesus, the precedent of archaic sculptures was followed. The column drums of the Artemision of Ephesus, built after the fire of 356, were again decorated, perhaps by Scopas (Pliny 36.95), though apparently with mythological not processional figures. It is now thought that the round reliefs were carved below the necks of the capitals, not on the bases.[34] During the classicistic revival around the middle of the second century B.C., inspired by the architect Hermogenes, the traditional Ionic figured frieze was brought back, though not very convincingly, as in the temple of Artemis at Magnesia.[35]

There was a much more sustained conviction that the altar at which the actual ritual took place deserved significant sculptured decoration. A monument of greatest importance for the future was the late classical altar of Artemis at
Fig. 57 Ephesus. In a somewhat involved passage, Strabo (14.641) who cites an earlier source, says that the "altar was pretty much [*schedon ti*] full of works by Praxiteles." It has been conjectured that these works by Praxiteles might have been

[31]E. V. Hansen, *Attalids*, pp. 289–90, 321.

[32]Hansen, *Attalids*, pp. 321–22 (statue of Athena in Library of Pergamon); A. H. Smith, *BMC* II (1900): 146, 152–53, no. 1150:1–4 (statue of Athena, Priene). It stood on a base dated by coins of Orophernes to 158 B.C. Left foot with join and bronze sandal straps, Society of Dilettanti, *Antiquities of Ionia* 4 (London: Macmillan, 1881), p. 31, fig. 17; O. Rayet and A. Thomas, *Milet et le Golfe Latmique* (Paris: J. Baudry, 1877), pl. 15, fig. 19.

[33]Pytheos, temple of Athena, Priene: Schede, *Ruinen*, p. 28, figs. 32, 34, 35; O. Bauer, "Vorlaufiger Bericht über die Neubearbeitung des Athenatempels zu Priene in der Jahren 1965/66," *IstMitt* 18 (1968): 212–20.

[34]A. Bammer, "Zum jüngeren Artemision," *JOAI* 47 (1964–65): 131–35, figs. 77, 79.

[35]C. Humann, *Magnesia am Maeander*, pp. 84–89, 184–85, figs. 35, 82–85; A. Schober, *Der Fries des Hekateions von Lagina, IstFo* 2 (1933): 89–90.

statues, not reliefs.[36] Recent Austrian excavations have begun to produce beautiful fragments of the architectural decoration of the altar.[37] There are also fragments of colossal statues, one possibly from an Amazon. A wonderful horsehead, probably from a processional chariot, combines superlative delicacy with fiery spirit.[38] This was part of a statuary group and A. Bammer (by letter, May 3, 1971) suggested that it may have stood separately on the roof of the colonnade around the altar. The excavators also believe that the altar was adorned with a figurative frieze, perhaps of Amazons. According to the local legend, the wounded Amazons had begged the Greeks for mercy at this very altar.[39]

Fig. 57

The motif of frontal figures in architectural compartments was resumed around the middle of the second century B.C. in the altar of the sanctuary of Athena in Priene. Most scholars assume that small panels with scenes from the gigantomachy held the place on the podium which the Amazons had on the altar in Ephesus, while large frontal figures perhaps of priestesses stood between the engaged Ionic columns of the upper story.[40] A similar arrangement occurred on the altar of the sanctuary of Artemis Leukophryene in Magnesia on the Maeander, where the design may have been made by the classicistic architect and theorist Hermogenes.[41] These altars, with their isolated, statuesque, frontal figures have

---

[36]Picard, *Manuel* 3:1 (1948), pp. 620–22.

[37]Fragments of altar: A. Bammer's latest report at hand, "Tempel und Altar der Artemis von Ephesos," *JOAI* Beiblatt 48 (1966–67): 22–43 states (p. 23) that he has "nothing to add to the proposed reconstruction (*Festschrift Eichler*, pp. 10–22) of the superstructure over the three wings of the altar which does include a *Figurenfries*." For the fragments of wonderful double maeanders with rosettes, insects, dolphins, and birds, cf. A. Bammer, *Festschrift Eichler*, figs. 3–12.

[38]Horse and chariot group: Bammer, *JOAI* Beibl. 48 (1966–67): 39, fig. 15; horse and altar view, *AJA* 74 (1970): 172, pl. 45:22. Over a dado course with upright lattice or pilaster motif similar to Ara Pacis was the maeander and above it the figurative frieze of Amazons. This part formed the podium for a wall with Ionic half-columns outside and (Ionic?) pteron inside, *JOAI* Beibl. 48 (1966–67): 24; *Festschrift Eichler*, pp. 20–21, fig. 13.

[39]For the legend, cf. Picard, *Manuel* 2:1 (1939), p. 300, n. 3.

[40]Altar, Priene: W. von Massow, *Führer durch das Pergamonmuseum*, p. 24, fig. 14; Schede, *Ruinen*, p. 36, figs. 44–48 (giants, female figure); A. H. Smith, *BMC* II (1900), nos. 1165–76. Fundamental treatment: P. Wolters, "Zur Gigantomachie von Priene," *JdI* 1 (1886): 56–64. Dating to

time of Orophernes, 158 B.C.: A. von Gerkan, "Der Altar des Athenatempels in Priene," *Bonner Jahrbücher* 129 (1924): 15–35. Detailed evaluation of gigantomachy and comparison with Pergamon frieze: A. Schober, "Zur Gigantomachie von Priene," *JOAI* 30 (1936): 28–49, figs. 3–10. C. Praschniker, "Die Gigantomachie-Reliefs von Priene," *ibid.*, pp. 45–49, suggests on the analogy of Belevi that the gigantomachy and possible amazonomachy reliefs from Priene were reliefs of coffered ceilings, and that the amazon scenes might belong to the time of Pytheos, the fourth century B.C. Praschniker's technical and other objections seem quite serious. He pointed out that according to Newton (*Antiquities of Ionia* IV, p. 33) the reliefs were found "in the ruins of the temple," according to Pullan, "in pronaos," (p. 29), and according to Rayet, "within the cella." G. Gruben in Berve-Gruben, pp. 478–80, is apparently unaware of Praschniker's objections.

[41]Magnesia: Podium reliefs never finished. Divinities in upper story: W. von Massow, *Führer durch das Pergamonmuseum*, p. 31, fig. 23; C. Humann, *Magnesia am Maeander*, pp. 91–102, fig. 93; A. von Gerkan, *Der Altar des Artemis-Tempels in Magnesia am Mäander* (Berlin, 1929), pp. 23–24, pls. XI, X; = Koldewey Gesellschaft, *Studien zur Bauforschung* I.

been thought to be conscious classicistic reactions to the Baroque exuberance of the great Altar of Zeus at Pergamon.

Figs. 58, 59   In the glorification of the altar against the temple and in the overabundance of figurative decoration, the great Altar of Zeus at Pergamon represents the culminating point. The very fact that an entire precinct was given to an altar without a temple makes the Altar of Zeus exceptional. So are its vast dimensions (120 feet by 112 feet; 36.4 meters by 34.2 meters). Almost unquestioningly, we take the Pergamon altar as a valid symbol of an entire age—*Aus der Welt des Pergamonaltars,* is the title of H. E. Stier's book concerned with the rise and fall of the entire Hellenistic age.[42]

Completed in a relatively short time (between 180–160 B.C.), the altar owed something to Eastern Greek-Anatolian tradition, for the Lydian mountain god[43] as well as the Hellenistic Zeus had his open-air altars on the mountain tops. Despite enormous mythological display, its essential meaning was propaganda for the royal house of Pergamon on whose behalf Athena and Zeus and the Olympian cohorts battled the giants around the podium; and whose descent from the divine hero Herakles via Telephos was described in the more intimate "interior" frieze around the altar itself.

The new intellectual world of literature and libraries joined the world of sculpture to create the encyclopaedic iconology of the battle of giants and gods. Classical Greek art and culture were invoked in the adoption of Phidian motifs and even more of the Phidian scale. But the larger than life colossality was reserved in the Parthenon for the highest zone of the pediments. The same scale and the loudest crescendo was "puffed up" and overextended in Pergamon by continuing the display in a frieze of even height only ten feet above the ground around three and a half sides of the altar.[44] (One is reminded of Wagner's youthful attempt to emulate Beethoven by having the kettledrums beating all through a symphony, *Eine Pilgerfahrt zu Beethoven.*)

Figs. 64, 66   Conversely, the elaborate mythological biography of the Telephos frieze may have owed something to the biographic-historic traditions developed on Anatolian dynastic monuments, such as the Nereid monument at Xanthos and *Fig. 71*   the Heroa of Trysa and Limyra, especially in battle and landing scenes and land-

[42]*Aus der Welt des Pergamonaltars* (Berlin: H. Keller, 1932).
[43]John H. Kroll, by letter, June, 1971, citing coins.
[44]E. Schmidt, *Great Altar of Pergamon;* H. Kähler, *Der grosse Fries von Pergamon;* G. Kleiner, "Die Istanbuler

Platte vom pergamenischen Gigantenfries," *IstMitt* 17 (1967): 168–72; A. Schober, *Die Kunst von Pergamon,* pp. 77–120.

scape elements.[45] But the closest and most obvious alliance of the Telephos frieze is with painting and possibly with book illustration. We know the same division of the wall in painting, and P. von Blanckenhagen has suggested that the Odyssey landscapes were derived from similar biographic cyclic prototypes.[46]

Here, as in the architecture of Pergamon, we deal with the highest and most intensive expression of the Helenistic age. We know that some of the leading sculptors of the altar were Rhodians, though others came from Asia Minor.[47] Yet was it by chance that not Egypt, nor Syria, nor mainland Greece but western Anatolia produced this most concentrated expression of dynamic colossality and Baroque élan, or was there, in the Anatolian population, not all of whom were yet fully Hellenized, something which responded to this particular image of reality and ideality?

In the remarks on the altars and their sculptures we pursued a traditional religious function of Greek sculpture. In the funerary monuments we encounter a type of architecture and sculpture which was clearly rooted in native Anatolian traditions.[48] It is especially the princes and dynasts of Lycia and Caria in south-western Asia Minor who had developed these fascinating monuments.

Known to Greeks since Homeric times, when Prince Bellerophon went to Xanthos and fought the fire-spitting Chimaira, Lycia paid tribute to Athens until ca. 440 B.C. From 440 to ca. 370 Persian sovereignty was imposed upon the local princes. From ca. 370 to 360 the remarkable Lycian ruler Perikles sought to create a large and unified Lycian state. He joined in a rebellion of Anatolian satraps against the Persian king in 364 B.C. but was then driven into exile. His competitor Maussolus of Caria became the satrap and trusted governor for the Persian king.[49]

Fig. 61

I shall now examine the Nereid monument of Xanthos, the Heroon of Limyra, the Maussoleum of Halikarnassus, and the Maussoleum of Belevi from two points of view. For our general theme, they represent varying dosages of Anatolian, Persian, and Greek elements. For the function of sculpture, they place before us a novel integration with architecture, which in formal effect and meaning is quite different from the traditional use of sculpture on Greek temples and altars.

Figs. 62, 63
Figs. 64, 66

---

[45]Telephos Frieze: M. Bieber, a*ScHell*, pp. 120–21, figs. 477–78. Xanthos, Trysa, and Limyra, cf. below, ns. 49 (Xanthos); 58 (Limyra); ch. I, n. 69 (Trysa).

[46]P. von Blanckenhagen, "The Odyssey Frieze," *RömMitt* 70 (1963): 100–46.

[47]D. Thimme, "The Masters of the Pergamon Gigantomachy," *AJA* 50 (1946): 345–57; Bieber, *ScHell*, p. 114.

[48]There were, of course, the more traditional, humbler, sepulchral monuments such as the funerary stelae of the fourth and third centuries B.C. See E. Pfuhl, "Spätjonische Plastik," *JdI* 50 (1935): 9–48, figs. 1–20, and for their continuation in the so-called "Eastern Greek Reliefs" of the Hellenistic and Roman ages, ch. 4, below.

[49]J. Borchhardt, *IstMitt* 17 (1967): 165–67.

Fig. 62

Fig. 64

Fig. 65

Figs. 66, 67, 68

The name of the owner of the Heroon of Xanthos[50] is not known but he must have ruled around 400 B.C. The location of his tomb in the rocky corner of the acropolis of Xanthos is superb. The podium, 6.28 meters by 9.60 meters at the base, rises to a beautiful egg and dart profile imitated from the Erechtheion in Athens, but doubled. Just below are two friezes. The larger, mythical frieze shows Greeks battling Amazons (?). The smaller frieze is historical; it shows the siege and surrender of a city.[51]

Mesopotamian and Persian iconography, or at least Persian concepts are adopted no doubt from the court art of the satraps.[52] These concepts are also found in scenes of tribute bearers and hunters on the top frieze and on a frieze of the interior. We have already mentioned in the first chapter the Oriental affinities of the funerary meal shown in the pediment and also within the shrine.[53]

The tall, tower-like podium is now generally believed to be derived from the elevated Lycian pillar monuments surmounted by house-like sarcophagi which were found on the same citadel of Xanthos.[54] The so-called monument "G" had a larger structure on a podium which was topped by a figurative frieze.[55] Several

[50]Discovered by Charles Fellows in 1828 and transported in part to the British Museum in 1843, C. Fellows, *The Xanthian Marbles, Their Acquisition and Transmission to England* (London: John Murray, 1843). For location cf. P. Demargne, *Fouilles de Xanthos* I and P. Demargne and P. Coupel, *Fouilles de Xanthos* III:1. Reconstructions of the Nereid monument: the most recent and reliable for architecture: Demargne and Coupel, *Xanthos* III; F. Krischen, *Weltwunder*, pp. 102–3, pl. 31; "Der Aufbau des Nereidenmonuments von Xanthos," *AthMitt* 48 (1923): 69–92, pls. 8–14; E. Reisch and G. Niemann, *Das Nereidenmonument von Xanthos*. For Nereids in intercolumniations: C. Fellows, "The Ionic Trophy Monument at Xanthus," in *Travels and Researches in Asia Minor* (London: John Murray, 1852), pp. 467–68 and fig. opp. p. 459, repeated in Smith, *BMC* 2 (1900), fig. 1 (lower frieze misplaced). Sculptures: Smith, *BMC* 2, pp. 12–46, nos. 850–944; W. R. Lethaby, "The Nereid Monument Re-examined," *JHS* 35 (1915): 208–24; Picard, *Manuel* 2:2 (1939), pp. 849–73, bibl. 850, n. 2; E. Akurgal, *KunstAnat*, p. 142, fig. 95.

[51]Surrender of city: "Satrap" seated on a throne under a parasol receives an embassy (either surrendering the city, or less likely, mediating the surrender): Smith, *BMC* 2, p. 24, no. 879, description; Krischen, *AthMitt* 48 (1923): 83, pl. 14, drawing with the context of frieze; Picard, *Manuel* 2:2 (1939), p. 870, fig. 353. Neo-Assyrian prototype: Assurnasirpal II standing under an umbrella, E. Strommenger, *Five Thousand Years of the Art of Mesopotamia* (New

York: Harry N. Abrams, 1964), pl. 204, bottom; Shalmaneser III seated under umbrella, *ibid.*, pl. 210 center; standing: pl. 213 bottom; Persian king under umbrella (walking): E. F. Schmidt, *Persepolis* I (Chicago, 1953), pp. 116–17, pls. 75–76; Persian king in audience scene, compositionally similar to satrap at Xanthos: Persepolis Treasury, R. Ghirshman, *Iran* (Harmondsworth: Penguin Books, 1954), pl. 19b; H. Luschey in Schefold, *Propylaeen*, p. 299, pl. 353b, bibl.

[52]Persian elements: G. Rodenwaldt, *SSBerlin*, pp. 1034, 1038, 1040–42.

[53]Funerary meal: cf. chapter 1, above, p. 19, n. 75; Smith, *BMC* 2, pp. 27–30, nos. 886, 895; W. H. Schuchhardt, "Die Friese des Nereiden-Monuments von Xanthos," *AthMitt* 52 (1927), Beil. XV, 885, 886, 893; Picard, *Manuel* 2:2, p. 863, fig. 347; Persian tribute bearers: Schmidt, *Persepolis* I pls. 27–49; on Persian motifs cf. Rodenwaldt, *SSBerlin*, above, n. 50.

[54]Pillar monuments: Akurgal, *KunstAnat*, pp. 122–27, figs. 77–80 and color pl. V, "Sarcophagus pillar," and "Harpy Monument."

[55]Monument "G": H. Metzger, P. Coupel, *Xanthos* II, ch. 5, "L'Édifice 'G' ", pp. 49–61, figs. 7–17. It already had an external frieze around the dado course and an internal frieze as well. Reconstruction: figs. 13, 14, 16. The date is ca. 460 B.C. Cf. B. S. Ridgway, *The Severe Style in Greek Sculpture* (Princeton: Princeton University Press, 1970), pp. 24–25, figs. 33, 34.

enigmatic towers built during Achaemenid times may be compared to its square form and elevation above ground but it seems that such tower monuments as the Zendan-i-Suleyman in Pasargadae were "foundation houses" to keep the sacred Avesta writing, not funerary buildings.[56]

There is no question that the top element imitates a classical Greek temple. So close is the architectural decoration to Attic work that the architect and the leading sculptors were surely Greeks—I believe, eastern Greeks who went to Athens to take part in the great Periklean building program, stayed to work on the Erechteion, then, when Athenian finances collapsed, returned to Asia Minor to find more remunerative employment. And surely they trained and employed a school of local assistants.

Quite novel, however, is the concept of Nereids or goddesses of the Sea Breezes (*Aurai*) flying from the back of a building along two sides toward the sea to bring the departed ruler (or perhaps the ruler and his wife) to the Isles of the Blessed.[57] These *fées de la mer,* as Picard calls them, "Faeries of the Sea," are placed between the columns as if they were real people running within the architecture, even though sea waves and dolphins sculpted under their feet show them to be over the sea at the same time. Thus, there is an ambiguity as to time and space. The design achieves a striking optic effect, but breaks down the strict architectural framework by which the statuesque figures of Greek pediments had been bound.

Discovered in 1966, the Heroon of Limyra near Finike, has been claimed as the burial monument of the most famous of Lycian princes, the dynast Perikles.[58] *Fig. 61* Sited below the acropolis, but high above the coastal plain on a rock-cut terrace, 19 meters long and 18 meters deep, the Limyra monument had virtually the same *Fig. 69* dimensions as the Nereid Tomb (10.4 by 6.8 meters). The burial chamber was accessible from the south.

In the front and back of the temple there were "Caryatids" imitated from the Erechtheion instead of columns. The Caryatids wear, however, an Anatolian

[56]Iranian towers: D. Stronach, "Excavations at Pasargadae: Architectural Survey of the Zendan," *Iran* 3 (1965): 11–17, fig. 3; E. Porada, *The Art of Ancient Iran* (New York: Crown Publishers, 1965), p. 146; A. U. Pope, *A Survey of Persian Art* IV (London, New York: Oxford University Press, 1938), pl. 79.

[57]Sea Breezes: Pindar *Olympia* 2. 71–72. *Okeanides Aurai* blow in the Isles of the Blessed. Description of "Nereids" *BMC* 2, pp. 33–38, nos. 909–23.

[58]Dynast Perikles: Coins, C. M. Kraay and M. Hirmer,

Greek Coins (New York: Harry N. Abrams, 1966), pp. 361–62, no. 660.0, pl. 191; Kaeppeli Coll., Basel, from El-mali hoard, overstruck on stater of Euagoras of Salamis. Kraay remarks that one of the most famous Greek die-cutters, Eukleides, might have fled from Sicily before the Carthaginians to Lycia, and cut this striking portrait head. Specimen in A. S. Dewing Numismatic Foundation, Fogg Art Museum: Silver Stater of Perikles, 380 B.C., no. 697a. R. P. Austin, "Athens and the Satraps' Revolt," *JHS* 64 (1944): 98–100.

Fig. 70   headgear with veil. The two long sides of the monument were adorned with
Fig. 71   friezes representing historical battles of King Perikles. We see the cavalry and massed infantry going into battle. The discoverer, J. Borchhardt, dates the monument and its sculptures at ca. 380 B.C.[59]

    The style of the Limyra sculptures is rather heavily tinged with Anatolian linearism and provincialism. The style is wholly Hellenic in the sculptures of the
Figs. 72–74   Maussoleum of Halikarnassus. Recent discoveries have enriched the two major
Fig. 72   friezes of the maussoleum, the one with the Amazons and the other with charioteers.[60] The new Amazonomachy fragment, now in the museum at Bodrum, joins an Amazon slab in The British Museum; our composite photograph shows the pieces in their proper position.

    Artemisia, the widow of Maussolus, who died in 353 B.C., wanted nothing but the best. The leading architect of the day, Pytheos, together with Satyros, designed the maussoleum and made the marble chariot on top. Either four or five of the most famous Greek sculptors worked on the decoration. The exact placing and distribution of statuary on the monument is a controversial matter. Thus, some scholars place the majestic figures of Maussolus and Artemisia in the entrance, some at bottom, some in the chariot.[61]

    There can be no doubt, however, that what one might call "semi-real" function of statuary was greatly enlarged with the many guardian lions and human statues placed all along the platform and along the approaches, the horsemen in intercolumniations, and quite possibly with a great number of statues along the roof.[62]

[59]Limyra: J. Borchhardt, *AnatSt* 20 (1970): 16–17; M. J. Mellink, *AJA* 74 (1970): 169–70; Borchhardt, *IstMitt* 17 (1967): 167 with illustrations of friezes, pls. 14–15 and peplos caryatid, pl. 16. The most extensive account is "Das Heroon von Limyra—Grabmal des lykischen Königs Perikles," *AA* (1970), part 3, pp. 353–90, figs. 2–47. Concerning the reconstruction sketch (*AA* [1970], fig. 2) Borchhardt observed (by letter) that instead of a victory the central acroterion showed a group of Perseus with the head of Medusa: "Limyra Bericht 1971," *Dergi* 20 (1973): 58, figs. 2–3; "Limyra," *AJA* 78 (1974): 119, pl. 27:8. I am greatly indebted to Dr. J. Borchhardt for some excellent photographs and a reconstruction sketch.

[60]D. Strong and K. Jeppesen, "Discoveries at Halicarnassus," *ActaA* 35 (1964): 195; Jeppesen, *ActaA* 38 (1967): 53, fig. 32. B. Ashmole, *Architect and Sculptor in Classical Greece* (New York: New York University Press, 1972), p. 178, figs. 209–11.

[61]On all of Maussoleum sculptures cf. Picard, *Manuel* 4:1 (1954), pp. 1–108. Late dating: R. Carpenter, *Greek Sculpture*, p. 214 and Havelock, *Hellenistic Art*, p. 36, pl. 18 with bibl. The scholars who placed the statues in the intercolumniations are enumerated by Picard, *Manuel* 4:1, p. 80, n. 1–2 (M. Collignon, E. A. Gardner, K. von Stradonitz, more recently, J. van Breen, Picard himself). On Maussolus and Artemisia, most recently, Havelock, *Studies Hanfmann*, pp. 55–67, pls. 22–24, whose dating to the second century B.C. does not persuade me.

[62]Positioning of statuary: cf. the reconstructions of the Maussoleum: Picard, *Manuel* 4:1 (1944), p. 25, n. 1, fig. 7, p. 19; H. W. Law, "The Maussoleum," *JHS* 59 (1939), pl. 9; F. Krischen, *Weltwunder*, pl. 26 (only lions in intercolumnia); K. Jeppesen, in addition to general views from *ActaA* 38 (1967): 29–58; Akurgal, *Civilizations*, p. 232, fig. 86b (east front). Cuttings for sculpture along foot of podium and on roof pyramid steps: K. Jeppesen, "The Site of the Maussoleum at Halicarnassus Reexcavated," *AJA* 77 (1973): 336.

The elevation of the king is in the spirit of the royal graves of Iran, where the king is raised above all subjects in the reliefs on the facade.[63] One might surmise that there was an Anatolian tradition in the importance of the queen—it may go back to the regard already shown by the Hittites to their queens. On the other hand, compared to the Nereid monument of Xanthos, the Iranian scenes, customs, and costumes are less prominent. Only the Iranian hairdo of Maussolus and the attire of some of his horsemen and servants are Persian traits.[64]

Fig. 73

Fig. 74

Some Persian elements make a comeback in the strange and controversial Maussoleum of Belevi, seven miles (11 km.) north of Ephesus.[65] If M. Theuer's reconstruction is correct, three pairs of lion-griffins, traditional Achaemenid symbols of regal dignity, were flanking a vase on each of the roof edges. Paired horses stood at each corner. Less certain is the position of the female, over-lifesize statues placed higher up, especially if the roof were really pyramidal. Most of the griffins and the frieze are in the Old Museum in Izmir. Inside the cult room was a painting of Phaethon, mourned by his sisters; a Greek inscription survives.

Figs. 75, 76

Fig. 75

Fig. 76

The remarkable coffered reliefs of the colonnade ceiling carried on the traditional motif of Greeks battling centaurs on three sides. The Greeks are real Hellenistic soldiers with swords, not legendary Lapiths who fought with bare hands. On the main (north) side were two wrestlers and an umpire bestowing the palm of victory upon an athlete, with another man, perhaps a trumpeter, standing by.[66] These are probably scenes of games given in honor of the deceased. Originally, these sculptures were placed overhead. This is a departure from Greek art and akin to the skyward projections of figured scenes in Baroque ceilings.

Fig. 77

Fig. 79

The colonnaded pyramid masked a block of rock into which was cut the grave chamber. The motif of Oriental banquet, traditionally represented in relief, was translated into a huge and imposing three-dimensional statue of the owner of the grave reclining on his couch. An Oriental servant, likewise fashioned in the round, stood by.[67] Here the realism of presence of the dead reaches a new stage.

Fig. 80

Fig. 81

[63]Rock cut graves in Iran with kings on top: Porada, *Art of Ancient Iran*, 147, fig. 81; E. F. Schmidt, *Persepolis* III (Chicago, 1970), pls. 18, 40, 41, 56, 63, 70; Pope, *Survey of Persian Art* IV, pl. 80 B.

[64]Maussolus, n. 61 above. For earlier portrayal of satraps cf. Tissaphernes and Pharnabazus, M. Bieber, *ScHell*, p. 71, fig. 243–44. "Oriental servant:" H. Möbius, "Zur Barbarenstatue von Halikarnass," *AthMitt* 50 (1925): 45–50, pl. 13; *Studia Varia* (1967): 47–50, pl. 13; Horseman: Picard, *Manuel* 4:2 (1963), pp. 97–98, fig. 47; Havelock, *Studies Hanfmann*, p. 61, pl. 25, with mid-Hellenistic dating.

[65]Maussoleum of Belevi: J. Keil, *Führer*, pp. 155–60; *JOAI* 28 (1933), Beibl. 28–43; *JOAI* 29 (1935), Beibl. 105–51; *JOAI* 30 (1937), Beibl. 173–93; C. Praschniker, "Die Datierung des Mausoleums von Belevi," *AnzWien* 85 (1948): 271–93.

[66]Frieze: Keil, *JOAI* 29 (1935), Beibl. 126–28; 30 (1937), Beibl. 182–89.

[67]Ruler on couch: Keil, *JOAI* 29 (1935), Beibl. 135–38, figs. 52–53. Oriental servant: *ibid.*, p. 139, fig. 54; Izmir, Old Museum, Basmane, no. 1084. This statue takes off from Lysippan style, cf. Picard, *Manuel* 4:2, p. 649, fig. 280.

J. Keil had proposed that the great general of the Persian king Artaxerxes Ochos (359–338 B.C.), a Rhodian Greek by the name of Memnon, or his brother Mentor, might have been buried in this striking maussoleum, which was never completed[68] because Alexander the Great had taken over Asia in 334 B.C. Keil's earlier proposal envisaged a Seleucid king, Antiochus the Second, who died at Ephesus in 246 B.C. as the tenant. I believe that the very knowing, intentionally simple, early Hellenistic style of sculptures and capitals favors this identification—unless the tenant was a local worthy unknown to literary sources. The Persian lion-griffins and Orientals were no doubt popularized as regal symbols by Alexander's court and must have been used often in the Seleucid Kingdom which reached from India across Iran to the Aegean. The lion-griffins still appear on Augustus's Altar of Peace.[69]

Xanthos and Limyra are within or next to parts of citadels; Trysa and Belevi lie outside citadels in the country. Clearly, in these Anatolian principalities, the major concentration of sculptured and painted arts was on commemorating and immortalizing the ruler in his funerary monument, wherever it may have been located.

If a creative combination of sculpture, architecture, and landscape was achieved in the regal Anatolian maussolea, sculpture invaded also the public civic areas of the Greek cities. We have relatively few actual statues preserved to illustrate this development, but we have a mass of inscriptions from lost statues. Sociologically, it is, indeed, a remarkable reversal. The Greeks had long insisted that a person must be dead before he could be honored by a statue—unless he won in athletic games. However, being honored by a statue during life became a standard formula reiterated by one honorary inscription after another: virtually each benefactor of a city "shall have free meals in the Prytaneion [city club] and his statue of bronze [sometimes even of silver or gold] shall be erected in the agora, and he shall be crowned with a gold wreath. . . ."[70]

We must realize that not only sanctuaries, but agoras, council houses, senates, and special halls of honor (like the *presbeutikon* in Sardis or *gerontikon* in Nysa

[68]Keil, *Führer*, p. 160.

[69]Lion-griffins: Keil, *JOAI* 29 (1935), Beibl. figs. 43, 50; 30 (1937), Beibl. figs. 61, 62. Altar of Peace: G. Moretti, *L'Ara Pacis Augustae* (Rome: Ministero della Educazione Nazionale, 1948), pp. 40–42; E. Nash, *Pictorial Dictionary of Ancient Rome* I (London: A. Zwemmer, 1961), fig. 71, bibl. p. 63.

[70]Honorific texts: for instance, Buckler and Robinson, *Sardis* VII.1, nos. 8, 27, the typical decrees for Menogenes and Iollas; the latter received two gilded wreaths, a gilded portrait effigy, a gilded colossal portrait effigy, a gilded equestrian portrait effigy, four bronze portrait effigies, three marble portrait images, and four painted portraits.

on Maeander)[71] were populated with masses of statues. The details of this development are not well known but characteristic examples of late Hellenistic statuary display occurred in the North Market of Miletus and the Agora of Priene.[72]

Fig. 82

The task thus set—that of purposeful combination of architecture and statuary—was also taken up for the theater so that we have, for instance, in Priene, plausible reasons for the presence of two honorary statues of distinguished citizens in the reconstruction.[73]

By the end of the Hellenistic period, the literary rhetorical theory of suitability (*to prepon*) was applied in a rather simple way to the placing of honorary statuary. Statues of lawyers were suitable for the agora, statues of athletes for the gymnasium. Thus the mathematician Licymnius warned the people of Tralles not to acquire a reputation of being fools like the people of Alabanda, where "in the gymnasium the statues were all of lawyers, and in the forum of athletes holding discus or running or playing ball. Thus the unsuitable placing of statues with respect to the proper function of places where they were displayed, gave in public a bad name to the city" (Vitruvius 7.5.6).

Sculpture thus became a popular adjunct of civic life without completely losing its original tie with religious dedication. The height of this penetration of urban life by sculpture occurred in Roman times.

⁓

The title of this Chapter was adapted from the title of a famous book *Mechanization Takes Command* by the Swiss architectural critic Siegfried Gidieon. By speaking of Hellenization taking command, I mean to convey that in the overall picture,

[71]Sardis: Buckler and Robinson, *Sardis* VII.1 no. 8, line 72. Nysa: Akurgal, *Civilizations*, pp. 234–36; Ward-Perkins in *ERA*, pp. 311, 395.

[72]Schede, *Ruinen*, p. 57, figs. 68, 69; North Market Miletus: Kleiner, *Ruinen*, p. 54.

[73]A. von Gerkan, *Das Theater von Priene*, pp. 73, 79–81, pl. 8. The two statues on circular bases in front of the second and tenth intercolumniations of the proskenion were honoring Apollodoros, son of Poseidonios, honored by the people for his virtue and good will towards them, ca. 170–150 B.C., and Thrasyboulos, son of Philios, honored by the people and by his wife Megiste, 150–130 B.C. The two bronze statues on the end piers of parodos walls were dedications by stephanophoros Kleandros Kallistratou to Zeus Oympios and the people; a third votive statue, to Dionysos, patron god of the theater, was given by Apollonios, son of Apollonios. "Later more honorary statues for the same two families were placed in the passages for the spectators, and finally in the central part before the proskenion." All statues are imaginary restorations; none was preserved.

Begun around 200 B.C. this build-up of statuary decoration is a good example of the way in which sculpture served both the traditional religious votive and the new honorary votive functions.

by midsecond century before Christ, the arts of western Asia Minor had become Greek in form and in most essentials of content.

I have chosen the altar on the Greek side and the maussoleum on the Anatolian-Iranian side as examples which have particularly rich and complex materials to illustrate the process of Hellenization. We have seen how the Iranian themes which were important ideological components in Xanthos around 400 B.C. became purely traditional, semi-ornamental motifs in Belevi a century later. We have seen how the Anatolian attitude toward life, death, and the ruler became completely clothed first in Greek style, and then in Pergamon, in Greek mythology. We might say that the Anatolian elements withdrew almost to the level of subconsciousness, to basic emotional predispositions. But on this level, Anatolian emotionalism did influence the Greek tradition. The picturesque, dramatic type of Greek literature and eloquence which the Greeks themselves called "Asianic" had its closest parallel in plastic and visual arts in the so-called Hellenistic Baroque. Both movements arose in western Asia Minor during the period we have considered, and both were in essence, manifestations of a new Graeco-Anatolian synthesis.

III: *Ad Claras Asiae Volemus Urbes:* Roman Governors and Urban Renewal

We do not know when the first Roman stepped on the soil of Asia Minor, but we know who brought the Romans into Asia Minor. The same kings of Pergamon who had made Pergamon the leading center of Hellenistic architecture and sculpture, made themselves faithful allies of Rome. To help Eumenes II, the ruler who built the altar of Pergamon, against the Seleucid king Antiochus III, the first Roman army arrived in western Asia Minor in 190 B.C. The Romans did much for Pergamon: the size of the kingdom increased tenfold. In return, Eumenes' son Attalus III (ruled 138–133 B.C.) left his kingdom to the Roman people.[1] A century of strife and decline for the cities of Asia Minor followed. King Mithradates VI of Pontos overran the country in the eighties; pirates plundered the coasts. In 75 B.C. pirates captured Julius Caesar just off Miletus; his ransom was paid by a wealthy Milesian named Eukrates.[2] Pompey's success in subduing the pirates (67 B.C.) was probably celebrated by the imposing, so-called "Big Harbor Monument" at Miletus. Pompey was honored by the Milesians in 63 B.C.[3] Showing the beginning artistic connections of Asia Minor with Rome, the Late Hellenistic Triton frieze of the Harbor Monument resembles another monument set up for the wars against the pirates—the marine frieze found near the Palazzo Sta. Croce in Rome, probably a work of Hellenistic sculptors.

Fig. 83

Figs. 84, 85

Fig. 85

Fig. 86

[1]Magie, *Roman Rule,* ch. 1, "The Bequest of Attalos," pp. 3–33.

[2]M. Gelzer, *Caesar, Politician and Statesman* (Cambridge, Mass.: Harvard University Press, 1968), pp. 23–24; G.

Kleiner, *Das römische Milet* (1970), p. 121; G. Bowersock, *Augustus,* p. 8; Magie, *Roman Rule,* ch. 8, pp. 177–98.

[3]Harbor Monument: Kleiner, *Das Römische Milet,* p. 9, pls. 4–5.

Under the Late Republic, thousands of Romans came as administrators, businessmen, and even tourists to Asia Minor, among them such literary figures as Cicero, who went in 51 as proconsul for Cilicia, and Catullus. Catullus lived in Nicaea, probably in 57–56 B.C., as a member of the entourage of the governor of Bithynia, the propraetor Caius Memmius. In the charming spring poem with which Catullus takes leave from Nicaea, I have found the theme of this chapter—"let us fly to the famous cities of Asia" (46:6). Catullus is here being technical—he is in Bithynia—the great cities are in the Roman province of Asia.[4]

For these splendid cities of the Roman province of Asia, for Ephesus, Sardis, Miletus, and Pergamon, there began with the emperor Augustus an era of reconstruction and prosperity[5] which continued to gain momentum through the first and second centuries A.D. until invasions of the Goths, Sassanian Persians, and Palmyrenes, after the middle of the third century broke the golden age of Roman peace.

(As we shall henceforth be largely speaking of our era, I shall skip the A.D. and only refer to B.C. dates when needed.)

The peaceful development was frequently disrupted by natural catastrophes. Disastrous earthquakes, such as the earthquake of 17 which ruined twelve cities or that of 178 which laid Smyrna low,[6] created urgent necessity of urban renewal. Tacitus (*Ann.* 2.47) vividly describes the disaster of 17: "In the same year twelve famous cities of Asia collapsed by an earthquake which struck at night . . . immense mountains settled, plains were heaved on high, fires broke out in the ruin. The disaster struck hardest at the Sardians. . . ." A senatorial commissioner, ex-praetor Marcus Ateius, was sent to inspect and rebuild Sardis.[7] The plan of the

Figs. 87, 106, 117

gymnasium area of Sardis, so thoroughly Roman in its massive symmetry, was probably the result of this mission.[8] In a marble base built into the synagogue we have found an eloquent footnote to the destruction and rebuilding. It says that

[4]C. J. Fordyce, *Catullus: A Commentary* (Oxford: Clarendon Press, 1961), pp. xi, 209.

[5]Bowersock, *Augustus,* pp. 99–100.

[6]Cadoux, *Smyrna,* pp. 279–84; Aristeides, *Or.* 41. 762–67; 21. 429–30; 22. 439.

[7]For earthquake of A.D. 17 cf. M. Hammond, "A Statue of Trajan Represented in the Anaglypha Triani," *MAAR* 21 (1953): 162–64 on the statue to Tiberius erected by 14 beneficiary cities. For the base at Puteoli (now in Naples) cf. E. Strong, *La scultura Romana* (Firenze: Fratelli Alinari,

1923), pp. 93–94.

[8]G. E. Bates, *Sardis* M 1 (1971), maps 3, 4. The planner may well have come from Rome with the senatorial emergency commissioner. For the imperial archive in Rome where plans of all Roman colonies were kept cf. G. Carettoni et al., *La pianta marmorea di Roma antica. Forma Urbis Romae* (Rome: Libraria dello State, 1960); Th. Mommsen in F. Blume, K. Lachmann, A. Rudorff, *Die Schriften der römischen Feldmesser* 2, p. 405.

Sokrates Polemaiou Pardalas, high priest of the goddess Roma and a man of highest standing in Sardis, had built a shrine and given an image of Hera. His granddaughter Julia Lydia piously restored both after the earthquake (*meta ton seismon*)—the Hera probably stood on this very base.[9]

In addition to earthquakes, the cities suffered from conflagrations comparable to those which swept Constantinople in later ages. The Younger Pliny mentions a fire which destroyed the senate, the temple of Isis, and many houses in the city of Nicomedia, later to become one of the capitals of the empire (*Letters* 10.33).[10] Such disasters called forth the aid of the emperors, who closely supervised the finances of the cities through governors and special financial officials. For instance, after the earthquake of 17, the emperor Tiberius granted ten million sesterces and five years tax exemption to the Sardians, and Emperor Claudius paid for their aqueduct.[11]

A large part of the great programs of urban expansion and renewal from the first through the early third centuries was paid for by the cities, and by the wealthy upper class families who had become part of Roman officialdom. In Ephesus, Tiberius Julius Celsus Polemaeanus, *consul suffectus* in 92, and his son Caius Julius Aquila, *consul suffectus* in 110, were the two responsible for the building of the famous library of Celsus, while Publius Vedius Antoninus, a friend of the emperor Antoninus Pius, built a tremendous gymnasium.[12] Perhaps a member of the same family, Claudia Antonia Sabina, *femina consularis*—wife or daughter of a consul—gave means for the gorgeous marble court of the gym-

Figs. 133, 134

Figs. 104, 105

---

[9]IN 63.123. Base with cutting for plinth of statue. Back roughly chiselled showing the statue stood against the wall. H. 0.435 m.; W. 0.70 m.; Depth: 0.63 m. Fine monumental writing, probably ca. A.D. 20–30. The base was found built into the late (fourth century A.D.?) wall of the synagogue at E 93/N 9, ca. *97.00. On Sokrates Polemaiou Pardalas cf. Buckler and Robinson, *Sardis* VII.1 (1932), nos. 22, 91, 122; *OGIS*, 437–92. Ioulia Lydia thus takes back to Tiberian age the impressive series of Sardian lady benefactresses.

[10]Pliny pleaded for the creation of a fire brigade of 150 men (*fabri*), but Trajan denied his request on the grounds that such associations had proved politically turbulent. R. MacMullen, "Urban Unrest," in *Enemies of the Roman Order* (Cambridge, Mass.: Harvard University Press, 1966), ch. 5, has made a general survey of the subject which provides

interesting background.

[11]Tiberius: Tacitus *Ann.* 2.47; Claudius *Sardis* VII.1, no. 39, p. 57. In general, R. MacMullen, *HSCP* 64 (1959): 200–10, 225 n. 28; *IGRR* 4:1431, from Smyrna for an unidentified public work, pavement of the basilica to be done by a private benefactor, other work "for as much money as we may obtain from the Lord Emperor Hadrian through Antonius Polemon."

[12]Upper class benefactions, Polemaeanus: Bowersock, *Augustus*, pp. 120, 142; MacMullen, *HSCP* 64 (1959): 207–8; *Sardis* VII.1, no. 45. Vedius: Bowersock, *Sophists*, p. 47. Bowersock's *Augustus* gives a comprehensive picture of the moneyed aristocratic friends of the Romans under the late Republic and early principate, and his *Sophists* depicts an influential group of later benefactors.

nasium at Sardis.[13] These benefactors had been successful; but even more instructive for the immensely competitive programs of urban aggrandizement—which were financed partly by municipal, partly by imperial, and partly by private funds—were the causes of real or alleged failure.

Dion Chrysostomus, "The Goldmouth," professor of eloquence, preacher, and politician, was a native of Prusa, the modern Bursa, the lovely city at the foot of the Bithynian Olympus. He had made his fortune in Rome, had become a friend of the emperors Nerva and Trajan, and after his return to his native city in 96, he conceived great plans for it. He planned to make Prusa the head of a federation of cities, increase its population by compelling other towns to join it, and, in his own words, he wished "not only to beautify the city and equip it with colonnades and water supply, but also to provide it with city walls, harbors, and shipyards . . ." a new bath and a library were also part of the program.[14]

Dion ran into great difficulties in carrying out his plan. Although his scheme was initially approved by the Roman governor who endorsed it to the city council of Prusa, Dion was accused by the anti-renewal party (1) of not keeping proper accounts; (2) proceeding in an arbitrary and dictatorial fashion; (3) committing treason and lèse-majesté crimes against the emperor Trajan by placing a statue of the emperor in the library of the same precinct in which Dion's wife and son had been buried—thus, defiling the sanctity of the emperor as pontifex maximus by contact with the dead.

Trajan answered that he was not worried about the contact of his statue with the dead; he was, however, concerned about the finances.[15] To clean up the

[13]Claudia Antonia Sabina: C. R. Morey, *Sardis* V.1 (1924); *BASOR* 177 (1965): 25, inscription of the "Marble Court of the Gymnasium, 211 A.D." Cf. also E. Groag, *PIR*[2], pp. 1070, 1071, Claudia Antonia Sabina, Claudia Antonia Tatiane. T. R. S. Broughton, "Roman Asia," in T. Frank, ed. *An Economic Survey of Ancient Rome* IV (Baltimore: Johns Hopkins University Press, 1938), p. 765.

[14]Dion *Discourses* 45.12–13, given in A.D. 101–2 outline and defense of the program; 47, a speech in the public assembly of Prusa, with further defense of his construction program, comparing himself with Herakles, Homer, Pythagoras, and Aristotle (who restored Stageira after destruction by Philip) and citing with approval the ambitious urban renewal programs of Antioch (especially the thirty-six stade colonnaded street), Tarsus, Nicaea, Nicomedia, and Kaisareia and commending the removal of sacred and cemetery sites to permit building over them (47.17): "The

people of Nicomedia passed a resolution to transfer their tombs; Makrinos . . . transferred from market place of Prusa the statue and tomb of founder King Prusias," (47.18): "Dion was accused of trying to act like a tyrant and dig down (*kataskaptein*) the city and all sacred places (*ta hiera panta*). . . ." Apparently he intended to use the site of the temple of Zeus which had burned down, "yet I saved the statues from the scrap pile and they are now placed in the most conspicuous place of the city . . ." (47.25): he concedes that he built his house in a luxurious style (*polytelōs*). H. Lamar Crosby, trans. *Dion Chrysostom* IV (Cambridge, Mass.: Harvard University Press, 1946), pp. 204–5, 243–45. On Dion in general, J. von Arnim, *Leben und Werke des Dio von Prusa*.

[15]Pliny *Letters* 10.81, "Your statue is in the library . . . the alleged burial place of Dion's son and wife is in an area surrounded by colonnades . . . presumably a peristyle

finances of this rich province, he took the province away from senatorial administration under imperial administration and sent Caius Plinius Caecilius Secundus, the Younger Pliny, to Bithynia in 110 as the new governor. Pliny's reports and Trajan's replies show conspiracy to defraud the public in Nicomedia where promoters spent over three million sesterces to build an aqueduct, then pulled it down and voted 200,000 more to build another, which they did not finish. In Nicaea, two architects were fighting with each other about an overambitious plan and poor construction materials for a gymnasium. In the same city, the construction of the theater allegedly cost the phenomenal sum of ten million sesterces, and Pliny observed that "this theater was sinking into the ground and displaying enormous cracks."[16]

Figs. 88–90

It is interesting to observe that this much maligned theater still stands. Unfortunately, it has never been excavated.[17] A view clearly shows the concrete walls around the auditorium, and A. M. Schneider's plan indicates the supporting vaults of powerful masonry. Its rubbled masonry parts are sturdily, although roughly built in part with reused spoils. Its facing masonry was very nicely finished. Apparently, the builders mended their ways after Pliny's criticism. The *porticus supra caveam*, "the colonnade above the auditorium," which according to Pliny, certain private donors had promised to build—but did not build—finally got built.

Fig. 90
Fig. 88
Fig. 89

We are fortunate in having reflected in the literary sources both the Greek and the Roman attitudes toward the urban renewal program. In the so-called sophists, that is, writers, orators, lobbyists, and public relations men, Dion of Prusa and

---

courtyard before the library. . . ." This is an interesting parallel and precedent for the Celsus library in Ephesus where Iulius Celsus was buried under the library (fig. 134). Trajan's reply, Pliny *Letters* 10.82: "You know well my purpose not to create fear or terror in people or acquire reverence of my nomen by *criminibus maiestatis* . . . Dion Cocceianus must submit accounts of all public works affected under his care [*cura*]."

[16]Pliny *Letters* 10.37 to Trajan on Nicomedia; 39 on Nicaea and Claudiopolis. "The present *architectus* who it must be owned is a rival to the one first employed on the theater of Nicaea asserts that the walls, though they are 22 feet (over 6 m.) thick, are not strong enough to support the superstructure *because their core is merely rubble* and they are *not faced* with brick . . ." (interesting professional condemnation of unfaced mortared rubble). In the last named, the bath, *depresso loco defodiunt* "are digging into a depression," *"imminente . . . monte . . ."* which is not "at the foot of a hill" as translated by Crosby; I take it to refer to the danger of landslides . . . "overhanging mountain." The two letters are very important for the careful way in which the Roman government controlled the urban programs. Pliny criticizes consecutively siting, planning, and construction (the gymnasium of Nicaea is *incompositum et sparsum*, "poorly designed and scattered"). From Trajan's reply it appears that it was "too overambitious."

[17]A. M. Schneider, *Die römischen und byzantinischen Denkmäler von Iznik-Nicaea*, IstFo 16 (1943): 9–10, figs. 2–3, plan 1, bibl.

Aelius Aristeides of Hadrianoutherai and Smyrna (who lived from 129–189) we find enthusiastic local Greek advocates of urban renewal, full of ambition and rhetoric, intolerably long-winded in their historical and mythological allusions to the past greatness of their home towns and of themselves, but unquestionably generous and devoted to their cities.

Although it covers only the brief span of two years, the correspondence of the Younger Pliny and the emperor Trajan is immensely revealing for the Roman attitude—businesslike and to the point. We have learned something of the Roman procedure in initiating financing and controlling urban development. The famous legal writer Ulpian wrote early in the third century: "The provincial governor ought to go round the temples and public works to examine whether they are in proper repair . . . if any are in course of construction, he ought to see that they are completed as far as the resources of the municipality permit. . . . He ought to appoint . . . superintendents of the works (*curatores operum*) . . . and if necessary, provide military assistants (i.e., technicians, *ministeria quoque militaria*) to support them" (*Digests* 1.6.7).[18]

As Pliny's letters show, all major public building projects were subject to careful hearings by Roman authorities. The presiding governors were no amateurs. Pliny himself had considerable experience in planning and building his own ambitious villas and he commented critically on such aspects as selection of site, design, plan, and construction techniques. He acted very much like an architectural critic on a jury today.[19]

Although Trajan steadfastly rejected Pliny's requests for Roman planners, architects, and engineers, Ulpian implies that it was customary to provide technical assistance. It was said of the emperor Hadrian, who did so much for the provinces, that he travelled around with a suite of "geometers, architects, and every sort of expert in construction and decoration . . . whom he enrolled by cohorts and centuries, on the model of the legions" (Aurelius Victor *Epitome* 14.5). It is, I think, safe to say that at least during the earlier phase of Roman domination, Roman-trained architects and engineers had direct influence upon the new type of urbanism in Asia Minor.

On the other hand, as Pliny's references to local architects indicate, the initiative, the overall design, and quite certainly the artistic styling often lay in the

---

[18]MacMullen, *HSCP* 64 (1959): 209–10.
[19]H. Tanzer, *The Villas of Pliny the Younger* (1924); G.

Becatti, "Plinio il Giovane," in *Arte e gusto negli scrittori Latini* (1951), ch. 13.

hands of Greek architects trained in Hellenistic traditions.[20] This was true even of the most ambitious projects. The architect of the largest temple built under the Romans in Asia Minor, the colossal temple to the emperor Hadrian at Kyzikos (on the Dardanelles) was a Greek architect named Aristainetos, famous enough to have his name inscribed on the temple. Unfortunately, the superstructure is known to us only from fifteenth century drawings and scanty fragments.[21] It had *Fig. 91* mythological friezes over the architrave, moulded arches—a novel motif—and seventy foot high columns, and a huge pediment with the bust of the emperor in the center.

These Greek architects were responsible for the decorative splendor of the newly formed, so-called Asiatic variety of Roman architecture. They may have brought it to Rome. Another anonymous architect of the Hadrianic era, the designer of the much admired temple to Zeus Philios and Trajan in Pergamon, is thought to have come to Rome to design for Hadrian the vast classicistic temple of Venus and Roma. It is not known whether the architect of the Traianeum was the same man as the architect Aelius Nikon, father of the famous physician Galen, who took an active part in the urban renewal of Pergamon and "seems to have worked on several great new buildings."[22]

When it came to practical execution of projects, the Romans were interested in fundamentals; efficient shipping and transportation was one. Trajan approved the canal to the Lake of Nicaea over which—among other products—marble and timber for construction were to be shipped.[23] Furthermore, the Romans gloried in road engineering. The same emperor, Trajan, wrote in an inscription about the road he built from Miletus to Didyma: "turning his attention to the road necessary for the sacred rites of Apollo [of Didyma], *he cut down the hills and filled in the valleys* and undertook, completed, and dedicated the road through Quintus Iulius Bal-

---

[20]G. Downey, "Byzantine Architects, Their Training and Methods," *Byzantion* 18 (1948): 99–118; MacMullen, *HSCP* 64 (1959): 211, 227. T. R. S. Broughton, *Economic Survey* IV (1938): 850 on public architects permanently in the service of communities. Nor should we forget that what we call urbanism or urban planning was already a specialized office in Hellenistic cities with such boards as the *Astynomoi* whose duties are described in a famous law code preserved in Pergamon: A. H. M. Jones, *Greek City*, p. 213, and bibl., p. 349, n. 5.

[21]B. Ashmole, "Cyriac of Ancona and the Temple of Hadrian at Cyzicus," *Journal of the Warburg and Courtauld Institutes* 19 (1956): 179–91, esp. 187–88, the inscription copied by Cyriacus of Ancona. C. C. Vermeule, *ImpArt* (1968): 256; Ward-Perkins, *ERA*, pp. 392, 573, bibl; F. Eichler, "Zum Partherdenkmal von Ephesos," *JOAI* 49 (1968–1971): 133, fig. 32. H. P. Laubscher, *IstMitt* 17 (1967): 211, pls. 22–23; F. Eichler, *JOAI* Beiheft 2 (1970): 133, fig. 32.

[22]Bowersock, *Sophists*, 60 = *PIR*² G 24.

[23]Canal Project: Pliny *Letters* 10.41; F. G. Moore, "Three Canal Projects, Roman and Byzantine," *AJA* 54 (1950): 97–111, fig. 1.

bus, the proconsul with Lucius Passerius Romulus, *legatus propraetore* in charge.''[24] This pride in great engineering feats, such as leveling mountains, echoes the famous inscription on the column of Trajan in Rome: "and to disclose how high a mountain was taken down."[25]

Public utilities were for the Romans a paramount concern. Already under Augustus, Ephesus received an aqueduct from Caius Sextius Pollio (4–14), a Romanized native; the emperor Claudius gave one to Sardis; Trajan approved the measures for water supply of Nicomedia; and Hadrian undertook to provide good water for Troy.[26] A typical Roman public fountain was built at Miletus around 100 to honor the father of Trajan. Three large vaulted chambers were fed by an aqueduct. Hidden behind a decorative facade, they provided the water for an open basin some fifty feet long and twenty wide (16.15 meters by 6.39 meters).[27]

Figs. 92, 93

Although for political reasons, Trajan denied the formation of a fire fighters association at Nicaea, he approved purchase of fire fighting equipment and enjoined fire prevention upon house owners.

The Greek cities, on the other hand, pushed for gymnasia, baths, and theaters as major status symbols—along with temples and shrines to emperors and the right of imperial cult. Trajan's amused but tolerant remark: "Our little Greeks (*Graeculi*) love gymnasia . . ." concerns that type of urban complex which was a major creative achievement of Asiatic urbanism, a synthesis of Hellenistic gymnasium and the Roman bath.[28] With its multiple functions as civic center, club house, leisure area, school, and place of worship of emperors, the gymnasium now replaced the palace and the temple as the major concern of Asiatic cities.

When we turn from written evidence to actual remains, it must first be said that Roman foundations of new cities were rare in western coastlands of Asia Minor and there was little opportunity to use the overall standard Roman colonial plan.[29] A small city like Priene retained a basically Hellenistic appearance until the Byzantine age. It is rather the enlargement and transformation of *existing* towns

[24]Kleiner, *Ruinen,* 29. *CIL* III 14 195[43] plus *CIL* III 7150 from Didyma. I owe the information and new translation to the kindness of T. R. S. Broughton.

[25]Inscription from Column of Trajan: *CIL* VI, 960. E. Nash, *Pictorial Dictionary* I, p. 286, fig. 337.

[26]C. Sextius Pollio: J. Keil, *Führer,* p. 133; *Forschungen in Ephesos* 3 (Vienna: Ed. Hölzel, 1923), p. 256, A.D. 4–14. Troy, MacMullen, *HSCP* 64 (1958): 207–8. In general, Jones, "The Public Services," *Greek City,* ch. 16.

[27]Nymphaeum. Miletus: Kleiner, *Ruinen,* figs. 85–86; J.

Hülsen, *Milet* I:5 (Berlin and Leipzig: Walter de Gruyter, 1919), pl. 48.

[28]Trajan in Pliny *Letters* 10.40. "*Gymnasiis indulgent Graeculi.* . . . Perhaps the Nicaeans were too big-hearted in tackling its construction. . . . They must be satisfied with what they can afford. . . ." On the development of gymnasia, J. Delorme, *Gymnasion* (Paris, 1960); Boëthius and Ward-Perkins in *ERA,* pp. 292, 399–403.

[29]Jones, *Greek City,* p. 61, lists the few Roman colonies and foundations known.

and cities, their expansion for a growing population, the raising of the standard of living through better supply system, utilities, and baths, the development of large facilities for social, intellectual, and leisure functions, and the expression of this revitalized, Romanized Greek polis in luxurious, nearly Baroque architectural forms—that made the cities of Asia the envy of the empire.[30]

A highly effective device in reshaping the cities was the colonnaded avenue. These were called "Syrian colonnades" because the earliest great example was built by Herod the Great at Syrian Antioch around 20 B.C., possibly on the occasion of a visit by Emperor Augustus. The earliest example in Asia Minor was perhaps the Main Avenue of Sardis, planned after the earthquake of 17. Eighty years later Dion enthusiastically recommended "Syrian colonnaded" streets for Prusa. These colonnades were a new synthesis from the Greek stoas and the new Roman *viae porticatae*.[31]

Figs. 87, 181

A second compositional device which helped shape the new image of the cities was the two- and three-storied so-called Asiatic facade. Introducing a vertical emphasis into the low contours of Greek cities, this new creation could be used with particular effect to provide stage-like monumentality to gates and fountains, as in the Nymphaeum of Miletus and to terminate long vistas, for instance, in the gate of the South Market in Miletus.[32]

Fig. 93

From general planning we now turn to housing. How big were these cities in terms of population? In the only ancient reference which specifically includes slaves and women, the famous physician Galen stated that his native city of Pergamon had 120,000 people in the second century. Other plausible guesses are: Ephesus, the largest city of the Roman province in Asia, perhaps had 200,000; Sardis was about the size of Pergamon; Smyrna had about 100,000 people (according to Cadoux).[33]

---

[30]Ward-Perkins in *ERA*, pp. 391–406, has a masterly account of architecture in "The Western Coastlands." To the literary and archaeological evidence for urban renewal must be added the interesting representations on coins, for which examples are given by P. R. Franke, *Kleinasien zur Römerzeit* (Munich: C. H. Beck, 1968), p. 15, figs. 71–84, 102, 201.

[31]Colonnades: Ward-Perkins, *ERA*, p. 417; Dion *Discourses* 47.16; G. Downey, *A History of Antioch in Syria* (1961), pp. 169, 173, figs. 6–11; D. Claude, (1969), pp. 245–46, pl. 4.

[32]"Asiatic Facade:" Ward-Perkins in *ERA*, pp. 405–6; Nymphaeum: Kleiner, *Ruinen*, pp. 144–48, fig. 85; Hülsen,

Milet I:5, pl. 63; South Market: H. Knackfuss, *Milet* I:7 (1924), p. 142, pl. 17, fig. 127 comments (pp. 51–58) on the combination of Hellenistic and Roman elements in the Roman design for the South Market.

[33]H. Rowell, *Rome in the Augustan Age* (1962), p. 103; Galen, *De cognoscendis curandisque animi morbis (Peri diagnoseos kai therapeias ton en tei hekastou psychei idion pathon)*, "On the diagnosis and cure of disturbances of the soul —particular to each person," ed. C. G. Kuhn, (Leipzig, 1823), vol. 5, ch. 9, p. 49: "If we now have about 40,000 citizens, and if you now add the women and the slaves, you will find twelve times 10,000 [i.e., 120,000] people . . . ," (literally, "you will find that you are richer than

Figs. 94, 95
Figs. 96, 97

How was the housing problem resulting from this increase of population solved? Only in recent years, when multiple-storied terraced apartment houses were found in Ephesus, has it become clear that as in Rome, Ostia, and Antioch, building upward must have prevailed in Asia Minor. Cumulatively, these "Houses on the Slope" in Ephesus reached a height of five stories, but the individual units were grouped in two stories around peristyle courts. No detailed analysis of the plans is yet available. It is clear, however, that these are real, continuous urban blocks, which developed from the individual peristyle house.[34] What was remarkable about these houses was the downward diffusion of palatial luxuries and their imitations in interiors and furnishings. In Ephesus these houses had excellent paintings such as the portrait of Sokrates of the first century, and the Muse Thallia (if it be she with two lambdas) of the third century.[35] Religious art

Fig. 98

Fig. 99

appears in charming domestic shrines[36] as that of Artemis and of hero reliefs for worship;[37] mosaics and statuettes of marble, alabaster, and ivory.[38]

All these furnishings reflect the same attempt to raise, if not mass-dwellings then at least the middle-class dwellings, to the same make-believe, pseudo-palatial splendor as in Rome, Pompeii, and Ostia. What characterizes the entire process of this urban program was that a genuine synthesis took place between the Hellenistic Greek and the Roman elements. This was true of planning; it was true of compositional units; it was also true of construction.

---

these 120,000 people"). Galen lived from A.D. 129–99. Cf. Bowersock, "The Prestige of Galen," *Sophists* 58–75. Other population data, Magie, *Roman Rule*, pp. 2, 144 n. 50; Cadoux, *Smyrna*, p. 186. For closely argued estimates of Ostia and Rome with only 27,000 for Ostia, cf. J. E. Packer, "The Insulae of Imperial Ostia," *MAAR* 31 (1971): 70. Cf. R. P. Duncan-Jones, "City Population in Roman Africa," *JRS* 53 (1963): 85–90 for North Africa. For the Byzantine period (6th century) see the much lower figures given by Claude (1969), pp. 163–64.

[34]Slope houses, Ephesus: General: Keil, *Führer* (1964), pp. 121–22, bibl., fig. 65 and plan of region. R. Meriç *Ephesus Guide* (1971), pp. 26–30; F. Eichler, *AnzWien* 100 (1963): 51–56, fig. 3; 101 (1964): 42–44; 102 (1965): 98–101; 103 (1966): 13–14; 105 (1968): 84–86, fig. 2, pl. I; H. Vetters, *AnzWien* 107 (1970): 7–13, figs. 1 (plan), 3, 4, detailed plan of Houses 1, 2, and elevation, fig. 7; pls. 3a–b; "Zum Stockwerkbau in Ephesus," *Mélanges Mansel* (Ankara, 1974), pp. 69–92, pls. 35–50. F. Fasolo, *L'architettura romana a Efeso* (1962), pp. 15–16, fig. 6, pointed out that the areas of ca. 100 hectares (ca. 250 acres) in the immediate urban

area would be insufficient for a population of 200,000. He thought the city might have spread into Selenus Valley.

[35]Sokrates: *AnzWien* 101 (1964): 44, pl. 4, first century of our era; Muse Klio, pl. 3 (with Artemis); paintings from Euripides' *Orestes* and *Iphigeneia* and Menander's *Sikyonioi* and *Perikeiromene*, *AnzWien* 105 (1968): 86–89, fig. 3, pl. 2. V. M. Strocka, "Theaterbilder aus Ephesos," *Gymnasium* 80 (1973): 362–80, pls. 16–20.

[36]Artemis: R. Fleischer, "Späthellenistische Gruppe vom Pollionymphaeum," *JOAI* 49 Beiheft 2 (1968–71): 176, fig. 14, ca. A.D. 150–200.

[37]Hero Relief: Eichler, *AnzWien* 107 (1970): 12–13, pl. 2c, Hellenistic, set into a wall of the third century A.D. A room perhaps devoted to the cult of the dead contained three "funerary meals" reliefs, one still in place in its niche, and had a painted red snake. Eichler, *AnzWien* 100 (1963): 54–55, pl. 2.

[38]Mosaics: *AnzWien* 107 (1970): 13, pl. 5, Nereid (or Venus) and Triton. Statuettes and reliefs, *ibid.*, pp. 14–19, pls. 6b–9b.

Inspired by the Roman use of concrete, the builders of Asia Minor developed a new building system which permitted adaptation—but not complete imitation—of Roman vaulted architecture. The new material in Asia was mortared rubble laid to form very thick walls (six feet are common); a variant with interven- *Fig. 100* ing bonding courses of brick was fully developed by the second century, the date of the central building of the gymnasium of Sardis. (At Sardis, the victory of mortared rubble over traditional Hellenistic masonry seems directly connected with the Roman-sponsored renewal program after the earthquake of 17.) In the fully developed Asiatic system, strong masonry piers linked by heavy stretches of rubble-and-brick walls carried the major loads. According to John Ward-Perkins, the Asiatic materials "lacked the strength needed for the creation of vaulting in a fully developed Roman manner,"[39] but quite sizeable spans *were* achieved with a sophisticated distribution of loads and stresses, as indicated by the 40-foot vaulted span over the swimming pool unit of the gymnasium at Ephesus.[40] *Fig. 101*

It was again Asia Minor that brought to highest pitch the use of marble revetments to cover the brick and rubble walls. Known as *skoutlosis,* a term derived from Latin *scutula,* "little shield," or "shield-like pattern of cut marble," the wall was sheathed with brilliant marble slabs hung from iron hooks over a thick layer of red cement grout.[41] Time and again, we read in inscriptions: "He gave the entire skoutlosis," (*ten skoutlosin pasan*), as in the earliest donor inscription of the Synagogue of Sardis.[42] We have sought to capture something of the coloristic effect in the actual reconstruction of a bay in the Main Hall of the Synagogue, but *Fig. 102* for the total impact of such an interior with marble walls and marble floor, we must rely on reconstructions in drawing, such as the view of the Hall for Imperial Cult, the *Kaisersaal* of the Harbor Baths in Ephesus (second century) in figure 139.[43] This is also a splendid example of the use of the niched aedicular Asiatic *Fig. 139* facade to decorate an *interior* space.

I alluded to the redistribution of major functions within the cities. Even on this small scale plan of Ephesus we can see that the traditional religious and civic *Fig. 103* political elements, the temples, the theater, and the agora, held their traditional

[39]Construction: Ward-Perkins, *ERA,* p. 387.

[40]F. Fasolo, "La Basilica del Consilio di Efeso," *Palladio* I–II, N.S., vol. 6 (1956), fig. 18. The subject of "Asiatic" construction is treated in greater detail in Fasolo, *L'architettura romana di Efeso,* p. 21.

[41]Skoutlosis: L. Robert, *NIS,* p. 50; Ward-Perkins, *ERA,* p. 411. Cf. G. Becatti, *Scavi di Ostia* VI (Rome, Libreria dello Stato, 1969), p. 128.

[42]Sardis Synagogue: L. Majewski, *BASOR* 187 (1967): 47–50; Robert, *NIS,* pp. 49–54.

[43]Harbor Baths: Miltner, *Ephesos,* fig. 35; Keil, *Führer,* pp. 80–83, fig. 40; *FoEphesos* I, pp. 182, 185. Cf. the discussion by Fasolo, *L'architettura romana di Efeso,* p. 29, fig. 15.

places, but up to eight percent of the city area was occupied by vast gymnasium-bath complexes.[44] It is interesting that even in antiquity, the Ephesians were reproved for the luxury of their baths by Apollonius of Tyana, who may have blamed these fashions on Roman customs.[45]

Fig. 105   In the plan of the Vedius Gymnasium the two component elements of this new type of social center may be clearly discerned—the Roman imperial bath on the left was added to the Greek athletic exercise ground, the palaestra, on the right. Opening onto the court was the Hall of Imperial Cult, which also served as a banquet hall. Roman Numeral VI was dressing rooms, IV was swimming pools, VII was a vast hall for general concourse and exercise, V was cold bath, XI was tepid bath, and XV-XIX were claimed as hot baths.[46]

Figs. 87, 106   To illustrate the artistic effect of these great civic monuments, let us examine Sardis where we have been restoring part of a gymnasium covering five acres. The central building of red brick dates before 166.[47] In our plan the rectangular palaestra is on the right; at the bottom right is the synagogue. Rising proudly between the palaestra and the central building is the so-called Marble

Fig. 107   Court, originally, perhaps, a Hall for Imperial Cult. We have just completed its partial restoration. Dated between February 211 and February 212, its dedicatory inscription celebrated the emperor Caracalla, his mother Julia Domna, and his brother Geta. Caracalla later, however, killed Geta, and Geta's name is erased from the dedication.[48]

This is an example of the rich Asiatic decorative style in full bloom. We have learned from the inscription that two noble ladies, Claudia Antonia Sabina and Flavia Politte helped the city to pay—*echryseothe de pan to ergon*, "and the entire work was gilded." Even if only the capitals and friezes were gilded, this must have been a staggering display of gold, quite in the tradition of Croesus.

The syncopated rhythm of the upper story, refinements, such as thicker and thinner columns alternating in centers of the three sides, prospects through screen colonnades and the vibrating liveliness of ornament—the latter strik-

[44]I owe the plan and marking to the kindness of A. Bammer, cf. *FoEphesos* VII.

[45]Philostratus *Vita Apollonii* 1.4, 1.13, 1.16.4 cited by C. P. Jones, *Plutarch and Rome*, p. 127. In contrast to H. Fuchs, *Der geistige Widerstand gegen Rom*, p. 49, Jones does not believe that an anti-Roman point was intended.

[46]Vedius Gymnasium: Keil, *Führer*, pp. 56–61, fig. 27, bibl.

[47]Lucius Verus Base: *BASOR* 154 (1959): 14, fig. 4; S. Johnson, *BASOR* 158 (1960): 7–10, figs. 2, 3 (inscription).

[48]Marble Court: *BASOR* 162 (1961): 40–41, *BASOR* 166 (1962): 46–48; 170 (1963): 37–38; 174 (1964): 25–30; 177 (1965): 21–27; 182 (1966): 32–34; 187 (1967): 52–60; 191 (1968): 34–35; 199 (1970): 43–44; 203 (1971): 18–20. Dedicatory inscription, *BASOR* 162 (1961): 42; 177 (1965): 24–25, fig. 23. For circulation of bathers compare Fig. 106.

Figs. 108, 109

ingly displayed in the head capitals of the colonnaded screen—made the
Sardis "Marble Court" a shining example of that great creation which I have
alluded to as the "Asiatic Facade."[49] Gymnasia, libraries, theaters, nymphaea,
and aqueducts were the amenities of civilized life looking for comfort and education which continued as the preponderant aspect of the cities of Roman Asia.

We may now briefly consider the architectural expressions of spiritual and
religious life which had become recessive or stagnant. Here a great cleavage and
conflict began to be felt as early as the first century. The theater changed from a
place of ritual performances in honor of the god of wine Dionysus to a place of
public performances of oratorical kind, such as the great show pieces of speeches
given by the sophists, and eventually it became a place of popular assembly even
for political matters, thus leading to the role assumed by the circus in Byzantine
times. It was in the theater of Ephesus[50] that the great riot took place, when the *Fig. 114*
people of Ephesus "with one voice for a space of two hours cried: Great is Diana
of the Ephesians" (*Acts* 19.18, 34). The outbreak was caused by Saint Paul who
had told the silversmith Demetrios that "they be no gods that are made with
hands."

Demetrios had been making little silver temples for Artemis of Ephesus; but
the time of the Grecian temple was passing. The last great structures of this
traditional type, such as the temple of Zeus and Mother of Gods, *Meter Steunene,*
at Aizani in Phrygia were built in the second century. The view of the Hadrianic
temple in Ionic style was taken before it was damaged by earthquake in 1970. The *Fig. 110*
bust in the foreground is an acroterion from the top of the temple, probably
showing the Mother of Gods.[51]

Already at the same time, the god who had really devout believers, the god of
healing Asclepius, was worshipped in an untraditional Pantheon-like rotunda in *Fig. 111*
Pergamon. This famous sanctuary was rebuilt by a Romanized local aristocrat,

---

[49]Ward-Perkins, *ERA,* pp. 405–6, figs. 152–53, pl. 211.

[50]Miltner, *Ephesos,* pp. 30–32 estimates the capacity of
the theater at 24,000. According to W. Alzinger, *Stadt,* p.
81, the earliest phase was Hellenistic, early third century
B.C.; change of stage building ca. early second century
B.C.; great Roman rebuilding, between A.D. 40 and 112.
Two-storied stage building finished by A.D. 66 was being
built in A.D. 57 during the riot in the theater against Paul.
Between A.D. 140 and 144 the front seats were removed for
better visibility. Midsecond century, third story added to
stage. Later repairs, third century A.D. and last rebuildings

already Byzantine. Alzinger has a good discussion, pp.
72–80. For discourses of sophists in the theater, cf.
Cadoux, *Smyrna,* p. 274, on Aristeides.

[51]Temple of Zeus at Aizani: R. Naumann, "Das Heilig-
tum der Meter Steuene," *IstMitt* 17 (1967): 218–47. According to Akurgal, *Civilizations,* pp. 268–69, Naumann has
proved that Kybele was worshipped in the barrel-vaulted
substructure of the temple. An inscription mentions Zeus
and Kybele together as major deities of Aizani. The central
acroterion was male over the pronaos (front porch) while
that over the opisthodomos was a female bust.

Lucius Cuspius Pactumeius Rufinus, consul in 142. The other circular building seen in the reconstruction was perhaps for the miraculous cures.[52] This was a non-Hellenistic type of structure. We may say that the untraditional cults, which were really alive, called for untraditional architecture. This is also true of the remarkable Serapeion of Miletus, a temple for the Egyptian gods. Serapis, a Greco-Egyptian agricultural divinity was apparently assimilated to the great Syrian Sun God who was one of the most vigorous competitors of Christ. The temple was given to Miletus around 270—280 by Julius Aurelius Menekles. The

Fig. 115   plan shows a classical porch with Ionic columns, but the shrine is a basilican hall about 75 feet by 40 feet (22.5 meters by 12.5 meters) with a small shrine on a platform at the back.[53] The front porch, called the "pronaon" in the temple inscription, had ceiling coffers with busts of gods, including the Apollo of Didyma,

Figs. 112, 113   Hermes, and the Muses, and a pediment with the Sun God-Sarapis in center.

Another important basilican hall of religious character, which probably existed in the late second and third centuries is the colossal Synagogue of Sardis, some 300 feet long. Like the Serapeion of Miletus it had little shrines at the back of the hall, but instead of one, it had two of them, one probably for keeping the

Figs. 116, 181, 184   Scriptures, the other perhaps for sacred utensils. We shall come back to the Synagogue when we speak of Constantinian buildings in chapter 5. Here I want

Fig. 116   to point out that the hall having started in Phase I as part of the gymnasium was either actually used or was about to be used as a civic Roman basilica, a court house in Phase II, when, perhaps with approval of the emperor Lucius Verus, it was turned over to the Jewish community.[54] The transfer to the Jews initiated Phase III, which lasted from possibly 166 to ca. 300 or even 350 of our era.

Its enormous size and capacity of at least a thousand people bespeaks a very large and influential Jewish community to whom, indirectly, the important early Christian church father Meliton addressed many admonitions in his homily on the Pascha. Meliton was active as a bishop of Sardis from ca. 140 to ca. 190. The Greek

[52]Bowersock, *Sophists,* pp. 60-61, "the Asclepieum was a well-known wonder in later antiquity and is several times alluded to as *Rouphinon alsos,* 'the grove of Rufinus,' in Byzantine epigrams." Ward-Perkins in *ERA,* pp. 388–89, 393–94, fig. 148 plan; pl. 206 second circular building. Aerial photograph: O. Ziegenhaus and G. de Luca, *Pergamon* XI.1, part 1, *Das Asklepieion,* pls. 1, 2.

[53]H. Knackfuss, *Milet* I:7, pp. 180–210; Kleiner, *Ruinen,* p. 46.

[54]Synagogue shrines: *BASOR* 170 (1963): 41, figs. 26, 31; 191 (1968): 31, fig. 25; 203 (1971): 17, fig. 11, after restoration; fig. 10, drawing of four phases of synagogue. For Hebrew inscription, possibly to emperor Verus, according to I. Rabinowitz, *BASOR* 187 (1967): 25. For description of synagogue, G. M. A. Hanfmann, "Ancient Synagogue of Sardis," Fourth World Congress of Jewish Studies, *Papers* 1 (1967): 37–42, figs. 1–15.

papyrus which has preserved his oration has been described by an eminent British church historian as "the most important find of patristic literature made in the 20th century." In view of the great wealth and power of the Jewish community of Sardis, it is perhaps not surprising that we find Meliton antagonistic, and indeed, accusing Israel of refusing and killing Christ.[55] The most extraordinary thing about the Sardis Synagogue is made evident in the birdseye view of the gym-   *Fig. 117*
nasium complex with the synagogue appearing as the basilican building on the left. We have here a huge Jewish assembly hall functioning as an integral part of a Roman-Asiatic gymnasium.

When in the time of the Maccabees (2.4.14) in the second century B.C., the high priest Jason and the liberals petitioned King Antiochus IV for a gymnasium, the truly religious Jews condemned this as "abominable and unheard of wicked-ness." In those days you were either a Jew or you went to the gymnasium, but not both. Now, three hundred years later, in the highly assimilated communities of Roman Asia Minor, the synagogue itself had become part of the gymnasium. We know from inscriptions that three members of the Jewish community were in the Roman imperial administration (of the province) and that at least nine were city councillors.[56] We must not forget, however, that not only the Jewish com-munities, but also the gymnasium had changed. Under the later Roman Empire, social, educational, and religious pursuits began to overshadow athletics. In Justin the Martyr's *Dialogue with Tryphon* (ca. A.D. 150), the Jew Tryphon and the Chris-tian Justin dispute about God while walking in the colonnade of a gymnasium at Ephesus.[57]

Let us again examine our original theme: what is Anatolian, what is Greek, what is Roman in this urban renewal and grandiose architecture of the Asiatic Baroque of the Roman era? The Anatolian element was by now fused with Hel-lenistic Greek and it had no formal equivalent (in architecture). It lay in the emotional approach to life, in the emergence of violent pagan and Christian sects, in the fragmentary survival of age-old religious beliefs, as witness, for instance,

[55]A. T. Kraabel, "Melito the Bishop and the Synagogue at Sardis: Text and Context," in *Studies Hanfmann*, pp. 77-85, with refs. For the Homily on the Passion cf. C. Bonner, *Studies and Documents*, ed. K. and S. Lake, p. xii. A Coptic papyrus has since appeared: W. H. Willis, Ninth International Congress of Papyrology, Oslo, 1958, *Proceed-ings*, p. 384.

[56]*BASOR* 187 (1967): 32, one procurator (*apo epitropon*) two *auditores tabularii;* since then a Jewish count (*comes*) has appeared on a mosaic found in 1971. For Jewish members of curia in the time of Justinian, Claude, p. 113, Justinian, *Novellae*, p. 45, a.537.

[57]Justin, *Dialogue with Trypho*. The location is given as Ephesus by Eusebius, *E.H.* 4:18. T. R. Glover, *The Conflict of Religions in the Early Roman Empire*, p. 176.

Fig. 118   the resurgence of the strange vegetation goddess, perhaps a pre-Greek "Artemis of the Swamps" on the small, fine temple of Hadrian at Ephesus.[58] One senses a correlation between this emotionalism and the pictorialism which distinguished the architecture and sculpture of Roman Asia Minor—as illustrated in the lux-
Fig. 117   uriant ornamentation of the temple of Hadrian.

I have stressed that urbanism and arts of Asia Minor under the Romans present a creative synthesis of Greek and Roman tradition. These two elements were held in balance during the Roman imperial age, but eventually, one element emerged as dominant. When we look at early Byzantine cities, at their public structures, at their synagogues and churches,[59] we see that Roman planning of vast symmetrical complexes, Roman composition of vaulted and domed spaces, and Roman-inspired construction technique of mortared rubble and brick had dominated the scene, while Hellenistic masonry construction, columnar facades, and colonnaded peristyle courts became integral but subordinate features.[60]

A parallel development had occurred in the general cultural situation. The wealthy educated class of the Greek citizens, as C. P. Jones has shown in his fine book on *Plutarch and Rome*,[61] sympathized with Rome, preached a lesson to the eastern cities which converged with Roman interest, and increasingly integrated itself not only politically and socially, but also ideologically into the overall framework of the Roman Empire. In early Byzantine times, from Constantine to Heraklios, the citizens of the cities of western Asia Minor continued to speak Greek but they called themselves *Rhomaioi*—"Romans."[62]

[58]Temple of Hadrian: Ward-Perkins in *ERA,* pp. 393, 408, frontispiece (color).

[59]D. Claude, "Monuments," part 1, ch. 3.

[60]Ward-Perkins, *ERA,* pp. 410–11, "The contribution of Asia Minor" seems to emphasize the element of Hellenistic survival and acknowledges the existence of Syro-

Hellenistic elements.

[61]C. P. Jones, *Plutarch and Rome,* pp. 129–30. He concludes that the Greek cities thus became part of "a system that preserved what it admired, and stayed alive."

[62]R. Jenkins, *Byzantium and Byzantinism,* Lectures in Memory of Louise Taft Semple (Cincinnati, 1963), pp. 6–7.

IV: The Social Role of Sculpture
in Roman Cities
of Western Asia Minor

In this chapter, I should like to attempt to sketch some aspects of the social distribution and functions of sculpture in that highly prosperous society which developed in Asia Minor in Hellenistic and Roman times. These aspects are: the social stratification of sculpture; the various functions of sculpture; and sculpture as reflection of ideology and social ideas.

For once, I should like to start not from the top but from the bottom—from the small towns and villages of the countryside. The modest dedication is to a very native god, the Moon God Mên Motelleites, by a woman Trophime for her adopted son Ioulianos, her *threptos,* or *alumnus*. It is dated to the year A.D. 228 (313 Sullan era). The classical figure, a distant descendent of late classical goddesses, has been flattened and has become almost a sign for emphatic gesture of prayer. The piece comes from Gölde in Maeonia, the volcanic region of so-called "Burned Lydia" to the east of Sardis. The donoress was underprivileged. Unlike the great majority she had not become a Roman citizeness in A.D. 212.[1] Here we are close to the native Anatolian undertow of rustic life. The form is Greek but nearly broken down. Socially, the reliefs are private communications from a person to his god, something that could occur on all social levels, but was particularly important and genuine in the lower classes of villages and small towns.

The other piece is from the gate jamb of a Roman estate in the plain of Sardis. It seems to show a snake-legged being and two dancing warriors, perhaps the

Fig. 119

Fig. 120

[1]Sardis Expedition, NoEx 62.26; L. Robert, *NIS* (1964): 35–36, pl. 3:1.

Kouretes.[2] The art and subject are perhaps somewhat more sophisticated; we may be moving here among substantial estate owners in the syncretistic circles where Mithraic-Iranian religious tradition survived in attenuated form.[3]

Native Anatolian cults, as J. Keil had once very plausibly shown for Lydia, survived into the Roman age under a thin veneer of Hellenization.[4] Although the Lydian tongue, according to Strabo (13.4.17; C 631) had died out by the time of Augustus, Phrygian had not; and when Saint Paul healed the cripple at Lystra the people "lifted up their voices in the speech of Lykaonia . . ." (*Acts* 14.11).[5]

It was the country of old and primitive rites and of mendicant priests of the Great Mother who cut and mutilated themselves. Even at the apogee of Roman power, life in rustic Asia was neither easy nor wholly safe. Although its locale is Thessaly, I always thought the vivid descriptions in "The Golden Ass" would apply equally to rural life in Roman Asia Minor—villagers turning out at night against would-be plunderers; robbers attacking travellers; Roman centurions bullying villagers; priests of Great Mother wandering about cheating—and there would have been rituals, miracles, and witches, though perhaps not as powerful as the famous witches of Thessaly.[6]

We must remember this hard side of native rustic life if we are to appreciate both the built-in resistance to Hellenization and the extraordinary degree to which Greek anthropomorphic art did penetrate the countryside under the Roman Empire. From the same small town as the votive of Trophime, from Gölde, came an unfinished torso of Herakles, a most explicit testimony that such a statue was made locally; and, one would have to say from its design, that it was made by a

---

[2]Sardis Expedition, NoEx 59.65. A giant seated on a rock supports two warriors with shields and helmets, who hold aloft a third figure. Provenance: Yilmaz Köy.

[3]A. Schober, *Der Fries des Hekataions von Lagina IstFo* 2 (1933). Kouretes: F. Cumont, *Oriental Religions*, pp. 65–66; F. Saxl, *Mithras* (Berlin: Verlag Heinrich Keller, 1931), pp. 88, 90; A. B. Cook, Zeus: *A Study in Ancient Religion* II.2, p. 1288 III.2, p. 1233 (Cambridge University Press, 1940).

[4]J. Keil, "Die Kulte Lydiens," *AnatSt Ramsay* (1923), pp. 239–66.

[5]K. Holl, "Das Fortleben der Volkssprachen in Kleinasien in nachchristlicher Zeit," *Hermes* 43 (1908): 240–54; A. H. M. Jones, *Greek City*, pp. 289–90; G. Neumann, *Weiterleben*, pp. 43, 106 is a comprehensive study of survival of Anatolian words. On p. 61 he cites a Lydian word in an inscription of 47 B.C., and agrees with

Holl that Isaurian (Lycaonian) lived on until at least the fifth century of our era.

[6]Apuleius *The Golden Ass* 1.7–13, 2.1. A lively picture of cities and sanctuaries of Roman Asia Minor appears in Philostratus, *Life oupollonius of Tyana* (for instance, 1.17, riots because of baths [Ephesus]; 4.10, death of an evil demon masquerading as old man [Ephesus]). For the hard realities of rural life, cf. Magie, *Roman Rule*, pp. 679–80 on complaints of the villagers of Araguë in Asia; and on soldiers, R. MacMullen, *Soldier and Civilian in the Later Roman Empire* (Cambridge, Mass.: Harvard University Press, 1963), ch. 4 "A Mixed Blessing," pp. 76–98, esp. p. 87 on a "shake down" (*diaseismos*) by *stationarii*. He cites "extortion, pillage, attacks, and beatings, theft of plough animals."

local artisan.[7] In the face of recent theories which postulate big, factory-like centralized sculptors' workshops for Asia Minor,[8] it is well to remember that these small-town or village sculptors were as necessary and as ubiquitous as nineteenth century village blacksmiths.

We seem to enter a somewhat higher level of attainment, of great interest for the survival and transformation of Hellenistic traditions when we examine the so-called Eastern Greek funerary reliefs.[9] One may well consider them manifestations of an expanding urban middle class.

The earlier of these reliefs still follow closely the tall form and simple setting of classical Attic grave stelae. Such is the stele of Matis found at Sardis. She hailed *Fig. 121* from Kelainai, the epigram tells us, was the wife of Andromenes, and left her husband, three sons, and one daughter when she died.[10] The date is mid-third century B.C. and the social ambient probably that of new Seleucid Greek settlers, that is, of veterans and officials who took pride in the trite Greek epigram and the Athens-like type of stele, "just like at home in Greece."

Most of these "Eastern Greek" reliefs can be dated on epigraphic grounds from ca. 200 B.C. to A.D. 100. The great majority of Eastern Greek reliefs includes both the continuation of the tall type of stele and the more original wide format resembling classical votive reliefs. They present a remarkable display of diverse *Figs. 122–127* elements of landscapes and sanctuaries, such as stelae, herms, statues, trees, curtains, and even complete architectural backgrounds. In the only comprehensive discussion of these reliefs published back in 1905, Ernst Pfuhl rightly remarked that such reliefs from western and southern Asia Minor as well as adjacent Greek islands (Lesbos, Samos, Kos) present a vivid picture of actual Hellenistic cemeteries, with their gates, funerary monuments, and sepulchral temples.

[7]Herakles Torso: Found in foundation of a house in village of Gölde, 1962. H. 0.83 m. Surface covered with rough chisel marks. A considerable collection of small-scale sculptures from one provincial workshop was found at Çavdarlı (Phrygia) and is now in the Museum at Afyon Karahisar. Pending its detailed publication, cf. S. Gönçer, *Afyon Ili Tarihi* (Izmir, 1971), pp. 196–98, figs. 69–71.

[8]G. Ferrari, *Commercio*, pp. 90–94; H. Wiegartz, "Lokalisierung der kleinasiatischen Säulensarkophage," *Mélanges Mansel* (Ankara, 1974), pp. 374–83.

[9]Unfortunately, the material has not been well collected. Ernst Pfuhl's great *Corpus of Eastern Greek Reliefs* begun early in this century is yet to be completed by Hans Möbius. In E. Pfuhl, "Spätjonische Plastik," *JdI* 50 (1935): 9–48, Pfuhl discussed a selection of what he considered

early examples of reliefs which he dated from late fourth through the third century B.C. The basic publication is still E. Pfuhl, "Das Beiwerk auf den ostgriechischen Grabreliefs," *JdI* 20 (1905): 47–96, figs. 1–19, I "Die Denkmäler," *ibid.*, 123–55, figs. 20–28, II "Die Bezirke und Bauten;" M. Bieber, *ScHell*, p. 125, fig. 489, p. 137, figs. 537–39, p. 152, figs. 646–47. N. Firatli and L. Robert, *Stèles de Byzance;* H. Möbius. "Hellenistische Grabreliefs," *AA* (1969): 507–10, figs. 1–6.

[10]G. M. A. Hanfmann and L. Robert, *AJA* 64 (1960): 49–56, pls. 9, 10:5. Similar in type and style: women and servant from Mylasa, H. Möbius, *AA* (1969): 509, fig. 6, in Izmir. Related examples are discussed by Pfuhl, *JdI* 50 (1935): 9–48.

They also illustrate a new Hellenistic use of sculpture to create a new "sacral landscape," a countryside adorned and hallowed by religious sculptures.

Fig. 122   In a typical Hellenistic relief from the city of Notion which dates to the early second century B.C., the dead woman is again being handed the jewelry box but the woman is now statuesque and large while the servant and the fan-bearing girl are much smaller. There is sky overhead and a tree on the left. Alluding to the possible survival of soul, a statue of Psyche is standing on a tall columnar base—a very interesting example for the way in which sculpture was displayed in Hellenistic times. The huge serpent spiralling around the column is the embodiment of a dead man who has become a helping hero, a "Dexios," perhaps the lady's husband.[11]

The style of the Pergamene Altar of Zeus with large bodies and swinging curves is echoed somewhat distantly in a remarkable relief in Izmir[12] perhaps of

Fig. 123   the late second century B.C. Two horsemen are shown as two hero snakes appear at both sides of the central tree. Perhaps the dead were brothers who fell in battle. Two little grooms lead the horses; one has put on his master's helmet.

Originally, it was the prerogative of the city to honor the brave men who had died fighting for their *polis,* but in Hellenistic times it is usually the family who regard the man as having become a hero, an immortal being who should be given offerings and prayed to, and who in turn will help his family.

This private survival of the public ideal of the *"polis* hero" changed when the Romans took over. In the rustic, linear representation of Marcus Antonios Fron-

Fig. 124   ton from the cemetery of Byzantium, the would-be hero is more concerned with the scholarly scroll in his hand than with the horse which the tiny groom leads past him.[13] The name of the dead man is Roman, and the relief dates to the early Roman Empire, probably to the first century of our era.

These were funerary reliefs, normally to be seen in the cemeteries. It is in-

[11]Relief from Notion in Izmir, International Fair Park Museum # 31, Aziz, *Guide,* pp. 17–18, from excavations of Istanbul Museums at Notion, 1906. Aziz calls the figure on the column Psyche-Nemesis and describes all small figures as servants. H. Möbius, by letter (January, 1972) cites Th. Macridy, "Antiquités de Notion, II," *JOAI* 15 (1912): 61–62, fig. 34, H. 1 m. Pfuhl, unpublished Corpus file, no. 280, dated the relief to mid-second century B.C. Möbius, 150–125 B.C. For Psyche-Nemesis, cf. W. H. Roscher, *MythLex* III.2 (Leipzig, 1902–9), p. 3250.

[12]Relief with two heroes, Izmir, International Fair Park Museum # 701: O. Walter, "Antikenbericht aus Smyrna," *JOAI* 21–22 (1922–24), Beiblatt, p. 238, fig. 135, H. 0.64 m., interprets the youths as dead assimilated to the Dioscuri. I owe the photograph to H. Möbius who dates the relief to 200–150 B.C.

[13]N. Firatli and L. Robert, *Stèles de Byzance,* pp. 112–13, no. 186, pl. 46, late first century A.D. Hellenistic, *ibid.,* no. 187. Objects in background include wax tablets, inkstand, *volumina.* Robert, pp. 141, 188, because of family name, the relief must date after 41–30 B.C.

teresting that a horseman hero relief, said to be Hellenistic, was found set into the   *Fig. 99*
wall of a Roman apartment house of the first century A.D. at Ephesus. It may have
been an heirloom, cherished and worshipped like a house icon.

We have previously discussed examples of the so-called funerary banquet
from the Persian era in the reliefs from Daskylion, Sardis, and Sidon. The idea   *Figs. 41, 42*
that the dead will go on feasting with their families forever became immensely
popular in Hellenistic and Roman funerary reliefs. In Byzantium alone, some
hundred relief stelae favored this subject. A very interesting relief from Smyrna in
Leiden clearly shows the influence of the votive reliefs.[14] Larger in stature, the   *Fig. 126*
Hades-like dead man is surrounded by worshipping survivors, no less than ten of
them. He reclines on a couch placed against the kind of wall with open balustrade
at top that has actually been found in second century B.C. houses in Delos and
Herculanum.[15] Shield, horsehead, and worshipping maidens appear between the
pilasters. The date may be between 150 and 100 B.C.

A relief in the Fitzwilliam Museum displays behind curtains the upper parts   *Fig. 125*
of three horsemen, quite in the manner of Hellenistic paintings. The two dead are
quaffing wine out of large cups, one of them pouring a new potion out of a Persian
style rhyton adorned with a goat or ibex protome.[16]

In a relief from Byzantium, Theodotos, son of Menephron, no longer drinks   *Fig. 127*
and makes merry. With thought-lined countenance he points to the celestial
globe. A sundial is shown over the sphinx at the left upper corner.[17] As in the
so-called third Pompeian style of painting, as in wall paintings of the House of
Livia in Rome, classicistic caryatids and fanciful sphinxes support the entablature of the house, indicating a date around the time of Augustus, the turn of our
era.[18] Outwardly, this is the same funerary meal, but ideologically a new theme is

[14]Museum van Oudheden pb 46. Pfuhl, *JdI* 20 (1905): 135, fig. 28. Votive reliefs: U. Hausmann, *Griechische Weihreliefs* (Berlin: Walter de Gruyter, 1960), figs. 12, 14, 15.

[15]Herculanum: cf. A. Maiuri, *Herculaneum*, ed. 6 (Rome, 1962), pp. 41–42, fig. 40, Samnite House "atrium." Delos: P. Brunneau, *et al. Exploration archéologique de Delos* 27: *L'Îlot de la Maison des Comédiens* (Paris: Editions E. de Boc-card, 1970), p. 34, figs. 29, 30.

[16]L. Budde and R. Nicholls, *Catalogue of Greek and Roman Sculpture in the Fitzwilliam Museum* (Cambridge, 1964), no. 64, hero relief of ca. first century B.C., pl. 20.

[17]Firatli, *Stèles de Byzance*, p. 54, no. 33, pl. 8; H. Möbius,

AA (1969): 508, figs. 3–4, and by letter (April, 1971) dates the relief to the first century B.C. L. Robert in *Stèles de Byzance*, p. 165, refers to H. Jongkees, *Archaeologica Trajec-tina* 1 (Greek Antiquities at Utrecht) (Groningen, 1957) for discussion of globe with seven wise men, and his own remarks on the Smyrna monument, *Bulletin épigraphique-REG* 73 (1961): 343.

[18]Caryatids and sphinxes in Third Style, which accord-ing to Vitruvius (7.5.5) was started by the painter Apaturius of Alabanda in Asia Minor, L. Curtius, *Die Wandmalerei Pompejis* (Cologne, 1929), pp. 130–35, figs. 61–62 (House of Livia).

sounded—the idea of intellectual immortality achieved through works of mind, such as philosophy and astronomy.

This then was the function of sculpture in serving the somewhat vague, private ambitions for immortality of the middle class in the cities of Asia Minor. The emphasis was on the family, house, important respectable status (indicated by *small* servants), and less strongly, on profession.[19]

We shall now interrupt our climb on the social ladder to consider briefly another aspect of our subject. Who were the sculptors who worked in western Anatolian cities in Hellenistic and Roman times? In discussing this matter we shall also examine something of the functions and patrons for whom the sculptors worked.

There is evidence to show that the initial artistic vocabulary of the "Eastern Greek" reliefs came from the so-called Hellenistic Rococo current of the late third and second centuries B.C. These workshops seem to have centered in the cities of the kingdom of Bithynia, cities such as Nicomedia, Prusias-ad-Hypium, and the geographically allied city of Kyzikos.[20]

The famous "Fighter Borghese" by Agasias, son of Dositheos of Ephesus is perhaps a copy from the first century B.C. rather than the original design. Inscriptions record the activity of Menophilos, before 110 B.C., and of Agasias, son of Menophilos who restored Nikai with Erotes and Anterotes and made many portraits of distinguished Romans beginning with Gaius Billienus (before 100 B.C.), and Marius (ca. 99 B.C.), and ending with P. Serveillius Isauricus, proconsul of Asia in 46 B.C.[21]

Even though these Ephesian sculptors worked abroad in Delos and on the Greek mainlands, they advertised the existence of a school at Ephesus; and they already worked for the Roman patrons. There may have been an atelier at Miletus, where inscriptions name Demetrios, son of Glaukos, who made portraits as well as statues of Apollo Delphinios and Lamp-Bearers for the Theaters of Miletus and Didyma; Ammonios and Perigenes, sons of Zopyros; and Lampitos, son of

[19]Pfuhl, *JdI* 20 (1905) 47–96. H. Möbius, *AA* (1969): 508; N. Firatli, *Stèles de Byzance,* pp. 30–36.

[20]Pfuhl, *JdI* 20 (1905): 152–53; A. Schober, "Vom griechischen zum römischen Relief," *JOAI* 27 (1932): 46–63; Bieber, *ScHell,* pp. 136–56, esp. pp. 152–55. Prusias ad Hypium: G. M. A. Hanfmann, "A Hellenistic Landscape Relief," *AJA* 70 (1966): 371.

[21]Marcadé, *Receuil* 2 (1957), II.1 (A. Dositheou), II:11 (A. Menophilou). If the statue of a fighting Gaul belongs to the monument of Marius (for his victories against Cimbers and Teutons, 101 B.C.), Agasias was still in the tradition of Pergamene Baroque, Marcadé, *Receuil,* II.5, pl. XXV, fig. *BrBr* pl. 9; Bieber, *ScHell,* pp. 162–63.

Apollonios.[22] Copying activities in Nicomedia seem to be attested for Menodotos and Diodotus, sons of Boethos of Chalkedon around 100 B.C., and Lippold substantiates a workshop in Tralles.[23]

We are singularly fortunate in having for Asia Minor good information about a well-known sculptors' workshop, and indeed, a regular sculptors' city at Aphrodisias in Caria, the city of Carian Aphrodite, somewhat south of the Maeander valley.[24]

The activity of the School of Aphrodisias began in the eighties of the first century B.C. under the patronage of the famous Roman general Sulla, who had just defeated King Mithradates of Pontus. A major monument ordered by the city and thus a public monument is a frieze honoring Gaius Julius Zoilos, priest of Aphrodite and a man wealthy and important enough to be called a friend by the then rulers of the world—the triumvirs Anthony and Octavian. In style, the transition from late Hellenistic to Roman art, the mixing of classicistic (so-called Neo-Attic) copying and Asiatic Baroque pictorialism, in content the remarkable allegorical mode, paralleled in the Asianic rhetoric, makes this frieze a key monument for understanding art and ideology of Asiatic cities during the transition from the late Hellenistic to Augustan Age.[25] The people are represented by the dignified bearded gentleman Demos who stands next to a Hermes herm of a famous classical type; "Honor," *Timé* in Greek, is a semi-nude lady who crowns Zoilos: Aphrodite, very vividly modelled, rushes into the scene to honor her priest; finally "Eternity," *Aion* looks on with thinker's gesture and prophetic gaze.

Figs. 128–131

Fig. 129
Fig. 130
Fig. 131

Most of the figures are abstract ideas given human form to celebrate the great contributions which Zoilos has made to his city. They are symbolized by the constant accompaniment of honorary wreaths hung up in the background. That all figures were inscribed is a clear indication that even the ancient spectator was not expected to understand this allegorical scene without some help.

[22]G. Lippold, *Plastik*, p. 372, with refs to *Milet* I:9, p. 159; *Milet* I:3, p. 409; Perigenes: *RE* XIX, p. 745; Lampitos: *RE* Suppl. V, p. 540, Nr. 2; *Milet* I:8, p. 182. Lippold has an excellent brief introduction to V, "Anfänge des Klassizmus," p. 364, "Kleinasien," pp. 371–75, and VI, "Ubergang zur römischen Kunst, 90–30 v. Chr.," pp. 379–80.

[23]Lippold, *Plastik*, p. 382, n. 9; G. P. Oikonomos, *Arch-Eph* (1923): 59–101. Apollonios and Tauriskos of Tralles who made one version of the "Farnese Bull" group were perhaps only copying an earlier bronze work in Tralles. The group mentioned by Pliny was in marble and trans-

ported from Rhodes; Richter thinks the original may have been in bronze.

[24]Bibl. C. C. Vermeule, *ImpArt*, p. 477; M. Squarciapino, *Scuola*; K. T. Erim, *National Geographic* 132:2 (August, 1967): 280–94.

[25]A. Giuliano, *Ritrattistica*, pp. 146, 192, 196, figs. 36–37; K. T. Erim, *National Geographic* 132:2 (August, 1967): 280–94; *AJA* 71 (1967): 233–43; F. Brommer, "Aion," *Marburger Winckelmannprogramm* (1967): 3, pl. 3. Date: L. Robert, "Inscriptions d'Aphrodisias," *AntCl* 35 (1966): 422–32; E. Rosenbaum-Alföldi, *Phoenix* 25 (1971): 180–81.

Another typical public display of sculpture commissioned by the people of Aphrodisias, i.e., by the city, was a frieze nearly a half-mile long dedicated to the city goddess Aphrodite, to the deified (i.e., dead) emperor Augustus, to Augustus's wife Livia, and Augustus's successor, Livia's son, the emperor Tiberius. It was executed between the death of Augustus (A.D. 14) and that of Livia (A.D. 29). In addition to the portraits of the imperial house and major divinities, the sculptors made a colossal display of heads copied from many famous Fig. 132 works of art of classical and Hellenistic times, perhaps to show off their knowledge of masterpieces of the past. The style is a rather wild, provincial expressionism.[26]

In Neronian and Flavian times, better balance and greater stylistic skill was achieved in presumably private orders such as the portrait statues of Flavian or Trajanic ladies in Istanbul or an athlete's statue, apparently designed as decorative sculpture, signed by the sculptor Koblanos and found in Italy at Sorrento, where the sculptor may have gone to make it.[27]

Subsequently, as attested by signatures, the School of Aphrodisias spread through the Mediterranean, and under Hadrian, it achieved imperial patronage. When its output is restudied it will present us with a model of the scope and activities of a sculptors' center from the first century B.C. through the fifth century A.D. Its production included city-commissioned monuments in monumental ensembles, such as the friezes just discussed, statues of emperors and benefactors, architectural decoration, and a remarkable number of decorative sculptures in the round.[28] I believe that there were similar ateliers in other cities of Asia Minor, often located near the marble quarries, such as at Dokimeion-Synnada in Phrygia or the island of Prokonnesos in the Sea of Marmara;[29] but they were also located in large cities like Ephesus, Smyrna, Tralles, and Sardis.

When we now turn to the role of sculpture in public buildings, we must recall that a very important compositional device for public displays of sculpture was

[26]Vermeule, *ImpArt,* pp. 53–54, figs. 55; G. Jacopi, *Mon-Ant* 38 (1939): 9–10, 209–10; K. T. Erim, "The School of Aphrodisias," *Archaeology* 20 (1967): 23, fig. 10.

[27]M. Squarciapino, *Scuola,* p. 16, no. 31, pp. 51–54, pls. 16–17; Erim, *Archaeology* 20 (1967): 18, fig. 2; Inan-Rosenbaum, pp. 172–73, nos. 229–30, pls. 124:1–2, 127.

[28]Squarciapino, *Scuola.* Inan-Rosenbaum, pp. 29–34; Erim, *Archaeology* 20 (1967): 18–27, figs. 2–17.

[29]On location of Turkish marbles cf. A. Tekvar, *Türkiye*

Mermer Envanteri, MTAE Publication no. 134; useful survey, bibl. in Ferrari, *Commercio,* ch. 1 "Il commercio dei marmi in età imperiale," pp. 17–23. On Dokimeion: J. Röder, *Dergi* 18 (1969): 111–16; on Prokonnesos: J. B. Ward-Perkins, "Four Roman Garland Sarcophagi in America," *Archaeology* 11 (1958): 98–104. We expect an up-to-date treatment of the subject by Ward-Perkins in the publication of his Jerome Lectures.

created in the so-called Asiatic aedicular facades. In a previous chapter we had considered these facades as elements of city planning. Their ultimate effect was achieved only in conjunction with sculpture through the statue niches, which were populated with statues. Architecture thus became much more anthropomorphic since it served as a framework for human figures.

In its original condition, the Library of Celsus at Ephesus was a fine example *Figs. 133, 134* of such public statuary display of ca. A.D. 125. Even though most of the statues are lost, we can reconstruct a very interesting ideological program from their inscribed bases. In the niches of the lower story stood the statues of "Sophia," "Arete," and "Episteme Kelsou": "Wisdom, Valor, and Knowledge of Celsus." This is, I believe, the first set of representations of Virtues known in ancient art. The fourth statue, "Insight of Philippos," was a later replacement. Two equestrian statues (lost except for their bases) were probably portraits of Celsus, consul in A.D. 92, and his son Aquila, consul in A.D. 110. A cuirass statue stood in the central niche of the upper story. Its identification oscillates between Tiberius Julius Celsus Polemaeanus, who is buried in a sarcophagus under the library, and *Fig. 134* Tiberius Julius Aquila Polemaeanus, who completed the building for his father. Having carefully looked at the statue in the Istanbul Museum, I think it is really a statue of the emperor Hadrian.[30]

The Library of Celsus presented us with the use of statuary on an external public facade, and the kind of statuary program which glorified the donor. As an example of interior decoration, we may take the statuary found in the Hall of Imperial Cult of the gymnasium which the millionaire Publius Vedius Antoninus, *Fig. 105* according to the dedicatory inscription, dedicated "with all its decoration to Artemis of Ephesus and the Emperor Aelius Hadrianus Antoninus Pius Augustus."

The statuary display must have been overwhelming. A colossal statue of the emperor served as the central cult image. Vedius, celebrated by his fellow citizens as "the Second Founder of Ephesus," had a statue at one end, which was balanced (at the other end?) by a statue of the mythical First Founder of the city, the hero Androklos, shown during the boar hunt which led him to the site of *Fig. 135* Ephesus. Some scholars discern in Androklos's handsome, individual counte-

---

[30]Library and statues: F. Eichler, *FoEph* V:1, pp. 57–59, figs. 95 ff., W. Alzinger, *Stadt*, pp. 108–21; Keil, *Führer*, pp. 105–8, figs. 57–58; Statue: Istanbul Archaeological Museums # 2453; Inan-Rosenbaum, p. 125, no. 144, pls. 82:2, 83:2, 84:1, 2. Dion Chrysostomus placed a statue of Trajan in his library; he also buried his wife and son in the library precinct as Aquila buried Celsus. Pliny *Letters* 10.81, 82. As H. North points out, statues of "four lifegiving virtues" were shown in Church of St. Basil in Caesarea, *Anthologia Palatina* I.93.

Fig. 136

Fig. 137

Fig. 138

nance a portrait of Hadrian's favorite, the Bithynian boy Antinous.[31] The portraits of the emperor and the donor were the only link with the Roman present. The rest of the statuary extolled the artistic and cultural past of Greece in general, and of Ephesus in particular. Famous writers, such as a poetess (who may be Sappho), famous athletes[32] alternated with gods, goddesses, and minor creatures of traditional Greek mythology to evoke a somewhat synthetic vision of the "Golden Age" of Greece as it applied to bathing. Satyrs and river gods, after Hellenistic models, often served as glorified faucets. Hermes was traditionally the patron god of the gymnasia. In the Vedius Gymnasium the entrance to a dressing room was flanked by two copies of the famous Hermes Before the Gate, "Propylaios," of which the classic original stood before the entrance to the Acropolis of Athens. The Ephesian herms were inscribed in verse: "I am not the work of someone who just happened to pass by but Alcamenes gave me this shape." If any visitor did not recognize the work of the most famous pupil of Phidias, the poem gracefully instructed him.[33]

Fig. 139

The great displays of statuary, on interiors, as in the Harbor Bath, on exteriors as in the Nymphaeum of Trajan[34] were a perpetual accompaniment to the daily life of the city. These sermons in stone were no longer religious but rather educational and aesthetic in content, and they did preach a definite ideology. While official acknowledgment was made to the ruling power of Rome, the main theme

[31]Vedius: Miltner, *Ephesos*, pp. 58–59, figs. 51–56. Statue: Inan-Rosenbaum, pp. 127–28, no. 150, pls. 83:3, 87:3, 4, apparently deny the identification. For a Vedius? head, *ibid.*, no. 182, p. 144, pl. 106:3, 4. Androklos = Antinous: W. Hahland, "Ebertöter Antinoos-Androklos," *JOAI* 41 (1956): 54–77, denied by F. Willemsen, "Aktaionbilder," *Jdl* 71 (1956): 34–35; accepted by Inan-Rosenbaum, pp. 73–74, no. 37, pl. 24, and C. Clairmont, *Antinous* (1966), p. 60, no. 66.

[32]The bronze athlete in figure 137 is illustrated here as a typical Roman bath athlete's statue; it comes from the Harbor Bath, not the Vedius Gymnasium. W. Alzinger, *Stadt*, figs. 105–6. S. Lattimore, "The Bronze Apoxyomenos from Ephesos," *AJA* 76 (1972): 13–16, pls. 7–8, bibl. Dates for the Greek original vary between mid-fourth century and early Hellenistic; most scholars consider the Ephesus bronze a Roman copy.

[33]Alcamenes herm: Izmir, Basmane Museum no. 675. Shaft rose way above spectator's head. Standing at the

doorway, the monument would have been very impressive. J. Keil, *JOAI* 24 (1929), Beiblatt, pp. 31–32, fig. 14; C. Praschniker, *JOAI* 29 (1935): 23–31, fig. 20; E. B. Harrison, *Agora* 11 (1965): 123; Picard, *Manuel* 2:2 (1939), pp. 554–58; J. R. McCredie, *AJA* 64 (1962): 87, pl. 56.

[34]Nymphaeum of Trajan: Miltner, *Ephesos*, pp. 50–51, fig. 39; Alzinger, *Stadt*, pp. 235–37; Miltner, *JOAI* 44 (1959), Beiblatt, pp. 326–46, figs. 171–86. Displays even more striking than those of Ephesus are better preserved at Side and Perge: A. M. Mansel, *Die Ruinen von Side*, pp. 24, 80–81, assigns some of these sculptures to the school of Aphrodisias. The Hall of Imperial cult at Side included Myron's Disk Thrower, Lysippan Sandal Binder (fig. 91), Ares Borghese (fig. 93), Herakles Farnese (fig. 90), Hermes of Stephanos (fig. 94), Late Classical Hygeia (fig. 95), Nemesis (fig. 97), as well as a Hellenistic type? Nike (fig. 96) and a cuirassed emperor (fig. 92) in the central niche. Cf. *Dergi* 17 (1968): 93–105, figs. 8–11, 18–20 (Perge statuary).

was a classicizing attempt to extol the past glories of the Greek mythical world, of the city's history, and of the Greek literary education and culture, *paideia,* while enjoying the benefits of the organizing ability and the comforts of the Roman present.[35]

Most of the public works were erected under the patronage of the aristocratic and wealthy families who had risen high in the Roman Empire.[36] The private dreams of this highest social class appear not on these buildings but on the very luxurious marble sarcophagi which seem to have been made in Asia Minor around the middle of the second century of our era. Although the name attested for antiquity is "Asianic," the eminent art historian, Charles Rufus Morey gave to these caskets of Roman times the name of "Asiatic" sarcophagi to indicate that they were made in Asia Minor.[37]

A comparison of the earliest known Asiatic sarcophagus, now at Melfi in Italy, and the reconstruction of the Library of Celsus illustrates the resemblances in architecture and in the placing of sculpture. The overall concept of such a sarcophagus was perhaps, as Hans Wiegartz has recently suggested, that of a Heroon or Maussoleum similar to the funerary monuments of kings and princes at Xanthos, Limyra, and Halikarnassos. Thus in death, all these affluent people became kings.

Figs. 140, 141

Fig. 133

Figs. 62, 63, 69, 75

Gods, such as Hermes, epic heroes, such as Meleager, Odysseus, and Diomed—the last two appear on the right end of the sarcophagus in Melfi—are sometimes depicted as statues, but usually rendered as actual living beings. Muses and literary luminaries, such as Homer, conjured the semi-mythical, semi-intellectual immortality which the heroized dead hoped to enjoy. The rare narrative themes have to do with attainment of immortality by active virtue, by *vita activa,* as in the deeds of Herakles, shown on an imposing casket found at Tiberiopolis near ancient Iconium, modern Konya in southern Asia Minor. In the later so-called Sidamaria group of sarcophagi, so termed after the findspot of a ten

Fig. 141

---

[35]Jones, *Plutarch and Rome,* ch. 5–6 and pp. 46, 109, has excellent discussion of the Greek attitudes. On p. 126 he remarks "Exaltation of Greek culture did not constitute rejection of the Roman present; archaism and antiquarianism were the fashion in both halves of the empire."

[36]Bowersock, *Sophists,* pp. 22–25, has much of interest on the subject.

[37]*TAM Patara* 2:1, no. 437, speaks of one local and one *Asianic* sarcophagus; J. Kubinska, *Les monuments funéraires dans les inscriptions grecques de l'Asie Mineure,* p. 41. C. R. Morey, *Sardis* 5:1 (1925): 21–28; Ferrari, *Commercio,* p. 75; H. Wiegartz, *Säulensarkophage,* pp. 48–50 opted for Perge or Side as *the* center of production. For the literary evidence on quarries at Dokimeion cf. L. Robert, "Lettres Byzantines," *Journal des Savants* (Jan.–June, 1962): 23–26, 45–51, and the survey by J. Röder, *Dergi* 18 (1969): 111–16.

foot high sarcophagus now in Istanbul, there appear heroic hunts. This too, was interpreted as symbolic of virtue combatting vice; it is so explained in the popular Stoic essay known as "The Painting of Cebes."[38]

The key figure for the understanding of the message of these sarcophagi is the seated philosopher often shown with a woman who either listens to him or inspires him (Muse? Sophia?). A particularly fine example of this group occurs on *Fig. 142* a sarcophagus from Dokimeion-Synnada, now in Ankara.[39]

The inspired philosopher or sage represents the Greek moral-intellectual tradition of immortality attained through life of mind. Subsequently, the type was adopted for the representation of the Evangelists. It is obvious how much early Byzantine art owed to this Romano-Asiatic art when we look at Saint Mark and the same female figure but signifying here perhaps Sophia, Divine Wisdom. The group is found in a miniature from the famous manuscript of the Gospels of the Rossano Cathedral; it may have been painted in Asia Minor during the sixth century.[40]

Contradictory concepts were sometimes fused in this funerary art. The sarcophagus is not only a regal maussoleum; it is also a couch on which the dead will *Fig. 140* either slumber eternally, as in Melfi, or enjoy perennial ease of the so-called funerary meal. We have already encountered Claudia Antonia Sabina, wife or daughter of a consul, as a benefactress of the Sardians who gave funds for the building of the gymnasium. Here she is with her nameless daughter reclining on *Fig. 143* her sarcophagus found at Sardis and now in the Museum at Istanbul. On a sarcophagus from Ephesus now in Izmir, we see Claudia Antonia Tatiane, from a similar noble family of Aphrodisias and Ephesus, reclining next to her *Fig. 144* husband.[41]

Leaders of the "Second Sophistic Movement," literary people and famous orators such as Antonius Polemon and Aelius Aristeides of Smyrna,[42] were inti-

[38]Interpretation of Asiatic sarcophagi: H. Wiegartz, *Säulensarkophage*, pp. 119–20; C. Praechter, ed. *Tabula Cebetis*, pp. 22–23; R. Parsons, ed. *Cebes' Tablet*, pp. 22–23, 35. Happiness crowns the virtuous man because he has been victorious in contests with the biggest beasts *(ta megista theria)*, Ignorance and Error.

[39]Ankara 10061; Ferrari, *Commercio*, pl. 6:2.

[40]Evangelists: A. M. Friend, Jr. "The Portraits of the Evangelists in the Greek and Roman Manuscripts," *Art Studies* 5 (1927): 115–47; 7 (1929): 3–29; C. R. Morey, *ECA* (1942): 108, 214, bibl., fig. 112. Rossanensis, fol. 121.

[41]Claudia Antonia Tatiane, according to inscription, ceded a sarcophagus to her brother Aemilius Aristeides in A.D. 204. J. Keil, *JOAI* 25 (1929), Beiblatt, pp. 46–48, fig. 26; and 26 (1930), Beiblatt, 11. For her statue cf. K. T. Erim, *Archaeology* 20 (1967): 22–25, fig. 7.

[42]Second Sophistic: A. Boulanger, *Aelius Aristide et la sophistique dans la province de l'Asie*; Cadoux, *Smyrna*, pp. 250–51; Antonius Polemon, friend of Hadrian, pp. 254–61; distinguished mathematician and Platonic philosopher Theon of Smyrna, pp. 261–62 (Fig. 148).

mate friends of the aristocrats buried in these sarcophagi. Pride in the traditional, especially local mythology, veneration of Greek literature and education, readiness to be uplifted and elevated by comparisons with mythical heroes and sages of old, and the belief that immortality can be attained through intellectual culture —that you can sit in a paradise of sages by the side of Homer, Socrates, and Plato—is the upper class ideal of immortality represented by the sarcophagi of Asia Minor.

We have now seen the role of sculpture in the private cemeteries and maussolea around the city and in the exteriors and interiors of the great public structures pertaining to daily life of the city, such as the baths and fountain houses. There was yet another important public use of sculpture which we have briefly noted in our discussion of the Hellenistic period: the displays of honorary statues in the open areas of civic centers, the agoras, and along the main avenues of the city. Very few such statues have survived in place. In a reconstruction of the North Market of Miletus, an attempt has been made to show the position of some *Fig. 145* honorary statues.[43] There is one statue still left in place along the Kuretes Street in Ephesus, that of the physician Alexandros. It is from hundreds of inscriptions, *Fig. 146* often found on statue bases, that we can evoke the picture of the staggering number of honorary sculptures which were produced in Roman times.

Franz Miltner has eloquently described this outburst of honorific activity in Ephesus: "The energies of the community urged eruptively a new shaping of their city. Builders, artisans, and sculptors were busy at every corner. Hundreds and hundreds of honorary statues were put up during the course of the second century in the colonnades of the Great Agora and in the Main Street. . . . This forest of statues belongs to the living image of the city; literary figures, orators, philosophers, priests, priestesses, and officials, municipal and Roman, all took part in this creative effort."[44]

To give just one example from inscriptions: in the South Agora of Miletus, in front of the internal columns of the huge East Hall, stood the statues of fifteen emperors, ranging from Domitian in the late first century through Septimius Severus in the early third. Ten additional statues honored outstanding citizens. Anticipating women's liberation, a remarkable lady of the early third century, whose name unfortunately is lost, held all major offices in the city and gave all the games. Perhaps most remarkable is the fact that she was Chairman-Gymnasiarch

[43]Kleiner, *Ruinen,* fig. 31; *Milet* I:6, pl. 28.   [44]Miltner, *Ephesos,* pp. 58–59.

of all three gymnasia for men; the Gymnasium of Boys, Gymnasium of Fathers, and the Gymnasium of Senior Citizens. Another celebrated citizen was a contractor who served without fee and built part of the famous Market Gate, now reconstructed in Berlin.[45]

Fig. 146
The effect of hundreds of these human presences startlingly lifelike in painted marble and bronze and standing close to, but above the beholder on their pedestals must have been considerable. Their intent was somewhat like that of a gallery of ancestors—a perennial parade in marble and bronze of citizens who had loved and served their city.

Just as the Dutch group portraits represent the social ideal of Holland in the seventeenth century, so do these honorary statues of the Roman era tell us how the leading citizens of western Anatolian cities wanted to be seen. Let us now examine this self-portrayal of "the living image of a city" in specific examples.

Fig. 148
One portrait of an intellectual can be identified with certainty, that of the mathematician, astronomer, and philosopher Theon of Smyrna (active ca. A.D. 115–140), whose writings on astronomy and on the use of mathematics in understanding Plato have been passed down to us. The inscription records that the portrait was given by the philosopher's son, a priest, in order "to honor Theon, Platonic philosopher."[46]

Derived from late classical sculpture, the bearded philosopher type is given individual overtones in the care-lined face, strained by intellectual effort.

A document of great importance for self-interpretation of the upper classes, is a sarcophagus from Aphrodisias. Its reliefs show the bust of Pereitas Kallimedes and his wife Tatia. Kallimedes held important offices in the city, and is made to

Fig. 147
look like a bearded philosopher on the relief. There are inscriptions for them and for their son, likewise a high official, who is described as "magistrate and True Philosopher."[47] Obviously, to be considered a philosopher was an integral part of the social ideal of the urban upper class.[48]

The statue found in the Marble Hall of the Vedius Baths has been claimed as a portrait of the millionaire Vedius, friend of Antoninus Pius, but other scholars deny the identification because the style of the portrait points to a later, Severan

[45]All numbers after A. Rehm, *Milet* I:7, pp. 309–19.

[46]Theon: G. M. A. Richter, *Portraits of the Greeks* III (London, 1965), p. 285, fig. 2038.

[47]Giuliano, *Ritrattistica*, p. 196, figs. 36–37, ca. A.D. 211–17.

[48]Bowersock, *Sophists*, pp. 10–11, on rivalry between professional "sophists" and "philosophers" and their claims to civic importance.

date.[49] There is something Zeus-like about his countenance; the traditional *pallium*, "cloak," claims for him the dignity of a classical citizen and philosopher.

The full assertiveness and amplitude of these leading citizens in the era of Roman prosperity appears impressively in the portrait of the son-in-law of Vedius, the sophist (which means man of letters and orator) Flavius Damianus[50] whose statue was found in the East Gymnasium of Ephesus. It stood in the Hall of the Imperial Cult. Over a laurel wreath he wears a strange crown with little busts, now broken off, which proves that he is shown as a priest of Imperial Cult. The wooden chest at his feet with a tablet for inscription may be envisaged as containing manuscripts of his speeches. The symbolic presence of the emperor—he was shown with the twelve gods in the little busts of the crown—is the one Roman element in this Greek-centered rendering of Zeus-like citizen philosopher. A Jovian questioner and judge, Damianus is not unworried by thought. In the refined interpretation of the individual likeness we see the contribution of the Roman concept of personality.

Fig. 149
Fig. 150a, b

Such then was the ideal of Asia Minor during the Roman peace; a man of substance and status, a philosophic citizen in the classical polis tradition, yet also a loyal Roman citizen, who piously combined the cult of the traditional twelve gods with the Thirteenth God, the *praesens divus*, "the ruling emperor." In sculpture, as in literature, "the vitality of the Greek Renaissance of the second and third centuries . . . owes much to the encouragement . . . fortuitous and deliberate . . . of Rome."[51]

In the ensuing time of crisis for the empire (ca. 235–285) this calm and self-assured ideal was invaded by an agony of spirit which could lead to creative synthesis of Roman individualism, and Greek intellectualism with the new spiritual call from the beyond. The bearded head found in the Main Avenue of Sardis, is such a superb "Soul Portrait" initiating the new, spiritualized concept of personality.[52]

Fig. 151

Having thus viewed the expression of the highest social stratum in sculpture, we should now ascend to the top rung of the social ladder, to the emperor himself. We have seen that traditionally the citizens' protecting gods and goddes-

[49]Inan-Rosenbaum, no. 150 (Izmir), pls. 83:3, 87:3–4.

[50]Inan-Rosenbaum, p. 128, no. 151, pl. 87:1–2; L. Robert, *Études anatoliennes*, p. 129. Bowersock, *Sophists*, pp. 27–28 details after Philostratus *Vitae Sophistarum*, p. 605, the great public works undertaken by Damianus.

[51]Jones, *Plutarch and Rome*, p. 109.

[52]Sardis "Saint": G. M. A. Hanfmann, *Roman Art*, p. 100, pl. 90. Inan-Rosenbaum, pp. 39, 41, 44, no. 220, pl. 180:3–4; Hanfmann, "On Late Roman and Early Byzantine Portraits from Sardis," *Hommages à Marcel Renard*, III, Collection Latomus 103 (1969): 288–95, pl. 113.

ses were the spiritual centers of the western Anatolian cities. Their images continued to be made under the Roman Empire in traditional, often bizarre Anatolian forms and costumes, as in the images of the Aphrodite of Aphrodisias and Ar-

Fig. 153   temis of Ephesus.[53]

Already, Hellenistic kings had sought to associate themselves with these divine protectors of urbanism by becoming their *paredroi* or *synnaoi*—literally those who "sit by the side" or "share the dwelling" of the god. These royal statues may have often been colossal.[54] A possible example may be the Hellenistic colossus

Fig. 155   from the Artemis temple at Sardis, hitherto regarded as that of Zeus assimilated to

Fig. 154   the ruler Achaeus but possibly intended from the start to represent the king.[55]

When Roman emperors became the central power, they also assumed the functions of resident divinities of the cities. The resident imperial divinity could receive its own cult temple and this *neokorate* was an honor much sought by the Greek cities of Asia Minor. The colossal size of the imperial images was derived from the tradition of colossal divine images in the temples of great Anatolian

Fig. 156a, b divinities. Thus a huge seated Domitian dwelled in his own temple at Ephesus.[56]

[53]Aphrodite of Aphrodisias: K. T. Erim, *National Geographic* 132:2 (August, 1967), fig. on p. 285; Artemis of Ephesus: F. Miltner, "Die neuen Artemisstatuen aus Ephesos," *Anatolia* 3 (1958): 21–34, pls. 5–12; G. M. A. Hanfmann, *Classical Sculpture,* p. 338, figs. 304–5; H. Thiersch, *Artemis Ephesia,* Gesellschaft der Wissenschaften zu Göttingen, *Abhandlungen* 3. Folge, no. 12. L. Lacroix, *Les réproductions des statues sur les monnaies grecques* (Liège: Faculté de Philosophie et Lettres, 1949), pp. 176–96, bibl. P. E. Arias, *EAA* I (Rome, 1958), s.v. Artemide, p. 694; W. Helbig and H. Speier, *Führer durch die öffentlichen Sammlungen klassischer Altertümer in Rom,* 4th ed. (Tübingen: E. Wasmuth, 1966), vol. 2, pp. 275–76, no. 1452. R. Fleischer, *Artemis von Ephesus und verwandte Kultstatuen aus Anatolien und Syrien* (Leiden: E. J. Brill, 1973).

[54]*Synnaoi, paredroi:* Fundamental,comprehensive treatment in "Synnaos Theos," *A. D. Nock, Essays on Religion and the Ancient World,* ed. Z. Stewart. Vol. I, Essay 11, pp. 202–51, esp. p. 219 ff., on Asia Minor, p. 231 f., on W. Ramsay's view of partial identity of local divinity and emperor. Cf. in general, C. Habicht, *Gottmenschentum und griechische Städte = Zetemata,* ed. E. Burck and H. Diller, Heft 14, esp. "Tempel, Altar, und Kultbild," pp. 141–44 and pp. 192–95 on the local city-conditioned character of the cults. Antiochus III and Laodike as *synnaoi* of Dionysus at Teos, ca. 200 B.C., P. Hermann, *Anatolia* 9 (1965): 43–44. Colossal statues: P. Bernard, "Fouilles d'Ai Khanoum," *CRAI* (1969): 338, has collected some examples. Cf. also G.

Daux, *BCH* 83 (1959): 625, figs. 13–14, Halicarnassus (Ares), Vitruvius 2:8:11. Athena Pergamon: F. Winter, *Pergamon* 7:1 (Berlin: Georg Reimer, 1908), pp. 33–46, pl. 8, ca. 160 B.C., 4.5 m. high. Athena Priene: Smith, *BMC* 2, 146, 152, no. 1150, ca. 150 B.C. Th. Wiegand and H. Schrader, *Priene,* pp. 110–11, ca. 6.5 m. high. Apollo, Artemis, Leto, Klaros: Apollo 7–8 m. high, Augustan: Akurgal, *Civilizations,* p. 137; L. Robert, *Les fouilles de Klaros* (Limoges, 1954); cf. *AJA* 59 (1955): 237; 60 (1956): 381; 62 (1958): 99. *Dergi* 7:1 (1957): 5; 7:2 (1957): 12–14. G. Roux, "Qu'est ce que un *kolossos,*" *REA* 62 (1960): 5–40 shows that the ancient word often does not mean a very large statue. P. Bernard kindly acquainted me with Roux's article.

[55]H. C. Butler, *Sardis* I (1922), p. 66, ill. 61. *BASOR* 166 (1962): 34–35, fig. 27. Achaeus coins: E. T. Newall, *Western Seleucid Mints* (1941), p. 265, pl. 60:1–2, and a new tetradrachm, Sardis Excavations: C 63.21.

[56]Inan-Rosenbaum, no. 27, p. 67, pl. 16:1. For emperors and imperial cults on coins of the cities cf. P. R. Franke, *Kleinasien zur Römerzeit,* pp. 11–13. According to A. Bammer, the colossus is identified as Titus rather than Domitian by G. Daltrop, V. Haussmann, and M. Wegner, *Die Flavier-Das römische Herrscherbild* 2:1 (Berlin: Mann, 1966): pp. 26, 38; similarly, already C. C. Vermeule, *ImpArt,* p. 232. On the basis of his recent field work, Bammer believes the statue stood in the open (oral communication, 1973).

If the emperor took over a pre-existing temple, was the previous possessor evicted or did the emperor join the traditional divinity? We used to think that at Sardis, for instance, the colossal images of Antoninus Pius and Faustina had superseded Zeus and Artemis upon the bestowal of the *neokorate* under Antoninus Pius (ca. A.D. 140). But a renewed examination of all colossal fragments indicates that both Zeus and Artemis were still represented by colossi in the temple. Joint protection by the emperor and the local divinity was certainly the emotional and ideological assumption expressed in the dedicatory inscriptions of public buildings. Thus in Ephesus the Nymphaeum was given to Artemis and Trajan and the Baths of Vedius to Artemis and Antoninus Pius.

Figs. 157, 158

Here an ideological synthesis of Anatolian Hellenism and Roman imperialism took place. By including the Roman emperor in their most cherished emotional traditions, the cities adjusted their spiritual focus. There were stern legal, and economic realities behind these sculptures and inscriptions. Saint Paul was a citizen of Tarsus; he was also a Roman citizen. It is as a Roman citizen that he could appeal directly to the emperor. Even before 212, increasing numbers of urban dwellers were becoming Roman citizens with Roman rights and responsibilities, and many Greek Asiatics became part of the Roman administrative system up to the consulate and thus partners in administering the empire.[57] The most cogent visual symbol of the justice, majesty, and authority of the Roman Empire was the statue of the Roman emperor.[58]

The last of the great imperial colossi of the middle empire seems to be the fierce and threatening head of Caracalla from Pergamon.[59] During the anarchical years when the disastrous defeat of Valerian by the Persians (258) and the Gothic and Palmyrene invasions had shaken Asia Minor to its foundations, the cities could neither afford colossi[60] nor did most emperors appear to be colossal to the citizens. Many of them did not last long enough to have authentic portraits reach Asia Minor. Only with the reconstruction of the empire by Diocletian and his institution of the Four Rulers, the Tetrarchs (284–285), did a new age begin.

Fig. 159

Both Caracalla and Diokles—Diocletian ("Famed of Zeus")—have the Zeus-

Fig. 160

---

[57]Jones, *Plutarch and Rome*, p. 46: "Asia Minor had already advanced in Plutarch's time to produce its first consuls and commanders of Roman armies."

[58]For the legal status of imperial images, including their role as recipients of loyalty oaths, cf. H. Kruse, *Studien zur offizielen Geltung des Kaiserbildes* (Bonn, 1934). H. C.

Niemeyer, *Studien*, pp. 18–26, bibl.

[59]Caracalla from Pergamon: Inan-Rosenbaum, p. 84, no. 60, pl. 38:1–2, A.D. 214.

[60]Cf. Magie, *Roman Rule*, pp. 708–9, 714–15 on economic decline of cities.

like formula of glowering glance under contracted eyebrows. There is, however, a striking difference between Caracalla's theatrical anger heightened by heavy features and frame of twisting hair and a new, superior, measuring assurance held by simple overall shape and flat, nearly linear work[61] in the head of the leading Tetrarch, from his new capital in Nicomedia. Here begins the new, late antique vision of a ruler.

It may be well to recapitulate our findings: never in the history of humanity was sculpture as abundant and all pervasive as it was in the Greek cities of the Roman Empire during the second and early third centuries of our era. Sculpture was spread through the entire life of the citizen from cradle to grave. It pervaded the city from private dwelling to public square, from the humble dedication of a slave to the colossal image of the emperor. Sculpture served not only as art, but as a prime vehicle of communication. Like posters, newspapers, and magazines today, it expressed and communicated private and public, social, religious, educational, and political concerns.

This was a unique situation in the history of urbanism and it was made possible by three factors. First, economic prosperity which permitted an enormous organization of marble trade and marble working. Second, the vast heritage of Greek sculpture had made available casts, copies, and adaptations, an enormous artistic vocabulary (*linguaggio*) to evoke the glories of Hellenic past and to celebrate the Graeco-Roman present. Finally, in ideology, the emotional appeal of the idea of the Greek city was still capable of exciting ardent loyalty in the citizens of Smyrna, Ephesus, Miletus, and Prusa. It was this vision of an ideal Greek city, integrated within the framework of the Roman Empire which evoked the great outpouring of sculptures. This outpouring was intended to show that the modern Roman cities of Asia Minor were steeped in glorious Hellenic art as much as, and even more than, the famous Greek cities of old. There was some pretense and artificiality in the cultural and artistic Renaissance of the Greek city under the Roman Empire, but it was based on living belief and genuine need. Until a crisis overtook the entire empire, the Greek city lived in its sculpture.

[61]Diocletian from Nicomedia: Istanbul #4864, Inan-Rosenbaum, p. 85, no. 61, pl. 39; 3–4; K. Bittel, *AA* (1939): 166, figs. 36–39; Vermeule, *ImpArt*, p. 330, fig. 169. On portraits of Diocletian: R. Calza, *Iconografia romana imperiale da Carausio a Giuliano* 3 (Rome: L'ERMA Bretschneider, 1972), pp. 14–16 (ancient sources) and pp. 89–117, figs. 6–51.

V: Instinctu Divinitatis:
The Tetrarchs, Constantine,
and Constantinople

In this final chapter, we shall first treat of the time of the Tetrarchs[1] and of the several cities in the western coastlands of Asia Minor which competed for the rank of the world capital. We shall then discuss Constantine's experience with urbanism and his use of it when he founded, in Constantinople, the first capital of a Christian empire.[2]

Let us recall that under the senior emperor Diocletian and his co-rulers a system of an empire ruled by four emperors lasted from 284–305. Born perhaps in 283, Constantine succeeded his father, Constantius Chlorus, as one of the rulers in 306. He then proceeded to eliminate the others. His last competitor, his brother-in-law Licinius, was defeated in a battle at Chrysopolis-Skutari across from Byzantium in 324. Constantine promptly began to build Constantinople in the same year.[3] He officially dedicated the new capital in 330 and died at Nicomedia in 337 while Constantinople was still abuilding. Constantine's official recognition of Christianity as state religion began in 313 but he was baptized only

[1]Tetrarchs: *CAH* 12 (Cambridge: Cambridge University Press, 1939), pp. 328–30; W. Seston, *Diocletian et la Tetrarchie* (Paris, 1946); H. P. L'Orange, "The Great Crisis and its Solution Under Diocletian," *Art Forms and Civic Life in the Later Roman Empire,* pp. 37–68 (historical, cultural, and artistic transformations).

[2]Constantine: H. M. Gwatkin, "Constantine and his City," *CMH* 1 (New York: The Macmillan Co., 1911), pp. 1–23; L. Voelkl, *Der Kaiser Konstantin;* J. Vogt, *Konstantin der Grosse und sein Jahrhundert;* J. Vogt, "Constantinus der Grosse," *RAC* 3 (1957): 306–79; R. MacMullen, *Constantine* (New York: The Dial Press, 1969); Mango, *Art,* pp. 3–6; "The Age of Constantine: Tradition and Innovation," *Dumbarton Oaks Papers* 21 (1967) contains a symposium summarized by A. R. Bellinger, pp. 287–89, with papers by A. Alföldi (unpublished), J. A. Straub, J. L. Teal, M. H. Shepherd, Jr., E. B. Harrison, I. Lavin, and R. Krautheimer, where earlier literature will be found.

[3]A. Alföldi, "On the Foundation of Constantinople," *JRS* 37 (1947): 10–16, discusses the background of the change.

on his deathbed, twenty-five years later. The phrase *Instinctu Divinitatis* comes from the inscription on the Arch of Constantine at Rome. It was Constantine's guiding theme in beginning the transformation of the cities and their arts from a Roman to a Christian world.

"In Bithynia alone Hellenism went deeper," said that great student of the Hellenistic Age W. W. Tarn.[4] The kings of Bithynia regarded themselves as rivals of the Attalids of Pergamon and founded many towns, usually to replace earlier Greek settlements; thus, Nicomedia (named after king Nicomedes I, 278–250 B.C.) replaced Astakos.[5]

Figs. 163, 164
Figs. 161, 162
Four cities of this key region between the Dardanelles and the Bosporus were to become imperial capitals: Nicomedia for Diocletian, Nicaea from 1204–1261 for the Byzantine Lascarids, Bursa (Prusa) for the early Ottomans, and Byzantium became Constantinople-Istanbul. Earlier, Daskylion had served as capital for the Third Satrapy of the Persians. Under Constantine, Nicaea achieved considerable importance. The First Ecumenical Council at which the orthodox Nicene Creed was formulated took place there in 325.

Fig. 161
Nicaeaque ager uber aestuosae, "the fertile land of burning Nicaea," which Catullus (46.5) was anxious to leave, is still hot, richly green and beautiful lying on the shore of the blue Ascanian Lake within its amazingly well-preserved, part Roman, part Byzantine city walls.[6]

Fig. 162
Nicaea was an interesting example of a Milesian Hellenistic grid plan with an axial cross. Strabo (12.4, 7.565) said that its circuit was 16 stadia, 2,893 meters, and rectangular in shape; and that "its streets are cut at right angles, so that the four gates can be seen from the middle of the gymnasium." Four gates can still be seen from the intersection at the ruin of the church (now museum) of Aya Sofya but they are not the same gates Strabo saw, and the walled circuit as preserved measures 4,970 meters. The outline became irregular when the city was enlarged by the Romans. Under the Flavian emperors, two marble gates were built by Proconsul Plancius Varus A.D. 78–79 (North or "Istanbul" Gate and East or "Lefke" or "White" Gate). Then, after the disastrous earthquake of A.D. 123, the emperor Hadrian built the other gates.[7]

[4]W. W. Tarn, *Hellenistic Civilization,* 2nd ed., p. 149; *RE* 5 (1897), s.v. "Bithynia," 507–39. Cf. also n. 12 below, literature on Nicomedia.

[5]J. Sölch, "Bithynische Städte im Altertum," *Klio* 19 (1925): 140–88. For the map compare Öztüre, p. 6.

[6]Schneider and Karnapp. The panorama, figure 161 is

from that publication.

[7]Strabo (63 B.C. to A.D. 23) must have seen the Hellenistic city walls. His visit cannot be closely dated but probably occurred before the beginning of our era, E. Honigmann, *RE* 7:2 (1931): 76–155; Varus and Hadrianic gates; Schneider and Karnapp, pp. 24–27, pls. 14–15.

Already under Trajan, during the governorship of the Younger Pliny (ca. 110), the city was engaged in a program of ambitious, if not always efficient, urban rebuilding. Of the buildings the Nicaeans were then striving to erect, the theater is still recognizable. The gymnasium may have been the successor to the one seen by Strabo. Trajan's aqueduct is attested by inscriptions.[8] Hadrian, celebrated by the Nicaeans as a second Dionysos and second founder gave to Nicaea agoras, colonnaded streets, and "walls toward Bithynia."[9]

Fig. 89

Nicaea had an imperial palace. According to Eusebius (*Vita Constantini* 3.10) the First Ecumenical Council met *"en mesaitatoi oikoi ton basileion,"* "in midst of the palace," and this palace was later repaired by Justinian. A possible location is a hillock named Treasure Hill (Mal Tepe), some 300 meters southwest of the East Gate where large unexcavated masonry walls are to be seen.[10]

Fortified by the emperor Claudius Gothicus after the invasion of the Goths in 253, Nicaea, whose defenses were considerably improved by the Byzantines, presented the appearance of a new type of a city—the militarized, castle-like, late antique, early medieval town.

At the East Gate, at the North Gate, and on top of the eastern wall, there are preserved several important reliefs from a Roman triumphal monument of the time of the Tetrarchs.[11] The slabs now immured on top of the eastern wall display the submission of a kneeling chieftain in front of a city wall with two towers. ALA/MANNIA, "Germany" is inscribed on one of the towers in irregular Latin letters. The city is perhaps Vindonissa—now Windisch in Switzerland. This slab is particularly badly weathered.

The reliefs on the East Gate preserve the lucid quality of marble and reveal some sophisticated details such as a sword overlapping a shield arranged in perspective. Massed infantry formations clash in the relief on the right. Animals and other booty are driven off over two superposed strips of ground and a bar-

---

[8]Trajan's aqueduct: Schneider and Karnapp, pp. 44, 47, nos. 10, 18. Theater: Schneider, pp. 8–9, figs. 2–3 (plan, sections); *Guide Bleu, Turquie,* p. 212. General bibl. on Nicaea in addition to above: W. Ruge, s.v. "Nikaia," *RE* 33:2 (1936), no. 7, pp. 226–43 (esp. history); C. A. Mango, "Iznik (Nicaea)," *Archaeology* 3 (1950): 106–9, and *Art,* p. 11; N. Firatli, *Guide to Iznik (Nicaea).* Translated by A. Mill (Istanbul: Istanbul matbasi, 1961). Vermeule, *ImpArt,* pp. 351, 453 (list of monuments, bibl.); Pliny's letters 10:39–40. Cf. also above ch. 3, ns. 16, 17.

[9]*Chronicon Paschale,* p. 475.

[10]K. Bittel, "Das Alamannia Relief in Nicaea (Bithyniae)," *Festschrift für Peter Goessler,* ed. W. Kimmig, pp. 21–22. Maltepe is described by Schneider, p. 19.

[11]The reliefs resist photography although they are quite readable in the original. Schneider and Karnapp, p. 44, no. 9, pls. 51, 52. Curiously, these reproductions, and Bittel's article, were unknown to B. Brenk, *IstMitt* 18 (1968): 241 when he wrote his study of Tetrarchic sculpture in Asia Minor. The major publication so far is Bittel, *Festschrift für Peter Goessler,* pp. 11–22, pls. 1–12, cited by Vermeule, *ImpArt,* p. 516, n. 9.

barian is being forced to his knees in the relief on the left (as the spectator faces the gate). Subjects and design of these reliefs are in the imperial Roman, not in the Hellenistic Greek tradition. The style is of the time of the Four Emperors or Tetrarchs (284–305). One of the Tetrarchs, Constantine's father, Constantius Chlorus defeated the Alamanni in 298 on the German frontier near Vindonissa. This must be the victory celebrated in the lost triumphal arch, one of the very rare examples of official Roman historic reliefs in Asia Minor.

Nicomedia, modern Izmit, city of Zeus Stratios, was the chosen capital of Diokles-Diocletian, "famed of Zeus," senior Tetrarch, who had assumed imperial dignity near Nicomedia in 284. In our time, Ataturk, too, had considered Izmit for the capital of Turkey. Diocletian wanted Nicomedia to rival Rome, *Romae coaequare* said Lactantius, (250–317), imperial professor and later a violent church father whom Diocletian had appointed to teach at Nicomedia.[12]

The famous pagan orator and professor Libanius, who lived at Nicomedia from 344–348, said that only four cities of the empire were bigger, and none more beautiful.[13] From his enthusiastic description we can envisage the busy waterfront

Fig. 164   sweeping around the crescent-shaped bay. It still sweeps around the bay and, as a Turkish friend put it, "all traffic of Asia and Europe still passes down this avenue . . . all honking their horns. . . ."

What comes as a surprise is the wonderful calm of the protected bay, where little boats can row freely; and the steep rise in two terraces from the waterfront

Fig. 163   up to the citadel hill (Orhan Mahalle). In its siting, Nicomedia is a magnificent example of the archaic Eastern Greek type—the harbor with acropolis.

The first phase of Roman urban renewal in which Pliny and Emperor Hadrian took part, left Nicomedia an Asiatic-Roman city with several agoras, colonnaded streets, gymnasia, and a huge bath built by Caracalla early in the third century.

[12]Lactantius *De mortibus persecutorum* 1.7.8–10, ed. J. Moreau, *Sources Chrétiennes* 29 (Paris: Éditions du Cerf, 1954), p. 86. Nicomedia: W. Ruge, s.v. "Nikomedeia," *RE* 33 (1936): 468–92; F. K. Dörner, *Inschriften und Denkmäler aus Bithynien, IstFo* 14 (1941): 44–51, sculpture, inscriptions; Guide Bleu, *Turquie*, pp. 194–96; R. Duyuran, "Izmit ve Silivri'de yapilan arkeolojik araştirmalar, 1947–48," *Belleten* 15 (1951): 213–19; R. Naumann, *AA* (1939): 156–71 with bibl. J. D. Ward-Perkins in D. Talbot Rice, ed. *The Great Palace of the Byzantine Emperors,* Second Report (Edinburgh: The University Press, 1958), p. 100; Inan-Rosenbaum, pp. 10–11, 19–20; N. Firatli, *Izmit (Nicomedie) Petit Guide.* Most up to date is N. Firatli, *Izmit Şehri ve Eski*

Eserleri Rehberi (Istanbul, 1971) with sketch plan of city and essential literature. There are many illustrations of the city and its antiquities (some otherwise unpublished) and an important plan which shows both the modern city and ruins underneath in Öztüre, see *Bibliography.*

[13]Libanius, *Oratio* 61:7. Other references, W. Ruge, *RE* 33:2 (1931): 490. On a bronze relief found in Croatia and datable after A.D. 350, *Nicomedia* is equal to *Constantinopolis,* both flanking *Roma;* the other two cities shown are Carthage and Siscia: J. M. C. Toynbee, "Roma and Constantinopolis in Late Antique Art," *JRS* 37 (1947): 142, pl. 7.

Diocletian reintroduced that element which had been missing from western Anatolian urban scene in Roman times, namely the Royal Palace. We hear that he had a palace of his own and that he also built palaces for his wife and daughter. He added yet another complex which was to become crucial in Constantinople —the Hippodrome (circus).[14]

This information comes from literary sources. There have been almost no regular excavations in the city[15] and owing to the vigorous expansion of modern Izmit from forty to one hundred thirty thousand inhabitants within the last fifteen years, building activities for the modern city are demolishing the scattered fragments of the ancient structures.

Both on the acropolis in the district Orhan Cami Mahallesi and around the city there are considerable remains of Roman, Byzantine, and possibly Hellenistic fortress walls. Their circuit has been traced.[16] Discovered recently at half-height on a platform against a steep rise of the citadel, the theater has some fine Hellenistic as well as Roman vaulted chambers of limestone masonry supporting the auditorium.[17] It opened to sweeping views on the southeastern part of the bay, including the site of Nicomedia's Greek predecessor, Astakos, on the sandspit projecting from what are now Kocaeli Fairgrounds. A nymphaeum of the second century of our era, one of the largest in Asia Minor, was on a slight rise (Tepecik), some 200 meters inland from the waterfront. In the west, near the waterfront, parts of colonnades were discovered during the construction of the huge modern SEKA paper factory and the equally modern State Supplies Office.[18] They have been interpreted by N. Firatli as parts of the agora. Very tentative reasons have been advanced for seeking the Palace of Diocletian in the western part of the city

Fig. 165

Fig. 164

Fig. 165.6

[14]Bath of Caracalla, Libanius *Oratio* 61.17; Procopius *De aedificiis* 5.3.7. Palaces, Hippodrome: Ruge, *RE* 33:2 (1931): 400–91 with ancient references. On its function: Claude, p. 77.

[15]Apparently some cleaning has been done at the Orhan Mahalle and at the theater, but otherwise the finds of buildings have come in the wake of modern building excavations. Guide Bleu, *Turquie*, pp. 194–95. Firatli, *Izmit*, p. 23, says that in the excavations by the Istanbul Museum in 1938 some fortress walls were found but no evidence to show that the Orhan Cami was preceded by a Christian church. Cf. R. Duyuran, *Belleten* 15 (1951): 213–19.

[16]Firatli, *Izmit*, pp. 11–12, figs. 13, 13a; cf. plan fig. 165.

[17]I am grateful to K. Kaval of the Izmit Museum for guidance to the theater at Kalemci sokak and other Izmit

sites. The theater is shown on Öztüre's, but not on Firatli's plan, fig. 165, no. 41. It also appears in C. Bosch's interesting attempt to reconstruct a plan of the major buildings of Nicomedia on the basis of coins. Unfortunately, this sketch cannot be usefully applied to the site as it exists. Firatli, *Izmit*, p. 7, fig. 2.

[18]Firatli, *Izmit*, p. 16, figs. 32–33 reports that a three-stepped marble structure going east-west was found in the garden of the *Devlet Malzeme Ofisi*. His plan, fig. 165:39, shows it turning a corner. He reproduces an Ionic column and a Corinthian capital. The structure was done away with by the builders and now only the Corinthian capital and column shafts (the latter in the embankment north of the State Supplies Office building) are to be seen.

Fig. 166 but farther uphill, inland.[19] An interesting testimony to the Hippodrome, possibly already that of Diocletian, is a relief with two charioteers which was found just outside the exit through the eastern city wall in Paç district.[20] There are vast cemeteries, mostly Roman, stretching to the east and west.[21]

Our lack of information is to be regretted even more since Nicomedia must have been crucial for Constantine's ideas about urbanism. He was sent there as a young man at the very time when Diocletian was rebuilding the city as a rival to Rome. The three ideological components of the later Byzantine capital, palace (*palatium*), temple (of Zeus—*sacerdotium*), and circus (hippodrome) were already united in Nicomedia. Only one ideologically important structure was missing. Diocletian had reserved his maussoleum to his militarily impregnable castle-palace at Spalato in Dalmatia.[22] His successor in Greece, Galerius, had also inte-

Fig. 167 grated his maussoleum with his palace complex in Thessalonike.[23]

From 296 to 306, Constantine, when he was in his twenties and early thirties, was at the court of Galerius. Here again, as at Nicomedia, was an opportunity to observe the rebuilding of a city as an imperial capital at close quarters and to learn about the administration of urban planning. Here again, as at Nicomedia, was a pool of skilled labor not too far from Constantinople, on which Constantine could later draw.

Finally there was Trier in Germany, the city that his father Constantius

Fig. 168 Chlorus and he himself had built. Chlorus restored the Barbara Baths and the

[19]I was told that the palace may have been inland at a street where a number of column capitals were allegedly found. I do not know the reason for the location of the palace on Öztüre's map (fig. 165 no. 5). He locates it at Eski Necatibey Okulu and says that ruins of it were observed during the construction of Sosyal Sigortalar Kurumu Hospital: Öztüre, p. 53, fig. 67, and a capital of much later date?, fig. 69.

[20]Firatli, *Izmit*, pp. 35–36, pl. 7:9, Izmit Museum, no. 53. Firatli dates it to the fourth century and notes that it was found with a small pediment, fig. 14. In front of the original, the dating seemed acceptable. Part of relief also Öztüre, p. 56, fig. 70. Öztüre suggests for the Hippodrome a location east of the city, southeast of Hayriseverler Cami which is no. 76 on his plan.

[21]Dörner, p. 56, sketch plan with cemetery near the paper factory and ostotheke of the second century. Firatli *Izmit*, pp. 16–17.

[22]T. Marasović et al. *Urbs* 4 (Split, 1961–62), devoted to problems of restoration and actual urban renewal and rehabilitation, contains also an English summary of recent

excavations within the maussoleum. See also J. and T. Marasović, *Diocletian Palace*, pl. 1 and plan fig. 34. For literature on the maussoleum, cf. S. McNally, "The Frieze of the Mausoleum in Split," *Studies Hanfmann*, p. 101. H. Kähler, "Domkirche," *Mélanges Mansel* (Ankara, 1974), pp. 803–20, fig. 99.

[23]Ward-Perkins, *ERA*, p. 524, fig. 198. E. Dyggve, "La région palatiale de Thessalonique," *Acta Congressus Madvigiani*, Proceedings of the Second International Congress of Classical Studies, I (Copenhagen: Ejnar Munksgaard, 1958), pp. 353–65 (also on hippodrome). *Deltion* 20 (1965): 407–12; N. Papahadjis, *The Monuments of Thessalonike*, pp. 4, 8. B. Brenk, *IstMitt* 18 (1968): 248–49, n. 29, pls. 74:2; 76:2; 80:2; 51:1; 83:1, capitals with sculptures from Galerius Palace. M. Vickers, *AnnIst* 15–16 (1969): 313–14 (hippodrome). L. Voelkl, *Der Kaiser Konstantin*, pp. 66–67, points out that Constantine continued the building activity at Thessalonike which Galerius had begun. Cf. also M. Vickers, "Observations on the Octagon at Thessaloniki," *JRS* 63 (1973): 110–20.

amphitheatre; and he constructed the Circus Maximus which was said to be similar to that of Rome. The gigantic Imperial Baths and the imposing new palace with the majestic palace audience hall, the *Aula Basilica* or *Aula Regia* were constructed by Constantine.[24]

Fig. 168.6, 168.5
Fig. 168.9, 168.3
Figs. 168.4, 169–170

It is to Trier, his father's favorite city and possibly his own that we must look if we want to know what Constantine's court art was like. What he liked on the Moselle, was likely to reappear on the Bosporus. Imperial architects and builders moved with the legions, and it was not much more time-consuming to bring them from Trier than from Rome.

Fig. 171

Fig. 172

When Constantine decided to found yet another new imperial capital he faced two major decisions: where to put it, and how to make it the capital of a totally new phenomenon—of a Christian empire. Byzantium was so clearly the key position between Europe and Asia, Mediterranean and Black Sea, that one really has to explain why it was *not* picked by the Hellenistic kings of Bithynia and by Diocletian.[25] The reason was presumably security; Constantine took the risks of a sudden attack from the Balkans to which Nicomedia, for instance, was less readily exposed.

As for the capital of a Christian empire, one may doubt how clearly anyone could foresee its character in 324, immediately after Constantine had defeated Licinius.[26] When he began building Constantinople, Constantine was not yet a baptized Christian. "The Highest Divinity has committed to my care . . . the government of all earthly things . . . I shall really and fully be able to feel secure and always hope for prosperity and happiness from the ready kindness of most mighty God, only when I see all venerating the most holy God in the proper cult of the Catholic religion with harmonious brotherhood of worship." This letter to his African prefect Aelafius states essentially the proposition of "one god, one emperor, one religion." Yet, as J. Straub has shown, there was constant improvisation, experimentation, and interchange between the empire and the church, and what each expected from the other.[27]

[24]Trier: M. Wheeler, *RAA*, pp. 71–76; W. Reusch, *Augusta Treverorum*; W. Reusch, *Aus der Schatzkammer des antiken Trier*; Th. K. Kempf and W. Reusch, eds., *Frühchristliche Zeugnisse im Einzugsgebiet von Rhein und Mosel*, esp. pp. 144–50 "Die Palastaula (sog. Basilika) in Trier," with bibl. E. M. Wightman, *Roman Trier and the Treveri* (London: Hart-Davis, 1970), pp. 58–62, 98–123, figs. 6–12, pls. 1–4, 8, 9.

[25]The outstanding position of Byzantium was recognized already by Herodotus 4.144 and Polybius 4.18. Cf.

V. P. Nevskaya, *Vizantiy v klassicheskuyu i ellinisticheskuyu epokhi*. German trans. by H. Bruschwitz, *Byzanz in der klassischen und hellenistischen Epoche* (Leipzig: Köhler and Amelung, 1955), pp. 21–30.

[26]A point emphasized by A. Alföldi, *JRS* 37 (1947): 10–16.

[27]J. Straub, *DOPapers* 21 (1967): 48; H. von Soden and H. von Campenhausen, *Urkunden zur Entstehung des Donatismus* (Berlin, 1950), no. 14, lines 65 ff. (Appendix to Optatus Milevitanus III, *CSEL* 26, for the letter to Aelafius.)

We tried to discern in our first chapter the liniaments of Croesus as an urban planner. Let us now describe Constantine as an urban planner. In seeking to meet the novel challenge of building a capital for a Christian empire, Constantine faced a fluid, experimental situation. Here, as in other fields, his actions were distinguished by grandeur of design and realistic pragmatism of execution. Thus, he did not try to found a completely new city or impose a completely new plan as Diocletian had done at Spalato. At Constantinople, as at Trier, Constantine the planner was satisfied to develop a pre-existing city with proven advantages of the site.

Byzantium had been destroyed by the emperor Septimius Severus in A.D. 196. He subsequently rebuilt it[28] and it became a modern city in terms of that Romano-Asiatic urbanism which we saw exemplified in Ephesus, Miletus, Sardis, and Nicaea.

The location of such major features as the ancient colonnaded ''Middle Avenue'' *(Mese)*; of the agora with four colonnades *(Tetrastoon)* an important public space which was used by Constantine for the piazza known as Augusteion; a major bath known as that of Zeuxippos (i.e., Zeus Hippios, a Thracian divinity)[29] and the siting of the hippodrome within the city, on its major north-south axis[30]

Fig. 173 were all features which Constantine developed from the Severan plan.

On the other hand, in the enlarged Constantinian city, he seems to have introduced a shift from the Severan plan, which was based on a rectangular
Fig. 174 intersection at the Tetrastoon, to a radial plan in the outer zone. Figure 174 shows a realistic assessment of the circulation pattern as the major *emboloi,* ''colonnaded streets'' seem to have followed the major pre-existing lines of traffic. The choice of a circular or oval *(kykloeides)* shape for his own forum and of the ''bent axis'' effect for the Mese Avenue were more original and possibly individual choices. Both effects had occurred in Roman cities in Syria and Jordan, for example, in Antioch and
Fig. 175, cf. 174, 179 Gerasa.[31] Constantine must have seen both on his early travels in Syria and Egypt.

---

[28]Janin (1964), p. 16. For pre-Severan and Severan Byzantium cf. Janin, ch. 1 ''Des origines à Constantin,'' plans I and II (fig. 173 below), and Mamboury, (1951), pp. 60–62 with plan, p. 64.

[29]Janin (1964), p. 16: Severus transferred a statue of Sol from the agora to the temple of Apollo. To compensate the Thracians in the populace, he built the Baths of Zeuxippos, southeast of the Tetrastoon. For a recent discussion of Baths of Zeuxippos, Augusteion, and Tetrastoon, cf. C. Mango, *Brazen House,* pp. 36–47, fig. 1. He suggests that

the Tetrastoon coincided in part with the Augusteion but occupied a larger area. F. Dirimtekin, ''The Augusteum,'' ''The Milion,'' *Ann. Aya Sofya Museum* 8 (1969): 24, plan. For a more concrete location of Milion, see below, n. 43.

[30]Mango, *Brazen House,* p. 37, with bibl. on the excavations 1950–52. Janin (1964), pp. 17, 183, 357. W. L. MacDonald, *The Hippodrome at Constantinople* (Ph.D. diss., Harvard University, 1956). Cf. in general Mango, *Art 3,* pp. 1–11, fig. 1.

[31]On circular central piazzas, D. Claude, pp. 63–64 with

Before proceeding further with our account of Constantinian Constantinople, it may be well to recall that in modern Istanbul very little from the time of Constantine is preserved and even less is visible. Sixteen hundred years of overbuilding have left the early city way below and mostly destroyed. The discussion that follows is based on literary traditions checked against relatively few valid topographical clues.

Turning to the ideological components of the city, what might seem the hardest problem, the Christianization of the city, was, for Constantine, relatively the easiest.[32] Thus the central ideological function, that is the divine protection of the city, was taken over from the pagan temples by the churches of Holy Wisdom, Aya Sophia, and Holy Peace, Aya Eirene. They would sound like familiar divinities to pagans. We have seen Sophia celebrated on the facade of the Celsus Library in Ephesus; and Eirene, "Peace," had been worshipped in Athens since

Fig. 133

---

bibl. Antioch, possibly under Diocletian; plan, Claude, pp. 245–46, pl. 4; Philippopolis (Shehba) possibly the earliest, under Philippus Arabs, pp. 244–49. Gerasa, C. H. Kraeling, *Gerasa* (New Haven: American Schools of Oriental Research, 1938), pp. 105, 115, pls. 19, 20, plan 12, 15; L. Crema, *L'Architettura Romana* (Rome, 1959), p. 349, figs. 401–30. M. Wheeler, *RAA*, p. 62, fig. 42 (fig. 175 below). On Philoppopolis Bibl. N. Duval, *Urbs* 4 (1961–1962): 69, n. 11. Damascus, too, had a circular piazza.

[32]The question whether Aya Sophia and Aya Eirene physically replaced pre-existing temples is unresolved. Ancient writers reported that Septimius Severus built a temple of Apollo on the Acropolis of Byzantium, which faced temples of Artemis and Aphrodite built by the legendary Byzas: *Chronicon Paschale* 1. 494.

In 1936, A. M. Schneider held that the temples were not under Aya Sophia but much farther north, n. 33, below. After his excavations of 1945–47 and 1949–50, M. Ramazanoğlu claimed that he had found between Aya Sophia and Aya Eirene evidence for a temple of Aphrodite and the Severan temple of Apollo. He also claimed that the porch of Theodosian Aya Sophia was partly identical with the Artemis temple. "Neue Forschungen zur Architekturgeschichte der Irenenkirche und des Komplexes der Sophienkirche," VIe Congrès International des études byzantines, *Actes* 2 (Paris: École des Hautes Etudes à la Sorbonne, 1951), pp. 347–57, esp. 347, 355; and "Neue Forschungen zur Architekturgeschichte der Irenenkirche und des Komplexes der Sophienkirche," VIII Congresso Internazionale di studi bizantini Palermo 2 *Atti* 2 (Roma· Associazione Nazionale per gli Studi Bizantini, 1953),

pp. 232–35, pls. 64–73. Mamboury, p. 61, accepted Ramazanoğlu's identifications for Aphrodite and Apollon temples but Janin (1964), p. 15, put the temple of Aphrodite near the column of Claudius Gothicus and the temple of Artemis "a little to the east," again away from the two great churches. Ramazanoğlu's successor as director of Aya Sophia Museum, F. Dirimtekin completely reinterpreted the excavations adding the results of additional digging in 1958–60. He considers the eastern part of structures excavated south of Aya Eirene as a Byzantine cistern and the western as a guesthouse *(xenodocheion)* of Samson built before Justinian. Cf. "Les fouilles faites en 1946–1947 et en 1958–1960 entre Sainte Sophie et Sainte Irene a Istanbul," *CahArch* 13 (1962): 161–85, pls. 1–2, figs. 1–2. For the *xenodocheion* of Samson, of which little is known, cf. Janin (1953), p. 574. Proposed with commendable caution, Dirimtekin's identification has found too hasty acceptance. Archaic, classical, Hellenistic, and Roman sherds and other objects were found in the excavations (e.g., Dirimtekin, fig. 22, Greek sherds dating from fifth to third century B.C.) and only a careful review of the entire evidence can determine whether any earlier structures might have existed within and below the early Byzantine stage. Cf. T. J. Mathews, n. 33, below.

For transformation of temples of Poseidon and Zeus into those of St. Menas and St. Menocius, G. Downey, *Constantinople in the Age of Justinian*. Cf. Nevskaya, pp. 148–49 for 29 sanctuaries listed by Dionysius of Byzantium in the second or third century A.D. along the Bosporus (with sketch of putative locations).

classical times.[33] They might appeal to pagans inclined to compromise. In a similar bid for "neutralism," a shrine of the great goddess Cybele was transformed into the shrine of the more abstract and allegorical Tyche—the Fortune of the City of Constantinople.[34]

The location of the palace and its relation to the main churches was more of a new challenge. How closely the church and the palace were linked in architecture at this early stage is difficult to say because both the Constantinian Palace and the Constantinian Santa Sophia with the palace of the Patriarch are very poorly known. Constantine's ecclesiastic advisor, Eusebius, pretended that Constantine "modelled, as it were, his very palace after the fashion of God's church," and that Constantine and his courtiers offered prayers regularly (*Vita Constantini* 4.17). This may be wishful thinking but Constantine's notion of the role of the Christian emperor as *Koinos Episkopos,* a general overseer of the church responsible for unity and harmony in religious matters,[35] would favor a palace plan with direct access to the central church of Aya Sophia. Accordingly, all recent reconstructions indicate that church and palace were planned with close reference to each other.[36]

Fig. 176 C. Vogt's reconstruction renders a later stage; but the essentials existed under Constantine—church and palace at equal height, opening as neighbors on the Augusteion piazza, but the church rising skyward, the palace descending down the slope.[37]

Fig. 177   Cyril Mango's plan of the situation at the time of Justinian shows the relation of the palace entrance, the *Chalke* or Brazen House, to Aya Sophia and the open

[33]Aya Sophia and Aya Eirene: Socrates *Historia Ecclesiastica* 2.16: "Constantius built the great church which is called Sophia and joined it to that called Eirene, and now both churches were included within one wall and had one title." For their early phases cf. A. M. Schneider, *BZ* 36 (1936): 77–85. T. J. Mathews, *The Early Churches of Constantinople* (University Park, Penn., 1971), pp. 11–19, figs. 1–4, pls. 1–2 ("The Old Hagia Sophia"), pp. 76–102, figs. 41, 48, pls. 60–61 (Hagia Eirene, the later Hagia Sophia), a careful, up-to-date discussion. He notes that according to Procopius, *De aedificiis* 1.2, 18–19: the two churches were dedicated to Christ under the titles of his divine attributes.

[34]Zosimus *Historia Nova* 2.31, on the two shrines built by Constantine, one for Tyche of Rome, the other for Rhea. Constantine removed the lions which this Rhea-Cybele previously held and restored her hands in an attitude of prayer as one "who oversees and takes care" of the city. J. M. C. Toynbee, *JRS* 37 (1947): 136–37; Janin (1964), pp. 24–25. Location of shrine: Mango, *Brazen House*, pp. 44–45.

[35]J. Straub, *DOPapers* 21 (1967): 51–53.

[36]A. M. Schneider, *BZ* 36 (1936): 78, 80, Hippodrome, palace, Augusteion, Aya Sophia planned as a unit. For history of research on the Great Palace and partial earlier plans (A. Labarte, 1861; Antoniades, 1907; J. Ebersolt, 1910; A. Vogt, 1935), cf. Mango, *Brazen House*. He remarks on the Constantinian palace: "The first period of the history of the Great Palace is scarcely known to us, yet it was at that time that many of the principal buildings were constructed and the basic layout established. . . ." Janin (1964), pp. 106, 117, discusses the Constantinian parts of the palace but gives no plan; cf. 106, n. 1–3 bibl. The most recent publications on the palace are Salvador Miranda, *Le Grand Palais de Constantinople* (Mexico City, 1964) and *Autour du Grand Palais de Constantinople* (Mexico City, 1968).

[37]A. Vogt, ed. *Constantin VII Porphyrogénète. Le Livre des cérémonies* (Paris, 1935) reconstruction, plan (fig. 176 below).

piazza of the Augusteion.[38] His plan also indicates the path of the formal processions of the emperor to the church, processions symbolic of the new unity of emperor and godhead which reached its culmination in the imperial attendance at the Divine Liturgy.

The new union of king and divinity was advertised in a painting over the entrance to the palace which showed Constantine as Defender of Faith overcoming the dragon of paganism—or so the Christians elected to think (Eusebius *Vita Constantini* 3.3).

Thus was resurrected the old Anatolian conjunction of the king living on the acropolis under the protection of a god or goddess. Contemporaries were conscious of reviving a native Anatolian tradition. "It was the custom of the ancients to build palaces on the acropolis," observed a Christian local writer; and they recalled that the mythical founder of Byzantium, King Byzas, had lived there and traced the area of his city (*Patria* 1.50).

In addition to the church and the palace a third urban component loomed large in Constantine's city—the hippodrome. Although its general location was determined by Severus, its inclusion in the palace complex area was due to Constantine. In those days of increasing social immobility, the hippodrome became a means of communication between the emperor and the urban populace of a city which eventually grew to 600,000. It was a substitute forum where people could vent their feelings not only on circus races but on social and political issues as well.

Fig. 176

Constantine obviously attributed great importance to this function.[39] Most of the official forty-day celebration of the founding of Constantinople in 330, took place in the hippodrome. The ceremonies included a public display of Constantine's statue, a ritual which he ordered repeated at subsequent celebrations of the city's birthday.[40]

In the hippodrome, the modern At Meydani, there is still to be seen the turning post *(spina)* of Constantine's circus around which the chariots turned during the races. An obelisk of masonry originally revetted with bronze, it was restored in the tenth century.[41]

---

[38]Mango, *Brazen House,* fig. 1.

[39]Cf. n. 30 above, for references; and on Nicomedia, ns. 14, 20. Claude, pp. 77–78, discusses the development of imperial prerogatives and duties with respect to the hippodrome and points for close connection of palace and hippodrome to Antioch and Thessalonike.

[40]*Chronicon Paschale* 1.527–30; *Patria* 2.45; Sherrard, p. 11. For bibl. on dedication, Janin (1964), p. 24, n. 6; Mango, *Art,* p. 10.

[41]Known as "colossus of Constantine Porphyrogennetos" from the mention of colossus of Rhodes in the poem about the restoration. Janin (1964), pp. 192–93 cau-

Prominent in the large-scale monumental planning, the Roman element was strongly advertised in official proclamations of the foundation. Constantinople was to be a "Second Rome," *Deutera Rome,* where Romans from Old Rome could feel at home. As at Rome, Constantinople had seven hills (originally six) and fourteen regions (originally thirteen). There was a capitol, a senate, a praetorium, and several fora.[42] Even the symbolic Golden Milestone of Rome, to which all

Fig. 178   roads of the empire led, was imitated in a structure known as the Milion. It was a construction with dome and arches, on top of which stood the statues of Constantine and Saint Helena holding a cross. Part of this Constantinian Milion, a marble pillar and a semicircular niche were discovered in 1967 about 200 meters west of Santa Sophia facing the Aya Sophia Square, which corresponds to the ancient Augusteion, and at the end of the modern Divan Yolu, which follows the direction of the ancient Mese Avenue.[43] Roma herself, no longer a goddess but still a potent symbol of the *imperium Romanum,* was given a special shrine.[44]

How did this "Second Rome," a mirror of Roman urbanism relate to *Constantinopolis Christiana,* the city that eventually came to contain 485 churches? Although some thirty churches were claimed by later chroniclers as Constantinian, the churches did not determine the divisions of the city; the Roman regions did.[45] Of more immediate importance in the picture of a Christian metropolis was the creation by Constantine of a second focal point of worship, at some distance from

Fig. 179   the palace complex. This was the cruciform church of Holy Apostles in the center

Fig. 197   of which the sarcophagus of Constantine was placed. To locate an imperial maussoleum within the palace area of an imperial city had the precedents of Diocletian in Spalato and Galerius in Thessalonike.[46] But to make his maussoleum into a major church was Constantine's imperial contribution to Christian urbanism. The Christians may have considered the building a *Martyrium,* a memorial church for an emperor who was "Isapostolos," equal to the apostles. Nevertheless, in 356 they moved Constantine from his central spot to a maussoleum annex, thus diminishing Constantine's claim to equality with Christ.[47]

---

tiously speaks of the possibility that the *colossus* may date before the fifth century.

[42]Janin (1964), p. 22, esp. p. 24.

[43]N. Firatli and T. Ergil, "The Milion Sounding," *AnnIst* 15–16 (1969): 208–12, figs. 1–6.

[44]Zosimus *Hist* 2.31. Toynbee, *JRS* 37 (1947): 136; Janin (1964), p. 25.

[45]Janin (1953), pp. 1–6; S. Eyice, *Petit Guide d'Istanbul à travers les monuments;* Mango, *Art,* pp. 10–11. On the

Christianization of ancient cities, cf. F. W. Deichmann, s.v. "Christianisierung, II," *RAC* 2 (1954): 1228–41; Claude, pp. 85–99. A new fundamental treatment: T. J. Mathews, *The Early Churches of Constantinople* (University Park, 1971).

[46]Cf. ns. 22, 23, above for references.

[47]Krautheimer, *ECBA,* 46–47 for an excellent summary. Janin (1953), pp. 36–55, with earlier bibl. G. Downey, *JHS* 79 (1959): 27–51, esp. pp. 42–43; *id.* "The Builder of the

Revival of Anatolian traditions and the conscious link with Troy; the heritage of Rome; and the new spiritual rule of Christ were the elements synthesized in Constantinople. Yet Hellenic culture was the all pervasive element. Byzantium had been a Greek polis with proud traditions of wealth and valor; and the Constantinopolitan legend depicts its new founder Constantine not as a new Romulus drawing city limits with a plough but as a Greek mythical city founder, a *ktistes,* striding vigorously, lance in hand, along the future boundaries of the city led by the Christian God.[48]

Such was Constantinople, then growing with might and main. This tremendous effort was draining away talent, means, and materials. We may now glance briefly at the situation of the other cities of the western coastlands of Asia Minor during this crucial period.

In general, the Tetrarchs and Constantine seem to have improved basic city matters. Roads were rebuilt and some important public buildings restored. In Ephesus, the great baths were repaired under Constantius (337–361) and henceforth called *Thermae Constantianae.*[49] A nymphaeum of the Marnas aqueduct was repaired and dedicated by Proconsul Lucius Caelius Montius. Montius also dedicated there two re-used cuirassed statues which stood in the structure, one of Constans, the other probably of Constantius.[50] Ephesus had heavily suffered from earthquakes in 358 and 363, and large-scale repair work was inevitable. Imperial aid was granted in 371–372 by Valens, Valentinian, and Gratian.[51] One has the feeling that similar activities possibly went on at Sardis, also because of earthquakes. That the urban renewal in western Asia Minor took final shape

---

Original Church of the Apostles at Constantinople," *DOPapers* 6 (1951): 51–80, and P. Grierson, "Tombs and Obits of Byzantine Emperors," *DOPapers* 16 (1962): 3–60, reject the tradition of *Vita Constantini,* pp. 58–60, 64–67, 70–71 and would make the church a work of Constantius II. Grierson, however, accepts the maussoleum as a work of Constantine.

[48]For the wealth of Byzantium and its courageous resistance to sieges from that of Philip II in 340 B.C. to that of Septimius Severus in A.D. 196 cf. Nevskaya, pp. 148–49. *RE* 5 (1897), s.v. "Byzantion," pp. 1116–59; Janin (1964), p. 11. For Constantine as *ktistes,* see Philostorgius *Historia ecclesiastica* 2.9, in J. Bidez, ed., *Kirchengeschichte, G.C.S.* 21 (1931): 21; and *Patria* 3.10, T. Preger, ed., vol. 2, p. 217. E. Gibbon, *The Decline and Fall of the Roman Empire* 1 (Modern Library Edition), ch. 17, 17.

[49]General situation: Vermeule, *ImpArt,* pp. 361-64 and material in the appendix, pp. 452-54 (milestones) from restored road. Ephesus, Thermae: Keil, *Führer,* pp. 76-79; *FoEph* 1 (Wien, 1906): 181. A statue base of Constans with a Latin dedication by Proconsul L. Caelius Montius, Eichler, *AnzWien* 100 (1963): 47.

[50]Nymphaeum: Keil, *Führer,* pp. 133-36, fig. 76. Eichler, *AnzWien* 100 (1963): 47, a new inscription by L. Caelius Montius. Statues: *JOAI* 15 (1912), Beiblatt, figs. 137-38. According to Vermeule, *ImpArt,* p. 465 and *Berytus* 13 (1959): 62, the cuirass statues came from the original nymphaeum of ca. A.D. 175.

[51]Keil, *Führer,* 115, inscriptions on the base of the Octagon Maussoleum. Cf. H. Vetters, *JOBG* 15 (1966): 273-87 who enumerates other building activities and statues.

Figs. 180, 181   around A.D. 400 is attested by the final form of such streets as the Arkadiane in Ephesus and the Main Avenue in Sardis.[52]

Among the buildings which were restored in provincial cities of Asia Minor during the fourth century, one has a special bearing on a very famous subject —that of the Constantinian basilicas.[53] As rebuilt in the fourth century, the huge Synagogue of Sardis had a porch, an atrium with a fountain, and an interior of basilican plan with powerful piers placed close to the long north and south

Figs. 116, 117, 183   walls.[54]

Fig. 182   The resemblance to old Saint Peter's, begun in 333 is plain.[55] A table decorated with Roman eagles stood where the altar stands in Christian churches, and the three benches for the Elders are the exact counterpart of the Christian Synthronon.[56] A beautiful mosaic in the apse had the "water of life" in a golden crater and a dedicatory inscription by two Flavian brothers Symphoros and

Fig. 184   Stratoneikianos.[57] The spatial effect of the interior of the main hall of the

Fig. 170   synagogue may have been not unlike that of the Constantinian basilica in Trier.[58]

The late Erwin Goodenough greeted the appearance of the "Eagle Table" and the apse as proof of a Hellenized sacramental-mystical Judaism, which, he maintained, had been suppressed by later orthodoxy.[59] Other scholars have raised the question whether the arrangement did not reflect the influence of Constantinian basilican churches.

---

[52]Both the Main Avenue (most recently, *BASOR* 203 [Oct., 1971]: 12–14, fig. 9; best plan *BASOR* 191 [Oct., 1968]: 40, fig. 36) and the colonnaded street which came from the Pactolus (*BASOR* 177 [Feb., 1965]: 14–17; 186 [April, 1967]: 24–25; 199 [Oct., 1970]: 29–30) were restored around A.D. 400. *Ananeosis* "renovation" is specifically attested by inscriptions both for the synagogue, where it may have lasted from mid to late fourth century, and parts of the gymnasium, which were restored by Severus Simplicius, a prefect of Lydia. *BASOR* 154 (April, 1959): 17; 166 (April, 1962): 44 (dating of Main Avenue and Byzantine Shops); Ananeosis inscriptions, synagogue: L. Robert, *NIS*, p. 53; *BASOR* 187 (Oct., 1967): 27. Severus Simplicius: *BASOR* 187 (Oct., 1967): 54, fig. 63. Arkadiane: Keil, *Führer*, pp. 71–73, 83–84 (column monument); fig. *FoEph* 1, p. 123. Claude, pp. 61–63, cites other colonnaded streets, and also gives examples of decline and decay through insertion of smaller structures.

[53]R. Krautheimer, "The Constantinian Basilica," *DOPapers* 21 (1967): 117–40. Cf. Mango, *Art*, p. 307.

[54]G. M. A. Hanfmann, "Ancient Synagogue of Sardis," 4th World Congress of Jewish Studies, *Papers* 1 (Jerusalem,

1967): 37–42, figs. 1–15. D. G. Mitten, *BA* 29 (1966): 63–66. The comparable elements are clearest in isometric view, originally designed by A. M. Shapiro, *BASOR* 187 (Oct., 1967): 61–62, fig. 70. Most recent reports: *BASOR* 191 (Oct., 1968): 31–32, figs. 18 (plan), 24–26; 199 (Oct., 1970): 47–51, figs. 36, 38, 40, 41; 203 (Oct., 1971): 12–18, figs. 9–11. Authoritative summary: A. R. Seager, "The Building History of the Sardis Synagogue," *AJA* 76 (1972): 425–35.

[55]Krautheimer, *ECBA*, pp. 32–35, fig. 14.

[56]Eagle table and benches: *BASOR* 174 (April, 1964): 36, fig. 19; 199 (Oct., 1970): 50–51, fig. 41. Tentative reconstruction by M. T. Ergene with Eagle Table, lions, benches, in Hanfmann, Fourth World Congress of Jewish Studies, *Papers* 1 (1967): 41, fig. 16. Other recent illustrations: Hanfmann, *Letters*, figs. 167–68, 199–200, 216–17.

[57]Mosaic: *BASOR* 174 (April, 1964): 30–33, fig. 17.

[58]Trier: W. Reusch, *Die Basilika in Trier 1856–1956*, p. 28, fig. 5, pl. 2. R. Krautheimer, *DOPapers* 21 (1967): 117–18, fig. 2.

[59]E. Goodenough, *Jewish Symbols in the Greco-Roman Period* 12 (New York, Pantheon Books, 1965), pp. 194–97.

In his article on the Constantinian basilicas, R. Krautheimer has rightly emphasized that there was much latitude and variety in the concept of a basilica. "At the upper end of the social scale the single-naved, apsed hall with marble-sheathed walls topped by painted plaster [and, as it happens at Sardis, glass mosaics] and with large windows was common in sumptuous public halls but is rarely used . . . by Constantine's architects." Disregarding the peculiarly narrowly placed piers, this is almost a description of the Sardis Synagogue. On the other hand, if we allow that there was an earlier columnar phase of the Sardis basilica, then the building shows much resemblance to imperial basilican plans such as those of the Antonine basilica in Smyrna and the Severan basilica in Lepcis, which, Krautheimer believes were intentionally revived by Constantinian architects to bestow proper imperial dignity upon the new houses of the Heavenly Ruler.[60]

Now that we know that the structure which became the Synagogue had gone through at least three phases prior to the fourth century,[61] it is even more difficult to judge whether the Jewish architects at Sardis had revised their interior arrangements in the light of such buildings as the new Aya Sophia at Constantinople (begun perhaps in 335). I believe that they imitated not churches but other large basilican synagogues.[62]

One matter is noteworthy: It was under the House of Constantine that the Jewish community of Sardis was permitted to use spoils from pagan temples in the renovation of the Synagogue.[63] This suggests a tolerant attitude on the part of the Christian authorities. In 330 Constantine did adopt a milder legislation toward the liability of the Jews to serve in curial offices by exempting the presidents of the

[60]R. Krautheimer, *DOPapers* 21 (1967): 130, 135–39.

[61]It started as a three-room part of gymnasium complex, then became a columnar basilican apsidal hall, possibly intended for a court basilica; and in the late second or early third century (possibly from 166 on) was turned into a synagogue. Detailed explanation by A. R. Seager, *AJA* 76 (1972): 425–35.

[62]At present it seems as if the renovation of the Sardis Synagogue, which certainly included the installation of the benches and the "Eagle Table," took place between 350 and 400. The existence of large basilican synagogues is, however, specifically attested for Alexandria, where the huge synagogue (*diplostoon*) was destroyed in A.D. 116. H. L. Gordon, "The Basilica and the Stoa in Early Rabbinical Literature," *Art Bull* 13 (1932): 360–61. R. Krautheimer, *DOPapers* 21 (1967): 123–24 is overly cautious. A. Grabar,

The Golden Age of Justinian (New York: Odyssey Press, 1967), pp. 57–58, believes that basilican synagogues are derived independently from Hellenistic halls. Cf. also S. Kraus, *Synagogale Altertümer* (Wien, 1922), pp. 261–62; E. Goodenough, *Jewish Symbols* 2, p. 85; R. Wischnitzer, *The Architecture of the European Synagogue* (Philadelphia: Jewish Publication Society of America, 1964), esp. pp. 11–13, synagogue at Elche, which also had an apse, and also had Elders (*presbyteroi*) as did Sardis. The arrangement of benches need not be imitated from Christians; it had probable precedent in the sanhedrin in Jerusalem.

[63]For the spoils cf. D. G. Mitten, *BASOR* 174 (April, 1964): 34–36. Many of them, including inscriptions, seem to come from a sanctuary of Cybele, later known as the Metroon.

synagogues from all public duties and taxes. If this legislation is correctly interpreted as a sign that Constantine came to view the Jewish religion as a source and forerunner of the *lex* of Christianity[64] then it would be understandable that provincial imperial authorities under Constantine's sons permitted the Jews of Sardis to restore their synagogue with great splendor in the most modern style of the religious structures of their day.

On sculpture, Constantine had important decisions to make which determined the role of sculpture in the Second Rome and in the new Christian Empire. By forbidding the worship of pagan images in Constantinople, he abolished a major incentive for making the statues of Greek gods and goddesses. On the other hand, he took no clear stand in the controversy about the images of Christ which was agitating the Christian church.

While cautious in matters of religious imagery, Constantine was determined and energetic in using plastic and pictorial arts to project his own image as that of the traditional omnipotent Roman emperor and as the new, divinely inspired overseer of the Christian church. A highlight of the foundation ceremonies in May, 330, was the raising of a statue of Constantine adorned with the seven-rayed crown of the Sun God on the 120 foot tall column, while assembled clerics sang "Kyrie Eleison."[65] Part of the column still stands in Istanbul in its ancient place in the Forum of Constantine. A simplified rendering of the lost statue has survived in the late Roman map known as Tabula Peutingeriana, dated A.D. 351.[66]

Fig. 185
Fig. 186

Previously, Constantine had presented the Sun God as his companion, as in the beautiful gold medallion from northern Italy coined at Ticinum in 313.[67] However, he himself now became the Sun with the rays of his crown containing a nail from the True Cross, and part of the Cross concealed within the statue. Hidden in the foundations and the base was the palladium which Aeneas brought to Rome from Anatolian Troy, the adze with which Noah had built the Ark, the rock from which Moses had struck water, and the remains of miraculous loaves with which Christ had fed the multitudes.

Fig. 189

[64]*Codex Theodosianus* 16.8.2. O. Seeck, *Regesten der Kaiser und Päpste für die Jahre 311 bis 476 n. Chr.* (Stuttgart: J. B. Metzlersche Verl., 1919), p. 180. L. Voelkl, *Der Kaiser Konstantin,* p. 185. Measures against building of new synagogues and conversion of synagogues into churches were frequent from Theodosius II on, cf. Claude, pp. 99–101.

[65]*Patria* 2.45, 49. *Chronikon Paschale* 1. 528–30; Sherrard (1965), p. 8. On the column, E. Mamboury, pp. 54, 264–66,

who excavated the base in 1929. C. Mango, *DOPapers* 17 (1963): 57, n. 13, bibl. Janin (1964), pp. 77–80 with references.

[66]J. M. C. Toynbee, *JRS* 37 (1947): 143, pl. 9:2.

[67]P. R. Franke and M. Hirmer, *Römische Kaiserporträts im Münzbild,* fig. 47. Ticinum Mint, A.D. 313. Gold Medallion. On Constantine's relation to Sol cf. J. Straub, *DOPapers* 21 (1967):43.

As a new sun, the Christian emperor was to unite in his new imperium the valor of Troy, the might of Rome, and the Old and New Law.[68]

It is very likely that Constantine supervised the manner in which his image appeared on coins. Thus, in a gold medallion of 325 and a gold coin of 335 struck at Nicomedia, where he often stayed, he is portrayed as supramundane ruler with heavenward gaze inspired by divinity.[69]

Figs. 187, 188

Constantine had to direct sculptural decoration in yet another capacity. As "exterior decorator" he imported dozens, if not hundreds of famous works of art to adorn Constantinople.[70] If Rome had collected thousands of masterpieces, the Second Rome could do no less. The Snake Column from Delphi, an early classical work of ca. 470 B.C. which still stands in the hippodrome,[71] and the famous horses of San Marco, probably late classical, which the Venetians brought from Constantinople,[72] are the best preserved of the vast number of statues that stood in the public places and buildings of Constantinople. They were living examples of Greek artistic tradition and an aspect of Greek *paideia*. They served occasionally as points of departure for classic revivals; but they came increasingly to be viewed as uncanny magic relics of a distant past rather than as beautiful works of art.[73]

Fig. 190

[68]A. Alföldi, *JRS* 37 (1947):11, rightly notes that the desire to make Anatolian Troy the ancestor of Constantinople stemmed from the wish to appropriate the legendary ancestor of Rome and thus make Constantinople more ancient and more eternal than the original Rome. The inscription of the "Burned Column" in which Constantine dedicates "your servant city and these sceptres and the might of Rome" to Christ is thought to be post-Constantinian by Janin (1964), p. 79.

[69]Eusebius *Vita Constantini* 4.9, "He had his image portrayed on gold coins in such a manner that he appeared to be gazing fixedly upward, as if praying to God," Mango, *Art*, p. 15. E. B. Harrison, *DOPapers* 21 (1967):90–91, fig. 35 (gold medallion), p. 37 (gold coin).

[70]*Patria* 2.73, states that sculptures were brought from a number of cities in Asia Minor including Nicomedia, Nicaea, Kyzikos, Tralles, Sardis, and Smyrna. C. A. Mango, *DOPapers* 17 (1963):57–59 with bibl. A. Cutler, "The *De Signis* of Nicetas Choniates, A Re-Appraisal," *AJA* 72 (1968):113–18. E. K. Gazda and G. M. A. Hanfmann, "Ancient Bronzes: Decline, Survival, Revival," in S. Doeringer et al. eds., *Art and Technology*, p. 247, ns. 22, 28. Brinkerhoff, *Collection*, pp. 55–59, 64–67, sets Constantine's collecting into the wider framework of collection and survival of ancient statuary in the fourth and

fifth century.

[71]P. Devambez, *Grands Bronzes du Musée de Stamboul*, pp. 9–12, pl. 2. Janin (1964), pp. 191–92, bibl. on history but without citing Devambez or F. Studniczka, "Zum platäischen Weihgeschenk in Delphi," *Festgabe Winckelmannsfeier* (Leipzig: Archäologische Seminar University, December 12, 1928).

[72]L. von Schlözer, "Die Rosse von San Marco," *RömMitt* 28 (1913):129–82. D. W. S. Hunt, "An Archaeological Survey of Chios," *BSA* 41 (1940–45):46–47, for provenance from Chios. Picard, *Manuel* 4:2 (1963), p. 534, figs. 223–24. One tradition would equate them with a quadriga by Lysippos which stood on a tower at the hippodrome of Constantinople. Nicetas, *De Manuele Comneno*, p. 156; *Patria* 2.87, near the spiral columns of the Neolaia, and above the *carceres* from which issued the race horses, Janin (1964), p. 194. For the theories that the horses are Constantinian originals or Constantinian casts after Lysippan originals see F. Magi, "La data dei cavalli di S. Marco," Pontificia Accademia Romana di Archeologia, *Rendiconti* 43 (1970–71):187–201, and G. Becatti, "Interrogativi sul problema dei cavalli di S. Marco," *ibid.*, pp. 203–6. The horses were transferred for repair and technical examination to Museo di San Marco in 1972.

[73]C. Mango, *DOPapers* 17 (1963):59.

Fig. 191

The adoption of Christianity and the founding of Constantinople resulted in great shifts of ideology and patronage. How did these changes affect the actual output and character of sculpture under the Tetrarchs and Constantine? In the late third century a strikingly abstract and pessimistic style arose at the Tetrarchic courts in the east. The prime example is the Tetrarchs themselves, the set of Four Rulers made of royal porphyry and now standing at the corner of San Marco, Venice. The group was at one time in Constantinople, for a foot fragment which fits has been recently found there. They do not represent, however, a style prevalent in Asia Minor.[74]

Fig. 192
Fig. 193

Much more local are some peculiar little friezes inserted into the temple of Hadrian at Ephesus.[75] They have been claimed as Tetrarchic because four bronze statues of the Tetrarchs were placed in front of the temple between 294 and 302 by Proconsul Junius Tiberianus; and the suggestion has been made that the friezes were done during a restoration at that time.[76] Among the subjects are Androklos hunting the boar before he founded Ephesus; Amazons fleeing before Herakles and an emperor or general sacrificing while being crowned by Victory; Amazons fleeing before Dionysus and his elephant; and a strangely stiff phalanx of gods, which includes the Artemis of Ephesus. After careful inspection I believe that the divine assembly is of the late fourth century, the other friezes of late third. These Tetrarchic reliefs attest the existence in western Asia Minor of a very uneven, partly "vernacular" classicism, with stylistic discrepancies as marked as in the contemporary Tetrarchic work in Rome.[77]

The uneven quality of these friezes, which must have belonged to an official imperial monument, points to a problem which became acute during the founding years of Constantinople. In edicts of 334 and 337, Constantine had complained about lack of competent architects.[78] It can hardly have been different with truly

[74]E. B. Harrison, *DOPapers* 21 (1967):84, figs. 20–21; Brinkerhoff, *Collection*, p. 22, on "Syro-Egyptian Tetrarchic style," figs. 26–27. The new fragment in R. Naumann, *AnnIst* 13–14 (1966):138–39.

[75]F. Miltner, *JOAI* 44 (1959), Beiblatt, pp. 264–66; Keil, *Führer*, pp. 118–19, fig. 64. N. Saporiti, "A Frieze from the Temple of Hadrian in Ephesus," *Essays in Memory of Karl Lehmann, Marsyas*, Suppl. 1 (1964), pp. 269–79, figs. 2, 5, 7, 9, with wrong (Severan) dating. R. Fleischer, "Der Fries des Hadrianstempels in Ephesos," *Festschrift Eichler*, pp. 23 ff., B. Brenk, *IstMitt* 18 (1968):239–58, pls. 79:1, 80:1. The reliefs are now in the Museum of Efes-Selçuk.

[76]By B. Brenk, *IstMitt* 18 (1968):250. For the pedestals cf. Vermeule, *ImpArt*, p. 333, fig. 141. Preserved are the bases

for Diocletian, Constantius, Galerius. Maximian was replaced by Theodosius. Date: B. Malcus, "Die Proconsuln von Asien von Diokletian bis Theodosius II," *OpusArch* 7 (1967):94, 119.

[77]Very striking on the Decennalia basis of A.D. 305. H. Kähler, *Das Fünfsäulendenkmal für die Tetrarchen auf dem Forum Romanum* (Cologne: Dumont Schauberg, 1964), p. 8, pls. 2–7. Brenk, n. 76 above, brings new interesting Tetrarchic material from Thessalonike. For Split cf. S. McNally in *Studies Hanfmann*, pp. 101–12.

[78]*Codex Theodosianus* 13.4.1 (334), 13.4 (337). Gibbon, *Decline and Fall* 1, p. 514 (Modern Library ed.). A. H. M. Jones, *The Later Roman Empire 284–602* 2, pp. 1013–14, n. 65. In the law of 337 Constantine encouraged sculptors "to

competent sculptors. To be sure, Constantine's personal artists produced portraits and paintings in a highly sophisticated court style, exemplified at his other residences by the bronze head from Naissus-Nish (his birth place)[79] and by the colorful paintings from the palace in Trier, the finest of which is the "Lady with the White Pearls," possibly the mother or the wife of Constantine.[80] In Constantinople (and Nicomedia as well) side by side with such fine court art, sculptures were made in local "rustic Bithynian" in fact, in provincial Anatolian folk style.[81]

Fig. 194

Figs. 198, 199

As A. Grabar has pointed out, in the same city quite different plastic traditions were being practised at different social levels.[82] For the higher levels of Constantinian art, the material from western regions is scanty.[83] Still, two imperial portraits, one of Constantine, the other probably of Constantine's third son, Emperor Constantius II, represent an impressive level of competence. The colossal head in the Istanbul Museum is just about the only head of Constantine, found so far in Constantinople.[84] Although poorly preserved, it strikes one in the original by its massive power and cubistic volume.

Figs. 195a, 195b

A colossal head in Izmir, well over twice lifesize, has not been hitherto recognized as a portrait of a ruler. It portrayed the emperor with toga drawn overhead, *capite velato*. Locks and large features fit only one ruler—the one we know from the colossal bronze head in Palazzo Conservatori in Rome —Constantius II, third son of Constantine, Emperor from 337–361, who had started his rule in the east. The fine marble head came to the Izmir Museum from the suburb of Bornova in 1926, but is conjectured to have been brought to Bornova from the sculptors' city of Aphrodisias.[85]

Fig. 196

---

become more skilled themselves and to teach their sons," Mango, *Art*, pp. 14–15.

[79]E. B. Harrison, *DOPapers* 21 (1967):81, figs. 1, 2 misjudges the piece as provincial. G. M. A. Hanfmann, *Roman Art* (Greenwich, Conn.: New York Graphic Society, 1964), p. 102, fig. 94.

[80]Kempf and Reusch, *Frühchristliche Zeugnisse*, p. 241, no. 40 a, Bild 8, color plate; pp. 244–46, identifications as Helena Sr. (Flavia Helena), Maxima Fausta, and Helena Junior, bride of Crispus. According to E. R. Alföldi, the date is 320–321.

[81]Izmit Museum, corner of sarcophagus lid from Çavdan. F. K. Dörner, pl. 22, no. 36. Cf. A. Grabar, *Sculptures byzantines*, pp. 37–39 on "rusticity." Cf. n. 87, 88, below.

[82]Grabar, *Sculptures byzantines*, p. 37.

[83]Imperial monuments and inscriptions have been collected by Vermeule, *ImpArt*, ch. 15 "The Tetrarchs" and 16

"Constantinus Magnus and His Successors," pp. 328–69 as well as in Appendices "Imperial Portraits," and "Works of Art and Inscriptions by Site," pp. 452–500. For portraits see Inan-Rosenbaum, "The Principal Centres of Portraiture in Asia Minor," pp. 19–38.

[84]Istanbul Archaeological Museums no. 5296. Vermeule, *ImpArt*, pp. 354, 516, fig. 177 with bibl. A rather crabbed female head from Nicomedia may represent a lady of the Constantinian house. Inan-Rosenbaum, pp. 99–100, no. 91, pl. 56 would date her to the late fourth century.

[85]Izmir (Old Archaeological Museum at Basmane) no. 173. For probable provenance from Aphrodisias see K. T. Erim, "De Aphrodisiade," *AJA* 71 (1967):240. It is not mentioned by Inan-Rosenbaum, nor by Vermeule, *Imp Art*, pp. 418–19 in his list of Roman "imperial" pieces in the Museum. Large-grained, fine (Parian?) marble. H. 0.68 m. W. 0.74 m. Back part unfinished, hence displayed against architectural background. Top of hand trimmed by

Fig. 197

Fig. 198

Fig. 199

Fig. 200

These two portraits were surely made by members of traditional, established ateliers. A guaranteed reflection of Constantine's own taste has been found in a fragment which had most immediate association with Constantine. This is the fragment of a porphyry sarcophagus in the Istanbul Museum, which J. Strzygowski, G. Mendel, A. Vassiliev and others have identified as part of the sarcophagus in which Constantine was buried. It exhibits the "neutral" imagery of garlands peopled with amorini, much in the manner of the school of Aphrodisias. The style is different, however, and the actual carving may have been done at the porphyry quarries in the Sinai, in Alexandrian ambient, rather than in Constantinople.[86] It makes a striking contrast with the fragment of a sarcophagus front in linear "Anatolian folk art" style; yet, the two may well be contemporary.[87]

Early Christian subjects now appear among the reliefs found at Constantinople, such as the charmingly naïve marble plaque with the prophet Jonah who first prays and then is swallowed up by a most amazing whale with shark-like head and lions paws.[88] Most of these Christian reliefs[89] are on folk art level—an indication that no specialized Christian sculptural workshops of high stylistic attainment had yet been formed.

A step higher socially and stylistically is the limestone "false" sarcophagus front of Flavios Eutyches, a kind of facade for a tomb otherwise built of masonry. The elaborate structure to which the relief belonged and the ambitious inscription in metal letters argue higher social aspirations. In a simplified but not incompetent classicizing style, Christ is shown between Peter and Paul. According to A. Grabar, the female figures symbolize the Church of the Circumcised and the

later hand. Nose and lips broken off. Damage to veil and front locks. A cleavage line goes through mid-face. The head was originally very carefully smoothed. It has powerfully cut eyes with deep pupils placed very high under the lids and surrounded by three pendant rings. The right eye also has drilled dots on either side of the pupil. Three soft folds of toga lie over the forehead. Bronze head of Constantius: F. Volbach and M. Hirmer, *Early Christian Art*, p. 316, pls. 18–19. R. Delbrueck, *Spätantike Kaiserporträts*, p. 139, pls. 52–54. Hanfmann, *Roman Art*, p. 102, fig. 95.

[86]J. Strzygowski, *Orient oder Rome. Beiträge zur Geschichte der spätantiken und frühchristlichen Kunst* (Leipzig: J. C. Hinrichs, 1901), p. 79. A. A. Vassiliev, "Imperial Porphyry Sarcophagi," *DOPapers* 4 (1948):14–15, 21–22, fig. 15, with bibl. Mendel, 2, pp. 447–48. Vassiliev also points out that according to one tradition, the empress Helena and Constantine were buried in the same sarcophagus by Con-

stantine II, after the Church of the Holy Apostles was completed.

[87]Relief from Çapa. Istanbul no. 4536. A. Grabar, *Sculptures byzantines*, pp. 41, 45, 128, pl. 13:3.

[88]Grabar, *Sculptures byzantines*, pp. 45–46, pl. 11:1, considers its "thoughtful iconography" the sign of "un atelier supérieur" in touch with classical tradition. N. Firatli, *CahArch* 11 (1960):82–83, 86, fig. 15. Something of fishermen's life on the Bosporus has carried over into the unusual scene.

[89]Such reliefs in the Istanbul Museum have now been collected by A. Grabar, *Sculptures byzantines*, pp. 16–19, 41, 45, esp. pls. 10:2; 11:2; 13:3; 12–14; 15; 16–17. The work of describing and collecting is yet to be done for other regions. Grabar, p. 41, rightly points to western Anatolian pagan antecedents in reliefs at Bursa and elsewhere.

Church of the Gentiles.⁹⁰ The busts of Eutyches and his wife are seen in the acroteria. The date might be around the middle of the fourth century.

Within the next two generations, the social and stylistic cleavages were partly overcome to create the first recognizable Constantinopolitan style, that of the so-called Theodosian Renaissance. It was reflected in workshops outside the capital. A fragment seen in 1971 at the church of Aya Sophia, Nicaea perhaps represents the Virgin rather than a youthful evangelist.⁹¹ It goes considerably beyond the sarcophagus front of Eutyches in achieving a well-rounded plastic quality. The apogee of this very consciously classical style is the sarcophagus of a child found in Constantinople.⁹² Classic and Christian aspects are programmatically conjoined as the front and back are adorned with angels or victories inspired by Roman triumphal arches, while on the ends apostles proclaim the victory of the Cross.

Fig. 201

Figs. 202, 203

We cannot survey here in detail the other sculptural centers of western Asia Minor. Unquestionably, there was a drastic reduction of sculptural output. Re-use and re-cutting of portrait statues became common practice: thus the two tetrarchic heads from Ephesus are said to be re-cut.⁹³ Still, portrait heads and portrait statues, such as that of a Consul Stephanos,⁹⁴ continued to be made for officials at Nicomedia, Nicaea, Ephesus, Aphrodisias, Sardis, and Smyrna⁹⁵ and displayed in public spaces well into the sixth century.

Fig. 204
Fig. 205
Cf. Fig. 146

⁹⁰Firatli, *CahArch* 11 (1960):77, fig. 4; Grabar, *Sculptures byzantines*, p. 36, pl. 9:1.

⁹¹No number. Found in 1968 built into the mihrab of the mosque which had succeeded the church. Marble, H. 0.55 m., Th. 0.09 m. Seated figure to right. R. arm veiled, bent, hand held something now broken off; left lowered, hand rests just above the knee. The folding chair stands on a "base line" of which the lower part is decorated with a pattern. The background is done with fine claw chisel. The rough-hewn but original edge is preserved on the left; it is treated for insertion into another piece. All other sides are broken but the piece was apparently a frieze, not a sarcophagus, unless it was a "false sarcophagus front" like the Eutyches relief, fig. 200. The head is broken except for the very charming right part of youthful face with one eye. There seems to be a bit of veil on the neck in which case the representation might be that of a female figure. While the other garment is treated with flat linearism, the undergarment has finer detail and the figure is well modelled.

⁹²The so-called "Prince's Sarcophagus," Istanbul Archaeological Museums; A. Grabar, *Sculptures byzantines*, pp. 30–32, pl. 7. Hanfmann, *Roman Art*, p. 125, fig. 143,

bibl. J. Beckwith, *The Art of Constantinople*, pp. 20–22, figs. 23–26. The style is very close to that of the "classicisme massive" of the Theodosius column base, even though the subject there was Roman-historical, Grabar, *ibid.*, pp. 25–29, pl. 5.

⁹³Inan-Rosenbaum, pp. 144–45, nos. 182–83, pls. 106–7, the re-cut fragment from Sardis, *Latomus* 103 (1969):290, pl. 104:3–4.

⁹⁴Stephanos: F. Miltner, *JOAI* 44 (1959):281, fig. 137; *Ephesos*, pp. 108–109, fig. 94; H. Vetters, *JOBG* 15 (1966):274, n. 3; F. Keil, *FoEph* 5:1, pp. 79–80, speak of the statue of Stephanos as found near its base. If this Stephanos was active in the late fourth century, when he transformed the Celsus library into a nymphaeum, either the statue or the head does not belong, for the style is of the sixth century, as W. Oberleitner, "Fragment eines spätantiken Porträtkopfes aus Ephesos," *JOAI* 44 (1959):86–89, figs. 60–62, has recognized. It is treated as an anonymous magistrate by Inan-Rosenbaum, pp. 157–58, no. 203, pls. 178:4, 186:4–5.

⁹⁵Inan-Rosenbaum, "Early Byzantine Portraits," pp. 19–20, 26–29, 38–44, pls. 175–86, show that active work-

A second branch of sculpture which continued to flourish was architectural decoration. The busts of divinities from the porch ceiling of the Serapeion in Miletus, dating in the late third century,[96] are perhaps among the last pagan anthropomorphic sets of such busts. The fine lion capital found in the Sardis synagogue probably belongs to the fourth century renovation.[97] Increasingly, human figures were eliminated while craters, doves, and animals remained. Emphasizing animals and plants, decorative sculpture was gradually transformed toward the semi-abstract beauty of early Byzantine ornamentation.[98]

In conclusion, taking a wide view, one might say that in the emergent Byzantine civilization and in early Byzantine urbanism, Greek tradition provided the general language of architectural decoration, Rome, the monumental organization and principles of construction, while Anatolian elements experienced a revival, both on the folk art level and in the social-psychological realm.[99] In a sense, the intensive veneration of images and the formation of monasteries were revivals of forms of religious life which had been practised at the great archaic sanctuaries of western Anatolia. At Ephesus, Artemis was succeeded by Virgin Mary. Many urban settlements declined, as did Ephesus, but others transformed themselves into "sacred fortresses," and many, like Nicaea remained sizeable and prosperous into the Middle Byzantine era.[100]

As a teeming megalopolis containing the court of King of Kings and the Patriarchate—the old Anatolian duality of *basileus* and *archiereus*—Constantinople, the "Czar-City," *Tsargrad* to the Slavs, was unique during the Dark

---

shops existed in Nicomedia, Nicaea, Ephesus, and Aphrodisias; to these must be added Sardis, and probably Smyrna. G. M. A. Hanfmann, "Late Roman and Early Byzantine Portraits from Sardis," *Latomus* 103 (1969):288, pls. 113–17. For Aphrodisias, K. T. Erim, "Two New Early Byzantine Statues from Aphrodisias," *DOPapers* 21 (1967):285–86, one of them (headless) Oikoumenios, *Praeses* (prefect) of Caria. Aziz, *Guide,* Izmir Museum no. 4, p. 76, ill. from Ephesus. Literary references: Mango, *Art,* pp. 46–49, 118–19.

[96]Serapeion: H. Knackfuss, *Milet* I:7, 180, Kleiner, *Ruinen,* p. 46, and ch. 3, above.

[97]*BASOR* 170 (April, 1963):44, fig. 34.

[98]Grabar, *Sculptures byzantines,* includes quite properly architectural and decorative sculpture of Constantinople in the second part of his work. At Sardis, the resulting contrast is very strikingly illustrated in the juxtaposition of anthropomorphic head capitals of the third century and beautiful early Byzantine Ionic "impost" capitals of the

fifth. D. G. Mitten, *BASOR* 182 (April, 1966):34–40, figs. 28–30. N. L. Hirschland, "The Head Capitals of Sardis," *BSR* 35 (1967):12–22.

[99]For architecture, cf. the assessment of Ward-Perkins, *ERA,* pp. 410–11. The interplay of traditional polis elements and the "East Roman" imperial legislation is analysed by Claude, ch. 2. "Die Verfassung der frühbyzantinischen Stadt." His book, though aimed at the situation under Justinian, constitutes a most valuable synthesis and contains materials for a developmental study from ca. A.D. 300 to 600.

[100]Cf. Claude, pp. 106 and 195–229, presents a careful analysis of different types of cities and sees "Christianization" and "militarization" as the two most clearly ascertainable factors: *ibid.,* pp. 208–19 on "Holy" cities. The expression "sacred fortress" was coined by O. von Simson for Ravenna, *Sacred Fortress: Byzantine Art and Statecraft in Ravenna* (Chicago: University of Chicago Press, 1948).

Ages and immediately thereafter. Its rivals were no longer the cities of the Greek East or European West but Damascus, Baghdad, and Cairo of the new Islamic world.

For the imperial court, ideology and iconography were a mixture of Roman and Greek elements, but something in the underlying psychological attitude toward power and toward its use and abuse seems to go back to Anatolian dispositions. There was a similar magnificent but somber coloration to the general tenor and to the particular intrigues and cruelties committed at the palace of the Lydian kings at Sardis and at the Great Palace of Constantinople.

I have put Croesus at the beginning and Constantine at the end and to them we now briefly return. The "portrait" of Croesus was made by an Athenian painter some fifty years after Croesus's death; the portrait of Constantine made at the height of his power, ca. 330, is from the great colossus in his basilica.[101]

Fig. 35

Figs. 206, 207

Both had little time as art patrons. Croesus ruled only 15 years. Constantine had only 13 years to build Constantinople. As persons and art patrons they had something fundamental in common. They both strove to discover and to serve the true god. Croesus trusted oracles and prophecies. Constantine trusted dreams and had a horoscope for Constantinople taken by an astrologer. Croesus sent out embassies to find out which god was truly inspired. He selected Apollo, who let him lose an empire. Constantine was told in a dream: "In this sign you will be victorious," and protected by Christ, he won an empire.

Croesus invented the gold standard and completed the economic revolution which gave the western coastlands of Asia Minor imperial leadership for two generations. Constantine founded Constantinople and through the new Christian synthesis of Anatolian, Greek, and Roman traditions, western Anatolia became the pivot of the medieval world and the center of the Byzantine Empire which lasted a thousand years.

[101]H. S. Jones, *Cat. Palazzo Conservatori,* pp. 5, 11–12, pl. 2. A. Minoprio, "A Restoration of the Basilica of Constantine, Rome." *BSR* 12 (1932):10–13, pl. 11 (reconstruction). Hanfmann, *Roman Art,* pp. 102–3, fig. 96. E. B. Harrison, *DOPapers* 21 (1967):92–95, figs. 3–4, 41–44 thinks an earlier imperial statue was re-used.

Bibliography

"The Age of Constantine: Tradition and Innovation." Symposium, 1966. Papers in *DOPapers* 21 (1967).

Åkerstrom, Å. *Die architektonischen Terrakotten Kleinasiens* (Lund: Gleerup, 1966).

Akurgal, E. *The Art of Greece: Its Origins in the Mediterranean and Near East* (New York: Crown Publishers, 1968).

———. *Ancient Civilizations and Ruins of Turkey* (Istanbul: Mobil Oil Turk, 1970).

———. *Die Kunst Anatoliens von Homer bis Alexander* (Berlin: Walter de Gruyter, 1961).

———. "Recherches faites à Cyzique et à Ergili," *Anatolia* 1 (1956):15–24.

Alföldi, A. "On the Foundation of Constantinople: A Few Notes," *JRS* 37 (1947):10–16.

———. "Die Geschichte des Throntabernakels," *La nouvelle Clio* 2 (1950):537–66.

Alzinger, W. *Die Stadt des siebenten Weltwunders: Die Wiederentdeckung von Ephesos* (Vienna: Wollzeilen, 1962).

Ashmole, B. *Architect and Sculptor in Classical Greece* (New York: New York University Press, 1972).

Aziz, A. *Guide du Musée de Smyrne,* new ed. Amis des antiquités de Smyrne et ses environs, *Publication* no. 9 (Istanbul, 1933).

Bammer, A. "Der Altar des jüngeren Artemisions von Ephesos," *AA* (1968):400–420.

———. *Zur Architektur des jüngeren Artemision von Ephesos* (Wiesbaden: Franz Steiner, 1972).

———. "Beiträge zur ephesischen Architektur," *JOAI* 49 (1968–71):1–40.

———. "Geometrie und Ornament als Antithese bei Doppelmäandern in Ephesos," *Festschrift Eichler,* pp. 10–22.

———. "Tempel und Altar der Artemis von Ephesos," *JOAI* Beiblatt 48 (1966–67):22–43.

———. "Zum jüngeren Artemision von Ephesos. Die Terrasse des jüngeren Artemisions und eustatische Schwankungen des Meersspiegels," *JOAI* 47 (1964–65):126–45.

———. "Zur Topographie und städtebaulichen Entwicklung von Ephesos," *JOAI* 46 (1961–63):136–57.

Baran, M. *Guide to Miletus* (Ankara Üniversitesi Basimevi, 1965).

Bates, G. E. *Sardis Monograph 1, Byzantine Coins* (Cambridge, Mass.: Harvard University Press, 1971).

Beckwith, J. *The Art of Constantinople: An Introduction to Byzantine Art 330–1453* (London: Phaidon, 1961).

Behr, C. *Aelius Aristeides and the Sacred Tales* (Amsterdam: A. M. Hakkert, 1968).

Berve, H., G. Gruben, and M. Hirmer. *Greek Temples, Theaters and Shrines* (New York: Harry N. Abrams, 1962).

Bieber, M. *The Sculpture of the Hellenistic Age,* 2nd ed. (New York: Columbia University Press, 1961).

Bittel, K. "Das Alamannia Relief in Nicaea (Bithyniae)," in W. Kimmig, ed. *Festschrift für Peter Goessler* (Stuttgart: W. Kohlhammer, 1954), pp. 11–22.

Boardman, J. "Pyramidal Stamp Seals in the Persian Empire," *Iran* 8 (1970):19–45.

Boethius, A., and J. B. Ward-Perkins. *Etruscan and Roman Architecture* (Baltimore: Penguin Books, 1970).

Böhlau, J., and K. Schefold. *Larisa am Hermus* I *Die Bauten* (Stockholm: Vitterhets Historie och Antikvitets Akademie, 1940).

Borchhardt, J. "Epichorische, gräko-persisch beeinflusste Reliefs in Kilikien," *IstMitt* 18 (1968):161–211.

———. "Das Heroon von Limyra—Grabmal des lykischen Königs Perikles," *AA* (1970):353–90.

———. "Limyra, Sitz des lykischen Dynasten Perikles," *IstMitt* 17 (1967):154–62.

———. "Limyra Bericht, 1971," *Dergi* 20 (1973):37–62.

von Bothmer, D. *Amazons in Greek Art* (Oxford: Clarendon Press, 1957).

Boulanger, A. *Aelius Aristide et la sophistique dans la province d'Asie au II_e siècle de notre ère* (Paris: E. de Boccard, 1923).

Bowersock, G. W. *Augustus and the Greek World* (Oxford: Clarendon Press, 1965).

———. *Greek Sophists in the Roman Empire* (Oxford: Clarendon Press, 1969).

Brenk, B. "Die Datierung des Reliefs am Hadrianstempel in Ephesos und das Problem der tetrarchischen Skulptur des Ostens," *IstMitt* 18 (1968):239–58.

Brinkerhoff, D. M. *A Collection of Sculpture in Classical and Early Christian Antioch* (New York: New York University Press, 1970).

Brommer, F. "Aion," *Marburger Winckelmannsprogramm* (1967), pp. 1–5.

———. "Neue pergamenische Köpfe," *Jahrbuch der Berliner Museen* 12 (1970):191–210.

Broughton, T. R. S. "New Evidence on Temple Estates in Asia Minor," in P. R. Coleman-Norton, ed. *Studies in Roman Economic and Social History in Honor of Allan Chester Johnson* (Princeton: Princeton University Press, 1951), pp. 236–50.

Bruun, P., in Bellinger, A. "Late Roman Gold and Silver Coins at Dumbarton Oaks, (Constantine)," *DOPapers* 18 (1964):176–84.

Buckler, W. H. *Sardis* VI.2 *Lydian Inscriptions* (Leyden: E. J. Brill, 1924).

Buckler, W. H., and W. M. Calder, eds. *Anatolian Studies Presented to Sir William Mitchell Ramsay* (Manchester, London, and New York: Manchester University Press, 1923).

Buckler, W. H., and D. M. Robinson. *Sardis* VII.1 *Greek and Latin Inscriptions* (Leyden: E. J. Brill, 1932).

Burn, A. R. *Persia and the Greeks c. 546–478* B.C. (London: Edward Arnold, 1962).

Cadoux, C. J. *Ancient Smyrna: A History of the City from the Earliest Times to 324* A.D. (Oxford: Basil Blackwell, 1938).

Calza, R. *Iconografia romana imperiale* 3 (Rome: "L'Erma" di Bretschneider, 1972).

Carettoni, G. et al. *La pianta marmorea di Roma antica. Forma Urbis Romae* (Rome: Libreria dello State, 1960).

Castagnoli, F. *Ippodamo di Mileto e l'urbanistica a pianta ortogonale* (Rome: De Luca, 1956).

———. *Orthogonal Town Planning in Antiquity* (Cambridge, Mass.: MIT Press, 1971).

Castelfranco, G. "L'arte della moneta nel Tardo Impero," *La Critica d'Arte* 2 (1937):11–21.

Claude, D. *Die byzantinische Stadt im 6. Jahrhundert* (Munich: C. H. Beck, 1969).

Codex Theodosianus, see Krueger, P.; Pharr, C.

Cook, J. M. *The Greeks in Ionia and the East* (New York and Washington: Praeger, 1963).

———. "Old Smyrna, 1948–1951," *BSA* 53–54 (1958–59):1–36.

Coupel, P., and P. Demargne. *Fouilles de Xanthos* 3, *Le Monument des Néreides. L'architecture* (Paris: Editions Klincksieck, 1969).

Cumont, F. *Oriental Religions in Roman Paganism* (New York: Dover Publishers, 1956).

Deichmann, F. W. "Frühchristliche Kirchen in antiken Heiligtümern," *JdI* 54 (1939):105–36.

Delorme, J. *Gymnasion* (Paris, 1960).

Dentzer, J. M. "Reliefs 'au banquet' dans l'Asie Mineure du Ve siecle av. J.-C.," *RA* (1971), fasc. 2, pp. 215–58.

Devambez, P. *Grands bronzes du Musée de Stamboul* (Paris: E. de Boccard, 1937).

Dindorf, L., ed. "Chronicon Paschale," *Corpus Scriptorum Historiae Byzantinae* (Bonn, 1832).

Dio Chrysostom, ed. and transl. by H. Lamar Crosby, *Loeb Classical Library* (Cambridge, Mass.: Harvard University Press, 1946).

Dörner, F. K. *Inschriften und Denkmäler aus Bithynien, IstFo* 14 (Berlin, 1941).

Dörner, F. K., and T. Goell. *Arsameia am Nymphaios: Die Ausgrabungen im Hierothesion des Mithradates Kallinikos von 1953–1956, IstFo* 23 (Berlin, 1963).

Downey, G. *Constantinople in the Age of Justinian* (Norman: University of Oklahoma Press, 1960).

———. "The Tombs of the Byzantine Emperors at the Church of the Holy Apostles in Constantinople," *JHS* 79 (1959):27–51.

Dressler, W. "Karoide Inschriften im Steinbruch von Belevi," *JOAI* 48 (1966–67):73–76.

Eichler, F. "Ephesos," *JOAI* 49 (1968–69):3–7.

———. *Die Reliefs des Heroon von Gjölbaschi-Trysa* (Wien: Deuticke, 1950).

———. "Ephesos, Grabungsbericht 1968," *AnzWien* 106 (1969):1–16.

———. "Die österreichischen Ausgrabungen in Ephesos im Jahre 1962," *AnzWien* 100 (1963):45–59.

———. "Die österreichischen Ausgrabungen in Ephesos im Jahre 1963," *AnzWien* 101 (1964):39–44.

———. "Die österreichischen Ausgrabungen in Ephesos im Jahre 1964," *AnzWien* 102 (1965):93–109.

———. "Die österreichischen Ausgrabungen in Ephesos im Jahre 1965," *AnzWien* 103 (1966):7–16.

———. "Die österreichischen Ausgrabungen in Ephesos im Jahre 1966," *AnzWien* 104 (1967):15–28.

———. "Die österreichischen Ausgrabungen in Ephesos im Jahre 1967," *AnzWien* 105 (1968):79–95.

———. *Festschrift*, see Österreichisches archäologisches Institute.

———. *Forschungen in Ephesos* V:1 *Die Bibliothek* (München and Wien: Rudolf M. Rohrer, 1944).

———. "Zum Partherdenkmal von Ephesos," *JOAI* 49 Suppl. 2 (1970):102–36.

Eiden, H. "Ausgrabungen im spätantiken Trier," in *Neue Ausgrabungen in Deutschland* (Berlin:

Römisch-Germanische Kommission des deutschen ärchäologischen Instituts, 1958), pp. 340–67.

Elderkin, G. W. "The Golden Lion of Croesus," *Archaeological Papers* 2 (1941):1–8.

Erim, K. T. "De Aphrodisiade," *AJA* 71 (1967):233–43.

———. "Aphrodisias: Results of the 1968 Campaign," *Dergi* 17 (1968):43–57.

———. "Aphrodisias. Excavations in the Roman and Byzantine City, Part 2. Buildings and Still More Statuary," *ILN* (Dec. 28, 1963):1066–69; Part 1 "The Mine of Statuary. The Temple and the Odeion," (Dec. 21, 1963):1028–31.

———. "Further Findings from the Carian 'Mine of Statuary' and the Discovery of the Unique Cult Statue of Aphrodisias," *ILN* (Jan. 5, 1963):20–23.

———. "The School of Aphrodisias," *Archaeology* 20 (1967):18–27.

Erim, K. T., and J. S. Blair. "Ancient Aphrodisias and its Marble Treasures," *The National Geographic* 132:2 (August, 1967):280–94.

Erim, K. T., and J. Reynolds. "A Letter of Gordian III from Aphrodisias in Caria," *JRS* 59 (1969):56–58.

Eyice, S. *Petit Guide d'Istanbul à travers les monuments* (Istanbul, 1955).

Fasolo, F. "L'architettura romana a Efeso" in *Bolletino del centro di studi per la storia dell'architettura* (Rome, 1962), pp. 1–92.

———. "La Basilica del Consilio di Efeso," *Palladio* 1–2, N.S. vol. 6 (1956):1–30.

Ferrari, G. *Il commercio dei sarcofagi asiatici* in *Studia Archaeologica* 7 (Rome, 1966).

Firatli, N. "Bitinya Araştirmalarina Birkaç Ilave," *Belleten* 17 (1953):15–25.

———. *Izmit Şehri ve Eski Eserleri Rehberi* (Istanbul: Milli Eğitim Basimevi, 1971).

———. *Iznik (Nicée). Son histoire, ses monuments* (Istanbul: Touring and Automobile Club of Turkey, 1959).

———. "Deux nouveaux reliefs funéraires d'Istanbul et les reliefs similaires," *CahArch* 11 (1960):73–92.

———. *Les stèles funéraires de Byzance gréco-romaine*. Bibliothèque archéologique et historique de l'institut français d'archéologie d'Istanbul 15 (1964), pp. 1–129.

Firatli, N., and T. Ergil, "The 'Milion' Sounding," *AnnIst* 15–16 (1969):208–12.

Firth, J. B. *Constantine the Great* (London: G. B. Putnam, 1904).

Fleischer, R. *Artemis von Ephesos und verwandte Kultstatuen aus Anatolien und Syrien* (Leiden: E. J. Brill, 1973).

———. "Der Fries des Hadrianstempels in Ephesos," *Festschrift Eichler*, pp. 23–71.

———. "Späthellenistische Gruppe vom Pollionymphaeum . . . mit dem Polyphemabenteuer des Odysseus; Aphroditetorso vom Pollionymphaeum in Ephesos; Artemisstatuette aus dem Hanghaus II in Ephesos," *JOAI* 49 (1968–69), Beiheft II, pp. 137–88.

Franke, P. R. *Kleinasien zur Römerzeit: Griechisches Leben im Spiegel der Münzen* (Munich: C. H. Beck, 1968).

Franke, P. R., and M. Hirmer. *Römische Kaiserporträts im Münzbild* (Munich: M. Hirmer, 1961).

Friend, A. M., Jr. "The Portraits of the Evangelists in Greek and Latin Manuscripts," I *Art Studies* 5 (1927):115–47; II *Art Studies* 7 (1929):3–29.

Gazda, E. K., and G. M. A. Hanfmann. "Ancient Bronzes: Decline, Survival, Revival," in S. Doeringer et al., eds. *Art and Technology* (Cambridge, Mass.: MIT Press, 1970), pp. 245–70.

Gerkan, A. von. *Von antiker Architektur und Topographie* (Stuttgart: Kohlhammer, 1959).

_____. "Der Altar des Athenatempels in Priene," *Bonner Jahrbücher* 129 (1924):15–35.

_____. "Die Datierung der Statuenbasen vor dem Proskenion in Priene," *AthMitt* 49 (1924):49–51.

_____. *Griechische Städteanlagen: Untersuchungen zur Entwicklung des Städtebaues in Altertum* (Berlin and Leipzig: Walter de Gruyter, 1924).

_____. *Milet, I:6 Der Nordmarkt und der Hafen an der Löwenbucht* (Berlin and Leipzig, 1922).

_____. *Das Theater von Priene* (Munich: Verlag für praktische Kunstwissenschaft, 1921).

Gerkan, A. von, and F. Krischen. *Milet* I:9 *Thermen und Palästren* (Berlin, 1929).

Giuliano, A. "Rilievo da Aphrodisias in onore di Zoilos," *ASAtene* 37–38 (1959–60):389–401.

_____. "La ritrattistica dell'Asia Minore dall' 89 A.C. al 211 D.C.," *Rivista dell'Instituto Nazionale d'Archeologia e Storia dell'Arte* N.S. 7 (Rome, 1959).

Glover, T. R. *The Conflict of Religions in the Early Roman Empire* (Boston: Beacon Press, 1961).

Grabar, A. *Sculptures byzantines de Constantinople (IVe–X siècles)* Bibliothèque archéologique et historique de l'institut français d'archéologie d'Istanbul 17 (Paris, 1963).

Greenewalt, C. H., Jr. "Lydian Vases from Western Asia Minor," *California Studies in Classical Antiquity* 1 (1968):140–54.

_____. "An Exhibitionist from Sardis," in *Studies Hanfmann,* pp. 29–46.

_____. "Orientalizing Pottery from Sardis: The Wild Goat Style," *California Studies in Classical Antiquity* 3 (1970):55–89.

Groag, E., A. Stein, and L. Petersen, eds. *Prosopographia Imperii Romani,* 2nd ed. (Berlin: Walter de Gruyter, 1933–70).

Gruben, G. "Beobachtungen zum Artemis-Tempel von Sardis," *AthMitt* 76 (1961):156–96.

_____. "Das archaische Didymaion," *JdI* 78 (1963):78–182.

Gusmani, R. *Lydisches Wörterbuch* (Heidelberg: Carl Winter, 1964).

Hanfmann, G. M. A. "The New Stelae from Daskylion," *BASOR* 184 (Dec. 1966):10–13.

_____. "On Late Roman and Early Byzantine Portraits from Sardis," *Hommages à Marcel Renard* III *Collection Latomus* 103 (Brussels, 1969).

_____. "A Pediment of the Persian Era from Sardis," *Mélanges Mansel* (Ankara, 1974), pp. 289–302.

_____. "Horsemen from Sardis," *AJA* 49 (1945):570–81.

_____. "Greece and Lydia: The Impact of Hellenic Culture," *Le Rayonnement des Civilizations Grecque et Romaine sur les Cultures Peripheriques,* 8ième Congrès International d'Archéologie Classique (1963) (Paris, 1965), pp. 491–99.

_____. *Letters from Sardis* (Cambridge, Mass.: Harvard University Press, 1972).

_____. "Sardis und Lydien," *Akademie der Wissenschaften und Literatur Mainz, Geistes-und sozialwissenschaftliche Klasse, Abhandlungen 1960,* Nr. 6 (1960).

Hanfmann, G. M. A., and K. Z. Polatkan. "Three Sculptures from Sardis in the Manisa Museum," *Anatolia* 4 (1959):57–65.

Hanfmann, G. M. A., K. Z. Polatkan, and L. Robert. "A Sepulchral Stele from Sardis. The Inscription of the Sepulchral Stele," *AJA* 64 (1960):49–56.

Hanfmann, G. M. A., and J. C. Waldbaum. "Kybebe and Artemis, Two Anatolian Goddesses at Sardis," *Archaeology* 22 (1969):264–69.

_____. "New Excavations at Sardis and Some Problems of Western Anatolian Archaeology," in J.

A. Sanders, ed. *Near Eastern Archaeology in the Twentieth Century Essays in Honor of Nelson Glueck* (Garden City, New York: Doubleday and Co., 1970), pp. 307–26.

———. "Sardis, 1969," *Archaeology* 23 (1970):251–53.

Hansen, E. V. *The Attalids of Pergamon,* 2nd ed. (Ithaca, New York: Cornell University Press, 1971).

Harrison, E. B. "The Constantinian Portrait," *DOPapers* 21 (1967):81–96.

Havelock, C. M. *Hellenistic Art* (Greenwich, Conn.: New York Graphic Society, 1971).

———. "Round Sculptures from the Mausoleum at Halicarnassos," *Studies Hanfmann,* pp. 55–64.

Herrmann, P. "Antiochos der Grosse und Teos," *Anatolia* 9 (1965):28–159.

Helbig, W., and H. Speier. *Führer durch die öffentlichen Sammlungen klassischer Altertümer in Rom,* 4th ed., vols. 1–4 (Tübingen: E. Wasmuth, 1963–72).

Hogarth, D. G. *Excavations at Ephesus. The Archaic Artemisia* (London: The British Museum, 1908).

Horn, R. *Stehende weibliche Gewandstatuen in der hellenistischen Plastik, RömMitt, Ergänzungsheft* 2 (Munich: Bruckmann, 1931).

Inan, J., and E. Rosenbaum. *Roman and Early Byzantine Portrait Sculpture in Asia Minor* (Oxford University Press, 1966).

Jacobsthal, P., and E. S. G. Robinson. "The Date of the Ephesian Foundation-Deposit," *JHS* 71 (1951):85–95.

Janin, R. *Constantinople byzantine: Developpement urbain et repertoire topographique,* 2nd ed. (Paris: Institut français d'études byzantines, 1964).

———. *La géographie écclesiastique de l'empire byzantin* 3, *Les Eglises et les Monastères* (Paris, 1953).

Jeppesen, K. "Explorations at Halicarnassus: Excavations at the Site of the Mausoleum," *ActaA* 38 (1967):27–58.

Jeppesen, K., and J. Zahle, "The Site of the Maussoleum of Halicarnassus Reexcavated," AJA 77 (1973):336–38.

Jones, A. H. M. *The Cities of the Eastern Roman Provinces* (Oxford: Clarendon Press, 1937).

———. *The Greek City from Alexander to Justinian* (Oxford: Clarendon Press, 1940).

———. *The Later Roman Empire 284–602. A Social, Economic and Administrative Survey* (Norman: University of Oklahoma Press, 1964).

Jones, C. P. *Plutarch and Rome* (Oxford: Clarendon Press, 1971).

Kähler, H. *Der grosse Fries von Pergamon* (Berlin: Mann, 1948).

———. *Seethiasos und Census: Die Reliefs aus dem Palazzo Santa Croce in Rom* (Berlin: *Monumenta Artis Romanae* VI, 1966).

Kawerau, G., and T. Wiegand. *Altertümer von Pergamon V:1 Die Paläste der Hochburg* (Berlin and Leipzig: Walter de Gruyter, 1930).

Keil, J. *Führer durch Ephesos* (Vienna, Österreichisches Archäologisches Institut, 1964).

———. "Die Kulte Lydiens," *AnatSt Ramsay,* pp. 239–66.

Kempf, T. K. "Konstantinische Deckenmalereien," in Kempf, T. K., and W. Reusch, eds. *Frühchristliche Zeugnisse im Einzugsgebiet von Rhein und Mosel* (Trier: Unitas-Trier, 1965), pp. 240–46.

Kleemann, I. "Der Satrapensarkophag aus Sidon," *IstFo* 20 (Berlin, 1958).

"Kleinasien und Byzanz," *IstFo* 17 (Berlin, 1950).

Kleiner, G. "Die Istanbuler Platte vom pergamenischen Gigantenfries," *IstMitt* 17 (1967):168–72.

————. *Das römische Milet*. Wissenschaftliche Gesellschaft an der Johann Wolfgang Goethe-Universität Frankfurt am Main, *Sitzungsberichte* 8:5 (1969) (Wiesbaden: Steiner, 1970).

————. *Die Ruinen von Milet* (Berlin: Walter de Gruyter, 1968).

Kleiss, W. *Topographisch-Archäologischer Plan von Istanbul* (Tübingen: E. Wasmuth, 1965).

Knackfuss, H. *Milet* I:7 *Der Südmarkt und die benachbarten Bauanlagen* (Berlin, 1924).

Kraabel, A. T. "Melito the Bishop and the Synagogue at Sardis, Text and Context," *Studies Hanfmann*, pp. 77–85.

————. "*Hypsistos* and the Synagogue at Sardis," *Greek, Roman and Byzantine Studies* (1969):81–93.

Krautheimer, R. "The Constantinian Basilica," *DOPapers* 21 (1967):117–40.

————. *Early Christian and Byzantine Architecture* (Baltimore: Penguin Books, 1965).

Krischen, F. "Der Aufbau des Nereidenmonumentes von Xanthos," *AthMitt* 48 (1923):69–92.

————. *Die griechische Stadt* (Berlin: Mann, 1938).

————. *Weltwunder der Baukunst in Babylonien und Ionien* (Tübingen: Ernst Wasmuth 1956).

Krueger, P., ed. *Codex Theodosianus* (Berlin: Weidmann, 1923–26).

Kubinska, J. *Les monuments funéraires dans les inscriptions grecques de l'Asie Mineure* Travaux du centre d'archéologie mediterranéenne de l'academie polonaise des sciences V.5 (Warsaw: Éditions Scientifiques de Pologne, 1968).

Lattimore, S. "The Bronze Apoxyomenos from Ephesos," *AJA* 76 (1972):13–16.

Laubscher, H. P. "Zum Fries des Hadrianstempels in Kyzikos," *IstMitt* 17 (1967):211–17.

Lawrence, A. W. *Greek Architecture* (Baltimore: Penguin Books, 1957).

————. *Later Greek Sculpture and Its Influence on East and West* (London: Jonathan Cape, 1927).

Lehmann, P. W. "The Setting of Hellenistic Temples," *JASAH* 13 (1954):15–20.

Lehmann-Hartleben, K. *Plinio il Giovane. Lettere scelte con commento archeologico* Testi della Scuola Normale Superiore di Pisa 3 (Florence, 1936).

Lippold, G. *Die griechische Plastik* (Munich: C. H. Beck, 1950).

L'Orange, H. P. *Art Forms and Civic Life in the Late Roman Empire* (Princeton: Princeton University Press, 1965).

McCredie, J. R. "Hippodamos of Miletus," *Studies Hanfmann*, pp. 95–100.

MacMullen, R. *Enemies of the Roman Order: Treason, Unrest, and Alienation in the Empire* (Cambridge, Mass.: Harvard University Press, 1966).

————. "Roman Imperial Building in the Provinces," *HSCP* 64 (1959):207–35.

————. *Soldier and Civilian in the Later Roman Empire* (Cambridge, Mass.: Harvard University Press, 1967).

McNally, S. "The Frieze of the Mausoleum at Split," *Studies Hanfmann*, pp. 101–12.

Macridy, T. "Antiquités de Notion, II," *JOAI* 15 (1912):61–62.

Magie, D. "Egyptian Deities in Asia Minor in Inscriptions and on Coins," *AJA* 57 (1953):163–87.

————. *Roman Rule in Asia Minor to the End of the Third Century After Christ* (Princeton, New Jersey, Princeton University Press, 1950).

Maj, B. M. F. *Iconografia romana imperiale da Severo Alessandro a M. Aurelio Carino (222–285 d. C.)*, Quaderni e Guide di Archeologia 2 (Rome, 1958).

Mamboury, E. *Istanbul Touristique* (Istanbul, 1951).

Mango, C. *The Art of the Byzantine Empire, Sources and Documents* (Englewood Cliffs, New Jersey: Prentice Hall, 1972).

———. *The Brazen House: A Study of the Vestibule of the Imperial Palace of Constantinople* (Copenhagen: Ejnar Munksgaard, 1959).

———. "Iznik (Nicaea)," *Archaeology* 3 (1950):106–9.

Mansel, A. M. "1968 Perge Kazisina Dair Önrapor," *Dergi* 17 (1968):93–105.

———. *Die Ruinen von Side* (Berlin: Walter de Gruyter, 1963).

———. *Mélanges Mansel-Mansel'e Armağan* (Ankara: Türk Tarih Kurumu Basimevi, 1974).

Marasović, J., and T. Marasović. *Diocletian Palace* (Zagreb: Zora, 1968).

Marasović, T., P. Pervan, and D. Sumić. "Istraživanje i Uredenje Dioklecijanove Palače," *Urbs* 4 (Split, 1961–62). Published 1965, with *Condensed English Version*.

Marcadé, J. *Recueil des signatures de sculpteurs grecs* 2 (Paris: E. de Boccard, 1957).

Martin, R. *L'Urbanisme dans la Grèce antique* (Paris, 1956).

Massow, W. von. *Führer durch das Pergamonmuseum* (Berlin, 1932).

Mathews, T. F. *The Early Churches of Constantinople: Architecture and Liturgy* (University Park, Penn. and London: The Pennsylvania State University Press, 1971).

Mellink, M. J. "Excavations at Karataş-Semayük and Elmali, Lycia, 1969," *AJA* 74 (1970):245–52.

———. "Excavations at Elmali, 1971," *AJA* 76 (1972):263–68.

———. "Excavations at Elmali, 1972," *AJA* 77 (1973):297–303.

———. "Notes on Anatolian Wall Painting," *Mélanges Mansel* (Ankara, 1974), pp. 543–46.

Meriç, R. *Ephesus Archaeological Guide* (Izmir, 1971).

Metzger, H. *Fouilles de Xanthos* 4 *Les céramiques archaiques et classiques et l'acropole lycienne* (Paris: C. Klincksieck, 1972).

Miltner, F. *Ephesos, Stadt der Artemis und des Johannes* (Wien: Franz Deuticke, 1958).

Miranda, S. *Grand palais de Constantinople* (Mexico City, 1964).

Mitchell, W. A. "Turkish Villages in Interior Anatolia and von Thunen's 'Isolated State,' " *The Middle East Journal* 25 (1971):355–69.

Mitten, D. G., and S. F. Doeringer. *Master Bronzes from the Classical World* (Cambridge, Mass.: The Fogg Art Museum, 1967).

Mitten, D. G., J. G. Pedley, and J. A. Scott. *Studies Presented to George M. A. Hanfmann* (Cambridge, Mass.: Fogg Art Museum, 1971).

Möbius, H. "Hellenistische Grabreliefs," *AA* (1969):507–10.

———. "Zu den Stelen von Daskyleion," *AA* (1971):442–55.

———. "Zur Barbarenstatue von Halikarnass," *AthMitt* 50 (1925):45–50.

Moore, F. G. "Three Canal Projects, Roman and Byzantine," *AJA* 54 (1950):97–111.

Morey, C. R. *Early Christian Art* (Princeton: Princeton University Press 1942).

———. *Sardis* V:1 *Roman and Christian Sculpture. The Sarcophagus of Claudia Antonia Sabina* (Princeton, 1924).

Muller, H. J. *The Loom of History* (New York: Harper and Brothers, 1958).

Naumann, R. *Architektur Kleinasiens von ihren Anfängen bis zum Ende der hethitischen Zeit*, 2nd ed. (Tübingen: Ernst Wasmuth, 1971).

Neumann, G. *Untersuchungen zum Weiterleben hethitischen und luwischen Sprachgutes in hellenistischer und römischer Zeit* (Wiesbaden: Otto Harassowitz, 1961).

Nevskaya, V. P. *Vizantiy v klassicheskuyu i ellinisticheskuyu epokhi* (Moscow: Akademiya Nauk SSSR, Institut Istoriyi, 1953).

Nicholls, R. V. "Old Smyrna, The Iron Age Fortifications and Associated Remains," *BSA* 53-54 (1958–59):37–137.

Niemeyer, H. G. *Studien zur statuarischen Darstellung der römischen Kaiser, Monumenta Artis Romanae* 7 (Berlin: Mann, 1968).

Nylander, C. *Ionians in Pasargadae* (Uppsala, 1970).

Oliver, J. H. "Marcus Aurelius: Aspects of Civic and Cultural Policy in the East," *Hesperia* Suppl. 13 (1970).

Österreichisches Archäologisches Institut, *Festschrift für Fritz Eichler zu dessen achtzigistem Geburtstag am 12. Oktober 1967 JOAI* Beiheft zum Band 48 (1966–67) (Vienna, 1967).

Ostrogorsky, G. *History of the Byzantine State* (New Brunswick, New Jersey: Rutgers University Press, 1957).

Öztüre, A. *Nicomedia-Izmit Tarihi* (Istanbul, 1969).

Packer, J. E. "Housing and Population in Imperial Ostia and Rome," *JRS* 57 (1967):80–95.

Page, D. L. "An Early Tragedy on the Fall of Croesus," *Proceedings of the Cambridge Philological Society*," 188 (1962):47–49.

Pedley, J. G. *Sardis in the Age of Croesus* (Norman: University of Oklahoma Press, 1968).

———. *Sardis Monograph 2 Ancient Literary Sources on Sardis* (Cambridge, Mass.: Harvard University Press, 1972).

Perrot, J. "Les fouilles de Suse," *CRAI* (1970):352–78.

Pfuhl, E. "Das Beiwerk auf den ostgriechischen Grabreliefs," *JdI* 20 (1905):47–96.

———. "Spätjonische Plastik," *JdI* 50 (1935):9–48.

Pharr, C., T. S. Davidson and M. B. Pharr, eds., *The Theodosian Code and Novels and the Sirmondian Constitutions* (Princeton: Princeton University Press, 1952).

Philostorgius, *Historia ecclesiastica* in J. Bidez, ed., *Philostorgius, Kirchengeschichte mit dem Leben des Lucian von Antiochien und den Fragmenten eines arianischen Historiographen* (Leipzig: J. C. Hinrichs, 1913).

Picard, C. *Manuel d'archéologie grecque: La sculpture* (Paris: Éditions A. and J. Picard et Cie, 1939–63).

Pliny the Younger, *Letters* 2 Loeb Classical Library (Cambridge, Mass.: Harvard University Press, 1963).

Polanyi, K., C. M. Arensberg, and H. W. Pearson, eds. *Trade and Market in the Early Empires* (Glencoe, Illinois: The Free Press, 1957).

Praschniker, C. "Die Datierung des Mausoleums von Belevi," *AnzWien* 85 (1948):271–93.

———. "Der Hermes des Alkamenes in Ephesos," *JOAI* 29 (1935):23–31.

Preger, T., ed. "Patria Konstantinopoleos" *Scriptores originum Constantinopolitarum*, 2 (Leipzig: G. B. Teubner, 1907).

Prosopographia Imperii Roman, see Groag, E. and A. Stein.

Pryce, F. N. *Catalogue of Sculpture, British Museum* I:1 *Prehellenic and Early Greek* (Oxford: Oxford University Press, 1928). I:2 *Cypriote and Etruscan* (Oxford University Press, 1931).

Radt, W. *Siedlung und Bauten auf der Halbinsel von Halikarnassos IstMitt*, suppl. 3 (Tübingen: E. Wasmuth, 1970).

Ramage, A. *Studies in Lydian Domestic and Commercial Architecture at Sardis* (Ph.D. diss., Harvard University, 1969).

Ramage, A., and N. H. Ramage. "The Siting of Lydian Burial Mounds," in *Studies Hanfmann,* pp. 143–60.

Ramsay, W. M. *Asianic Elements in Greek Civilization* (New Haven: Yale University Press, 1928).

Reusch, W. *Augusta Treverorum* (Trier: Paulinus Verlag, 1968).

―――. *Aus der Schatzkammer des antiken Trier* (Trier: Paulinus, 1959).

Reusch, W. et al. *Die Basilika in Trier, 1856–1956. Festschrift zur Wiederherstellung 9. Dezember 1956* (Trier: Paulinus, 1956).

Richter, G. M. A. *The Portraits of the Greeks* 3 (London: Phaidon Press, 1965).

Ridgway, B. S. "A Story of Five Amazons," *AJA* 78 (1974):1–17.

Robert, L. "D'Aphrodisias à la Lycaonie," *Hellenica* 13 (1965).

―――. "Inscriptions d'Aphrodisias," *L'antiquité classique* 35 (1966):377–432.

―――. *Noms indigènes dans l'Asie Mineure gréco-romaine* Bibliothèque archéologique et historique de l'institut français d'archéologie d'Istanbul 13 (Paris, 1963).

―――. "Édition et index commenté des epitaphes," in Firatli, *Stèles de Byzance,* Bibliothèque archéologique et historique de l'institut français d'archéologie d'Istanbul 15 (Paris, 1964), pp. 131–89.

―――. *Nouvelles inscriptions de Sardes* (Paris: Librarie d'Amerique et d'Orient Adrien Maisonneuve, 1964).

―――. "Sur des inscriptions d'Ephese; Fêtes, Athlètes, Empereurs, Epigrammes," *RevPhil* 41 (1967):7–84.

Robinson, E. S. G. "The Coins from the Ephesian Artemision Reconsidered," *JHS* 71 (1951):156–67.

Rodenwaldt, G. "Griechische Reliefs in Lykien," Akademie der Wissenschaften, Berlin, Phil. Hist. Klasse, *Sitzungsberichte* (1933):1028–55.

Röder, J. "Bericht über Arbeiten in den antiken Steinbrüchen von Iscehisar (Dokimeion)," *Dergi* 18 (1969):111–16.

Roebuck, C. "The Economic Development of Ionia," *CP* 48 (1953):9–16.

―――. *Ionian Trade and Colonization* (New York: Archaeological Institute of America, 1959).

Rostovtzeff, M. I. *Social and Economic History of the Roman Empire* (Oxford: Clarendon Press, 1926).

Roux, G. "Qu'est ce que un kolossos," *REG* 62 (1960):5–40.

Rumpf, A. *Stilphasen der spätantiken Kunst, ein Versuch* Arbeitsgemeinschaft für Forschung des Landes Nordrhein-Westfalen, Geisteswissenschaften *Abhandlung* 44 (1955).

Runciman, S. *Byzantine Civilization* (Cleveland and New York: The World Publishing Co., 1933).

Schede, M. *Die Ruinen von Priene,* 2nd ed. (Berlin: Walter de Gruyter, 1964).

Schefold, K. "Xanthos und Südanatolien," *Antike Kunst* 13 (1970):79–84.

―――. *Die Griechen und ihre Nachbarn,* Propyläen Kunstgeschichte 1 (Berlin, 1967).

Schlumberger, D. *L'orient hellenisé* (Paris: Éditions Albin Michel, 1970).

Schmidt, Erich F. *Persepolis* 1 *OIP* 68 (Chicago: University of Chicago Press, 1953).

Schmidt, Evamaria. *The Great Altar of Pergamon* (Boston: Boston Art and Book Shop, 1965).

Schneider, A. M. *Die römischen und byzantinischen Denkmäler von Iznik-Nicaea, IstFo* 16 (Berlin, 1943).

―――. Konstantinopel. *Geschichte und Gestalt einer geschichtlichen Weltmetropole* (Berlin: Florian Kupferberg, 1956).

————. "Die vorjustinianische Sophienkirche," *BZ* 36 (1936):77–85.

Schneider, A. M., and W. Karnapp. *Die Stadtmauer von Iznik (Nicaea), IstFo* 9 (Berlin, 1938).

Schober, A. *Der Fries des Hekateions von Lagina, IstFo* 2 (1933).

————. *Die Kunst von Pergamon* (Vienna, Innsbruck, and Wiesbaden: Margarete Friedrich Rohrer Verlag, 1951).

Seager, A. R. "The Building History of the Sardis Synagogue," *AJA* 76 (1972):425–35.

Sherrard, P. *Constantinople: Iconography of a Sacred City* (London: Oxford University Press, 1965).

Sherwin-White, A. N. "Trajan's Replies to Pliny: Authorship Necessity," *JRS* 52 (1962):114–25.

Smith, A. H. The British Museum, *A Catalogue of Sculpture in the Department of Greek and Roman Antiquities* 2 (London, 1900); 3 (London, 1901).

Smithsonian Institution, *Art Treasures of Turkey* (Washington, D. C., 1966).

Socrates (Scholasticus), *Historia Ecclesiastica* in *Patrologia Graeca,* ed. Migne, vol. 67 (1878), pp. 9-842; trans. R. Hussey (Oxford, 1853, reprint W. Bright, 1878).

Squarciapino, M. *La scuola di Afrodisia* (Rome: Studi e materiali del Museo dell'Impero Romano, 1943).

Stier, H. E. "Aus der Welt des Pergamonaltars," (Berlin: Heinrich Keller, 1932).

Straub, J. A. "Constantine as Koinos Episkopos," *DOPapers* 21 (1967):39–55.

Stronach, D. B. "A Circular Symbol on the Tomb of Cyrus," *Iran* 9 (1971):155–58.

————. "Excavations at Pasargadae: Second Preliminary Report," *Iran* 2(1964):21–36.

————. "Excavations at Pasargadae: Third Preliminary Report," *Iran* 3 (1965):9–40.

Strong, D., and K. Jeppesen. "Discoveries at Halicarnassus," *ActaA* 35 (1964):195–203.

Tarn, W. W. *Hellenistic Civilization,* 2nd ed. (London: Edward Arnold, 1936).

Teall, J. L. "The Age of Constantine: Change and Continuity in Administration and Economy," *DOPapers* 21 (1967):13–36.

Tekvar, A. *Türkiye Mermer Envanteri* (Ankara: Publications of the Minerals Research Institute, no. 134, 1966).

Toynbee, J. M. C. "Roma and Constantinopolis in Late Antique Art from 312 to 365 A.D.," *JRS* 37 (1947):135–44.

Tuchelt, K. "Die archaischen Skulpturen von Didyma (Beiträge zur frühgriechischen Plastik in Kleinasien)," *IstFo* 27 (Berlin, 1970).

Vermeule, C. C. "Dated Monuments of Hellenistic and Graeco-Roman Popular Art in Asia Minor: Pontus Through Mysia," in *Studies Hanfmann,* pp. 169–76.

————. *Roman Imperial Art in Greece and Asia Minor* (Cambridge, Mass.: Harvard University Press, 1968).

Vetters, H. "Ephesos: Vorläufiger Grabungsbericht 1969," *AnzWien* 107 (1970):1–19.

————. "Ephesos: Vorläufiger Grabungsbericht 1972," *AnzWien* 110 (1973): 175–94.

————. "Zum byzantinischen Ephesos," *JOBG* 15 (1966):273–87.

————. "Zum Stockwerkbau in Ephesus," *Mélanges Mansel* (Ankara, 1974), pp. 69–92.

Vickers, M. "The Date of the Walls of Thessalonica," *AnnIst* 15–16 (1969):313–18.

Voelkl, L. *Der Kaiser Konstantin. Annalen einer Zeitenwende 306–337* (Munich: Prestel, 1957).

Vogt, J. *Constantin der Grosse und sein Jahrhundert* (Munich: F. Bruckmann, 1949/1969).

Walter, O. "Antikenbericht aus Smyrna," *JOAI* 21–22 (1922–24):223–59.

Ward-Perkins, J. B. "Four Roman Garland Sarcophagi in America," *Archaeology* 11 (1958):98–104.

Welles, C. B. "Die hellenistische Welt," *Propyläen Weltgeschichte* (Berlin, n.d.).

Wheeler, Sir M. *Roman Art and Architecture* (New York: Frederick A. Praeger, 1964).

Wiegand, T. "Reisen in Mysien," *AthMitt* (1904):254–339.

Wiegand, T., and H. Schrader. *Priene: Ergebnisse der Ausgrabungen und Untersuchungen in den Jahren 1895–1898* (Berlin: Georg Reimer, 1904).

Wiegartz, H. *Kleinasiatische Säulensarkophage: Untersuchungen zum Sarkophagtypus und zu den figürlichen Darstellungen, IstFo* 26 (Berlin: Mann, 1965).

Winter, F. E. *Greek Fortifications* (Toronto: University of Toronto Press, 1971).

Yassihöyük: A Village Study (Ankara: Middle East Technical University, 1965).

Young, R. S. "Making History at Gordion," *Archaeology* 6 (1953):164–65.

Zosimus, *Historia Nova,* text ed. L. Mendelssohn (Leipzig: 1887).

Illustrations

41 Stele with funerary meal from Daskylion. Istanbul Archaeological Museums. Courtesy Deutsches Archäologisches Institut, Istanbul.

42 Pediment with funerary meal from Sardis. Manisa Museum. Courtesy Archaeological Exploration of Sardis.

43 Pyramidal seal with Lydian inscription and griffin. Paris. Bibliothèque Nationale. Photo Courtesy John Boardman.

44 Pyramidal seal with Lydian inscription and two royal sphinxes. Leningrad. Hermitage. Photo Courtesy John Boardman.

45 Wall painting. Kizilbel Tomb. Detail of south wall with Pegasus and Chrysaor. Courtesy M. J. Mellink.

46 Amazon from Villa of Hadrian, Tivoli. Photo Deutsches Archäologisches Institut, Rome.

47 Wounded Amazon. The Metropolitan Museum of Art. Gift of John D. Rockefeller, Jr. 1932.

48 Amazon in Museo Capitolino, Rome. Photo Anderson.

49 New foundations of Hellenistic cities. After C. B. Welles, *Die hellenistische Welt,* Propyläen Weltgeschichte map opp. p. 512.

50 Miletus. Plan after G. Kleiner, *Ruinen,* fig. 14.

51 Bird's-eye view of ancient Miletus looking southwest. By Charles A. Blessing. On the right, the Lion Harbor with Theater Hill above. The city center includes on the left; Delphinion, North Market, and South Market. On the right, Stadium and West Market. In upper center, Sacred Road leading to Didyma. Courtesy Charles A. Blessing.

52 Priene. Central part of city. Model by H. Schleif. Courtesy Staatliche Museen zu Berlin, Antiken-Sammlung.

53 Priene. House XXXIII. Reconstruction of original state. After M. Schede, *Ruinen,* fig. 118.

54 View of Halicarnassus with site of Maussoleum. Photo copyright Niels Hannestad.

55 Halicarnassus. View from the sea. After Krischen, *Griechische Stadt,* pl. I.

56 Pergamon. West side of upper city. Model by H. Schleif. Courtesy Staatliche Museen zu Berlin, Antiken-Sammlung.

57 Ephesus. Altar of Artemis. Reconstruction by A. Bammer.

58 Pergamon. View of Altar of Zeus looking west.

59 Pergamon. Altar of Zeus, gigantomachy frieze: Nyx, new fragment of giant, Moira. Courtesy Staatliche Museen zu Berlin, Antiken-Sammlung.

60 Lycia. Sketch map of ancient sites. After F. Eichler, *Die Reliefs des Heroons von Gjölbaschi Trysa,* fig. 19.

61 Silver stater of Perikles of Lycia. Dewing Numismatic Foundation No. 697 a.

62 Xanthos, Nereid monument. Reconstruction by Krischen, *Weltwunder,* pl. 31.

63 Xanthos, Nereid monument. Reconstruction of facade. After Coupel and Demargne, *Xanthos* 3, pl. 98.

64 Xanthos, Nereid monument. Ruler accepts surrender of a city. Courtesy Trustees of The British Museum.

65 Assyrian relief, Nineveh. Surrender of Lachish to Sennacherib. Courtesy Trustees of The British Museum.

66 Xanthos, Nereid monument. Small frieze. Tribute bearers. Courtesy Trustees of The British Museum.

67 Persepolis, Palace of Darius, western flight of southern stairway. File of servants on inner face of parapet. Courtesy the Oriental Institute, University of Chicago.

68 Persepolis, Apadana, eastern stairway. Cappadocian tribute bearers. Courtesy the Oriental Institute, University of Chicago.

69 Limyra, Heroon. Preliminary reconstruction sketch by J. Borchhardt.

70 Limyra, Heroon. Caryatid. Courtesy Deutsches Archäologisches Institut, Istanbul.

71 Limyra, Heroon. Frieze of horsemen. Courtesy Deutsches Archäologisches Institut, Istanbul.

72 Maussoleum of Halicarnassus, Amazon frieze. Block recomposed of parts in The British Museum (left) and Bodrum (right). Courtesy K. Jeppesen.

73 a, b Maussoleum of Halicarnassus. Statues of Maussolus (a) and Artemisia (b). Courtesy Trustees of The British Museum.

74 Maussoleum of Halicarnassus. Squatting Oriental. Izmir, Fuari Museum.

75 Maussoleum of Belevi. Reconstructed by M. Theuer. After J. Keil, *Führer,* fig. 89.

76 Maussoleum of Belevi. Lion-griffins flanking crater. Izmir, Fuari Museum.

77 Maussoleum of Belevi. Coffer frieze. Centauromachy. Izmir, Fuari Museum.

78 Maussoleum of Belevi. Coffer frieze. Centauromachy. Izmir, Fuari Museum.

79 Maussoleum of Belevi. Coffer frieze. Wrestlers and umpire. Athlete crowned. Izmir, Fuari Museum.

80 Maussoleum of Belevi. Ruler reclining on couch. Taken *in situ*. Courtesy Österreichisches Archäologisches Institut, Wien.

81 Maussoleum of Belevi. Statue of Oriental servant. Izmir, Fuari Museum.

82 Priene. Hypothetical reconstruction of statues in the agora. After Krischen, *Griechische Stadt,* pl. 22.

83 Map of Roman Asia Minor. After C. C. Vermeule, *ImpArt,* end paper.

84 Miletus. Great Harbor Monument. Reconstruction after Kleiner, *Ruinen,* fig. 34.

85 Miletus. Great Harbor Monument. Relief with Triton and dolphins. Courtesy G. Kleiner.

86 Relief from Palazzo Santa Croce, Rome, in Munich, Antikensammlung-Glyptothek. Poseidon, Amphitrite, and Marine Thiasus.

87 Sardis. Plan of Roman Gymnasium-Bath complex. Courtesy Archaeological Exploration of Sardis.

88 Theater of Nicaea. Sketch plan. After A. M. Schneider, *IstFo* 16 (1943), fig. 2.

89 Theater of Nicaea. View of substructures. Courtesy Deutsches Archäologisches Institut, Istanbul.

90 Theater of Nicaea. Southeast pier. Detail of masonry and cemented rubble construction.

91 Temple of Hadrian at Kyzikos. Drawings by Cyriacus of Ancona. Courtesy Stiftung Preussischer Kulturbesitz: Staatliche Museen Berlin, Kunstbibliothek.

92 Miletus. Plan of Nymphaeum. After Kleiner, *Ruinen,* fig. 86.

93 Miletus. Reconstruction of Nymphaeum by C. R. Hülsen. After Kleiner, *Ruinen,* fig. 85.

94 Ephesus. Slope Houses. Plan of first and second phases. Courtesy Österreichisches Archäologisches Institut, Wien.

95 Ephesus. Slope Houses. Looking south. Courtesy R. Meriç.

96 Ephesus. Slope House. Peristyle SR 22–23 looking west. Note mosaic (left), marble floor, marble revetments, and frescoes (upper right). Courtesy R. Meriç.

97 Ephesus. Slope House. Peristyle SR 22–23, east, south, west elevations. Courtesy Österreichisches Archäologisches Institut, Wien.

98 Ephesus. Slope House. View of Artemis Shrine *in situ*. Courtesy Österreichisches Archäologisches Institut, Wien.

99 Ephesus. Hellenistic hero relief found in Slope House. Courtesy Österreichisches Archäologisches Institut, Wien.

100 Sardis. Central unit (BC Hall) of gymnasium building. West wall showing construction of cemented rubble and brick bonded masonry (looking south). Courtesy Archaeological Exploration of Sardis.

101 Ephesus. Baths of Vedius Gymnasium. Reconstruction of structural system. After F. Fasolo, *Palladio* 1–2 (1956), fig. 18.

102 Sardis. Synagogue main hall with skoutlosis (right). Courtesy Archaeological Exploration of Sardis.

103 Ephesus. Plan showing locations of baths and gymnasia. Courtesy A. Bammer.

104 Ephesus. Vedius Gymnasium. Reconstruction. Courtesy Österreichisches Archäologisches Institut, Wien.

105 Ephesus. Vedius Gymnasium. Plan. Courtesy Österreichisches Archäologisches Institut, Wien.

106 Sardis. Gymnasium-Bath complex. Tentative plan of circulation by F. K. Yeğül. Courtesy Archaeological Exploration of Sardis.

107 Sardis. Gymnasium. "Marble Court." Looking northwest. Courtesy Archaeological Exploration of Sardis.

108 Sardis. Gymnasium. Detail of head capital from screen colonnade of Marble Court. Courtesy Archaeological Exploration of Sardis.

109 Sardis. Gymnasium. North side of Marble Court. Detail of ornamentation of entablature with part of dedicatory inscription. Courtesy Archaeological Exploration of Sardis.

110 Temple at Aezani. View of west side with acroterion depicting Meter Steunene. Courtesy Deutsches Archäologisches Institut, Istanbul.

111 Pergamon. Model of Sanctuary of Asclepius by H. Schleif. Courtesy Staatliche Museen zu Berlin, Antiken-Sammlung.

112 Miletus. Temple of Serapis. Reconstructed view of front porch. After *Milet* I:7, fig. 218.

113 Miletus. Temple of Serapis. View of pediment. Courtesy G. Kleiner.

114 Ephesus. View of theater, city and bay. Looking northeast. Courtesy R. Meriç.

115 Miletus. Plan and Section of Temple of Serapis. After *Milet* I:7, fig. 193.

116 Sardis. Synagogue. Conjectural building history. Courtesy Archaeological Exploration of Sardis.

117 Sardis. Synagogue and gymnasium. Bird's-eye view toward southwest. Courtesy Archaeological Exploration of Sardis.

118 Ephesus. Temple of Hadrian. Detail of facade and inner pediment with parts of frieze at lower right. Courtesy Österreichisches Archäologisches Institut, Wien.

119 Stele of Trophime from Gölde. Manisa Museum. Courtesy Archaeological Exploration of Sardis.

120 Door jamb from Yilmaz Köy near Sardis with relief of Zeus and Kouretes(?) Manisa Museum. Courtesy Archaeological Exploration of Sardis.

121 Stele of Matis from Sardis. Detail. Manisa Museum. Courtesy Archaeological Exploration of Sardis.

122 Stele from Notion. Izmir, Fuari Museum. Courtesy H. Möbius.

123 Horsemen relief in Izmir, Fuari Museum. Courtesy H. Möbius.

124 Stele of Marcus Antonios Fronton, Byzantium. Istanbul Archaeological Museums. Courtesy N. Dolunay.

125 Hero relief. Trinity College Collection on permanent loan to the Fitzwilliam Museum, Cambridge. Photo courtesy The Fitzwilliam Museum.

126 Relief with funerary meal from Smyrna. Leiden, Museum van Oudheden. Courtesy Museum van Oudheden.

127 Funerary stele of Theodotos from Byzantium. Istanbul Archaeological Museums. Courtesy Istanbul Archaeological Museums.

128 Aphrodisias. Preliminary drawing of Zoilos frieze by Simonetti. After A. Giuliano, *ASAtene* 37–38 (1959–60), fig. 12.

129 Aphrodisias. Zoilos frieze. Demos and Herm. Courtesy K. T. Erim.

130 Aphrodisias. Zoilos frieze. Head of Zoilos with new fragment. After *AJA* 74 (1970), pl. 46:30.

131 Aphrodisias. Zoilos frieze. *Aion.* After Akurgal, *Civilizations*, fig. 63.

132 Aphrodisias. Frieze from Ionic portico dedicated to Tiberius and Livia. Detail. Bearded head. After K. T. Erim, *Archaeology* 20 (1967), fig. 10.

133 Ephesus. Library of Celsus. Restored facade with statues. After W. Wilberg, *FoEph* V:1, pl. 1.

134 Ephesus. Library of Celsus. Cross section. After W. Wilberg, *FoEph* V:1, fig. 78.

135 Ephesus. Antinoos as Androklos from Vedius Gymnasium. Izmir, Fuari Museum. Courtesy Deutsches Archäologisches Institut, Istanbul.

136 Ephesus. Vedius Gymnasium. Sappho(?) Izmir. Courtesy Österreichisches Archäologisches Institut, Wien.

137 Ephesus. Bronze athlete from Harbor Baths. Kunsthistorisches Museum, Vienna. Courtesy Österreichisches Archäologisches Institut, Wien.

138 Ephesus. Rivergod Maeander from Vedius Gymnasium. Izmir, Fuari Museum. Courtesy Österreichisches Archäologisches Institut, Wien.

139 Ephesus. Harbor Baths. Restoration of the Hall of Imperial Cult. Courtesy Österreichisches Archäologisches Institut, Wien.

140 "Asiatic" sarcophagus in Melfi. Front view. Courtesy Deutsches Archäologisches Institut, Rome.

141 Sarcophagus in Melfi. Lateral face. Odysseus and Diomed. Courtesy Deutsches Archäologisches Institut, Rome.

142 Sarcophagus from Dokimeion-Synnada in Ankara. Woman and sage. Courtesy Deutsches Archäologisches Institut, Istanbul.

143 Sarcophagus lid from Sardis. Claudia Antonia Sabina and daughter. Istanbul Archaeological Museums. Courtesy Princeton University Department of Art and Archaeology, Sardis Archives.

144 Sarcophagus lid from Ephesus. Claudia Antonia Tatiane and her husband. Izmir, Basmane Museum. Courtesy Österreichisches Archäologisches Institut, Wien.

145 Miletus. North Market. Reconstruction of second century A.D. state. After Kleiner, *Ruinen*, fig. 31.

146 Ephesus. Kuretes Street with statue of physician Alexandros (right). Courtesy R. Meriç.

147 Aphrodisias. Sarcophagus of Marcus Aurelius Diodorus Kallimedes. Detail: Busts of Kallimedes and his wife Tatia. Courtesy A. Giuliano.

148 Bust of Theon from Smyrna. Museo Capitolino, Rome. After G. M. A. Richter, *Portraits*, fig. 2038.

149 Statue of Flavius Damianus from Ephesus. Izmir, Fuari Museum. Courtesy E. Rosenbaum-Alföldi and the Warburg Institute.

150 a, b Head of Flavius Damianus, Ephesus. Details. Courtesy E. Rosenbaum-Alföldi and the Warburg Institute.

151 Head of bearded man from Sardis. Manisa Museum. Courtesy Archaeological Exploration of Sardis.

152 Statue of Aphrodite of Aphrodisias. Roman Copy. Courtesy K. T. Erim.

153 Aphrodisias. Aphrodite from the Zoilos frieze. © 1967 National Geographic Society.

154 Coin of Achaeus from Sardis. Courtesy Archaeological Exploration of Sardis.

155 Fragment of colossal head of Zeus from Artemis Temple, Sardis. Courtesy Archaeological Exploration of Sardis.

156 a, b Ephesus. (a) Colossal head of Domitian(?) from his temple. Courtesy E. Rosenbaum-Alföldi and the Warburg Institute. (b) Colossal arm of Domitian(?). Izmir, Fuari Museum. Courtesy Österreichisches Archäologisches Institut, Wien.

157 Colossal head of Antoninus Pius from the Artemis Temple, Sardis. Courtesy Archaeological Exploration of Sardis.

158 Colossal head of Faustina from the Artemis Temple, Sardis. Courtesy Trustees of The British Museum.

159 Colossal head of Caracalla from Pergamon. Bergama Museum. Courtesy Deutsches Archäologisches Institut, Istanbul.

160 Head of Diocletian from Nicomedia. Istanbul Archaeological Museums. Courtesy Deutsches Archäologisches Institut, Istanbul.

161 Nicaea-Iznik panorama. Courtesy Deutsches Archäologisches Institut, Istanbul.

162 Nicaea-Iznik. Plan of ancient city. After A. M. Schneider, *IstFo* 9 (1938), map.

163 Nicomedia-Izmit. View of citadel from the bay. Courtesy Turkish Tourism and Information Office, New York City.

164 Nicomedia-Izmit. View from the theater toward eastern part of the bay.

165 Nicomedia-Izmit. Plan. After A. Öztüre. *Nicomedia: Izmit Tarihi* (1969), map.

166 Circus relief from the Paç region, Nicomedia. Izmit Museum.

167 Thessalonike. Mausoleum of Galerius and entrance to palace. Hypothetical sketch. After Ward-Perkins, *ERA*, fig. 198.

168 Roman Trier, city plan. After H. Eiden, "Ausgrabungen im spätantiken Trier," in *Neue Ausgrabungen in Deutschland* (Berlin, 1958), fig. 1.

169 Trier. Restoration of palace hall (Basilica). Photo Landesmuseum Trier. Courtesy W. Reusch.

170 Trier. Interior of palace hall (Basilica). After W. Reusch, *Die Basilika in Trier* (1956), fig. 5.

171 Trier. Aerial view. Photo Landesmuseum, Trier. Courtesy W. Reusch.

172 Istanbul. Aerial view looking across Golden Horn toward Beyoğlu-Galata. Courtesy Turkish Tourism and Information Office, New York City.

173 Plan of Pre-Constantinian Byzantium. After Janin, (1964) plan II.

174 Constantinople. Public spaces and major roads. After Janin, (1964), plan V.

175 Gerasa. Oval piazza. Courtesy Yale University.

176 The Great Palace at Constantinople. Reconstruction by C. Vogt from A. Vogt, ed., *Constantin VII Porphyrogénète. Le Livre des cérémonies* (Paris, 1935).

177 Constantinople. Great Palace. Conjectural reconstruction of approach. After C. Mango, *Brazen House,* fig. 1.

178 Istanbul. The Milion. Courtesy N. Firatli.

179 Plan of Constantinople with monuments and churches. Courtesy C. Mango.

180 Ephesus. Arkadiane Avenue. Reconstruction. After Miltner, *Ephesos,* fig. 91. Courtesy Österreichisches Archäologisches Institut, Wien.

181 Sardis. Synagogue and surroundings. Restored plan. Courtesy Archaeological Exploration of Sardis.

182 Rome. Old St. Peter's. After Krautheimer, *ECBA,* fig. 14.

183 Sardis. Synagogue. Isometric reconstruction by A. R. Seager. Courtesy Archaeological Exploration of Sardis.

184 Sardis. Synagogue. Interior of main hall looking north. Tentative restoration by A. M. Shapiro. Courtesy Archaeological Exploration of Sardis.

185 Istanbul. Column of Constantine. Photo G. M. A. Hanfmann.

186 *Constantinopolis* from *Tabula Peutingeriana,* Vienna, Staatsbibliothek. After J. M. C. Toynbee, *JRS* 37 (1947), pl. 9. Courtesy Österreichische Nationalbibliothek, Vienna. Bildarchiv und Porträtsammlung.

187 Gold medallion of Constantine from Nicomedia, A.D. 325. Dumbarton Oaks. Courtesy Dumbarton Oaks Collection.

188 Gold coin of Constantine from Nicomedia, A.D. 335. Dumbarton Oaks. Courtesy Dumbarton Oaks Collection.

189 Gold medallion. Constantine and Sol. Mint of Ticinum, A.D. 313. Paris. Cabinet de Médailles. Photo Hirmer Fotoarchiv München.

190 Venice. Horses of San Marco. Alinari.

191 Venice. Corner of Basilica of San Marco. Tetrarchs. Anderson.

192 Ephesus. Tetrarchic(?) frieze from Temple of Hadrian. General sacrificing, Herakles and Amazons. Original relief in Selçuk (Efes) Museum. Courtesy Österreichisches Archäologisches Institut, Wien.

193 Ephesus. Temple of Hadrian. Drawing of Tetrarchic(?) frieze. Dionysus; emperor and gods. Courtesy Österreichisches Archäologisches Institut, Wien.

194 Trier. Painted ceiling from Constantinian Palace under the cathedral. Bischöfliches Museum, Trier. Woman with veil and crown of pearls. After W. Reusch, *Frühchristliche Zeugnisse,* pl. 40 A. Courtesy T. K. Kempf, Bischöfliches Museum, Trier.

195 a, b. Head of Constantine from Constantinople, front and profile. Istanbul Archaeological Museums. Courtesy N. Dolunay.

196 Head of Constantius II(?) from Aphrodisias. Izmir, Basmane Museum.

197 Fragment of porphyry sarcophagus of Constantine(?) Istanbul Archaeological Museums. Courtesy Deutsches Archäologisches Institut, Istanbul.

198 Relief from Çapa. Istanbul Archaeological Museums. After N. Firatli, *Cahiers archéologiques* 11 (1960), p. 82, fig. 13. Courtesy N. Dolunay.

199 Jonah relief from Constantinople. Istanbul Archaeological Museums. Courtesy N. Dolunay.

200 Relief of Flavius Eutyches from Constantinople (Taş Kasap). Istanbul Archaeological Museums. Courtesy N. Dolunay.

201 Relief with seated figure found in church of Aya Sophia, Nicaea. Photo G. M. A. Hanfmann.

202 "Prince's Sarcophagus" from Constantinople. Lateral face. Apostles flanking cross. Istanbul Archaeological Museums. Courtesy Deutsches Archäologisches Institut, Istanbul.

203 "Prince's Sarcophagus." Front. Angel-victories. Courtesy Deutsches Archäologisches Institut, Istanbul.

204 Ephesus. Kuretes Street. Consul Stephanos(?) as found. Courtesy Österreichisches Archäologisches Institut, Wien.

205 Ephesus. Early Byzantine official. Izmir, Basmane Museum.

206 Rome. Basilica of Constantine with restored colossus of Constantine. After A. Minoprio, *BSR* 12 (1932), pl. 9.

207 Head of colossus of Constantine from his basilica. Rome, Palazzo dei Conservatori. Alinari.

Index

Plates

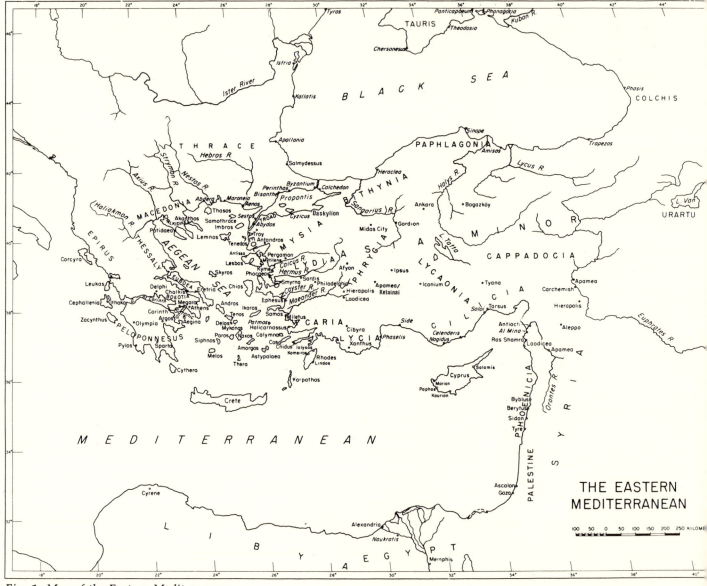

Fig. 1. Map of the Eastern Mediterranean

Fig. 2. View of Lydian mounds at Durasalli

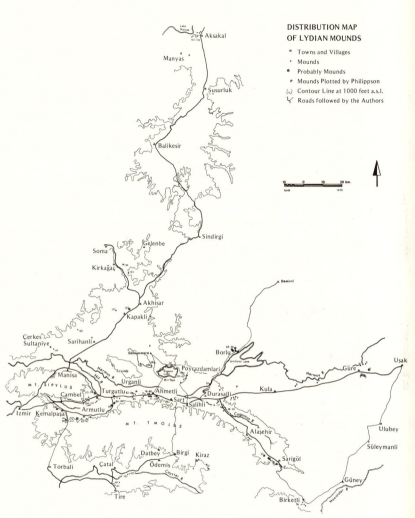

Fig. 3. Distribution map of Lydian mounds

Fig. 4. View of modern houses at Sart Mustafa village

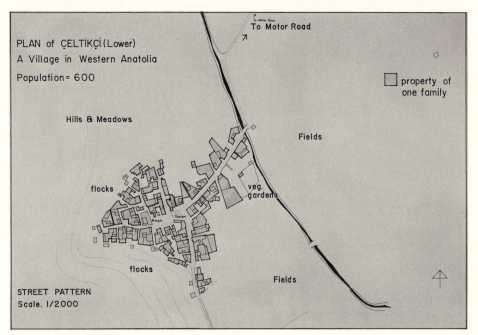

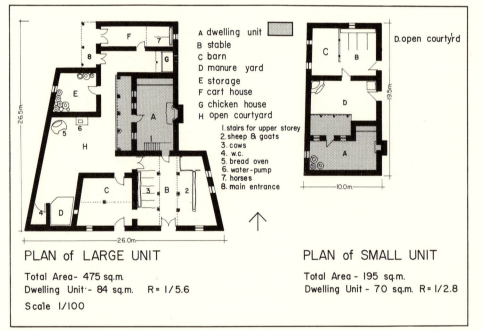

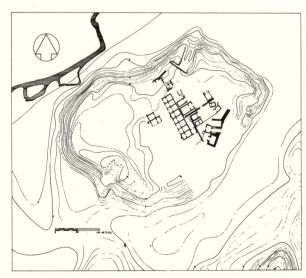

Fig. 5. Plan of Çeltikci village street pattern

Fig. 6. Çeltikci village, house plans

Fig. 7. Restored plan of Phrygian level at Gordion

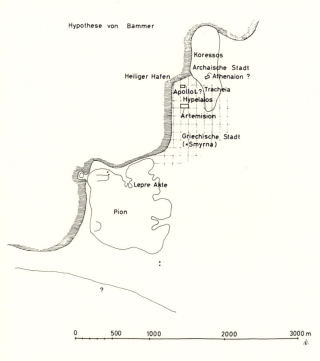

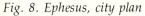

0   500   1000   2000   3000 m

Fig. 8. Ephesus, city plan

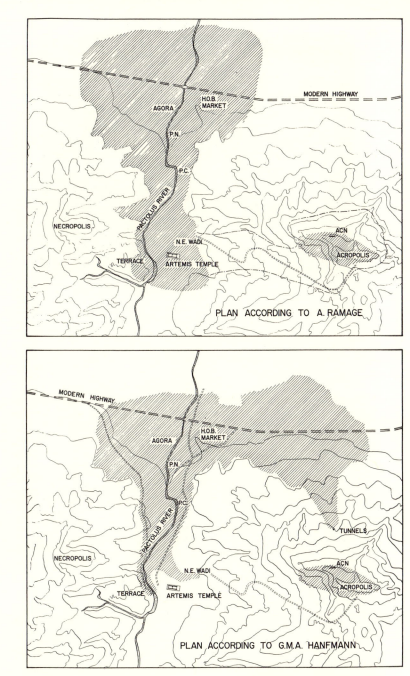

Fig. 9. Sardis, city plans

Fig. 10. View of sector PN with altar, Sardis

Fig. 11. Pitted flake of gold foil from sector PN, Sardis

Fig. 12. Large gold stater of Croesus

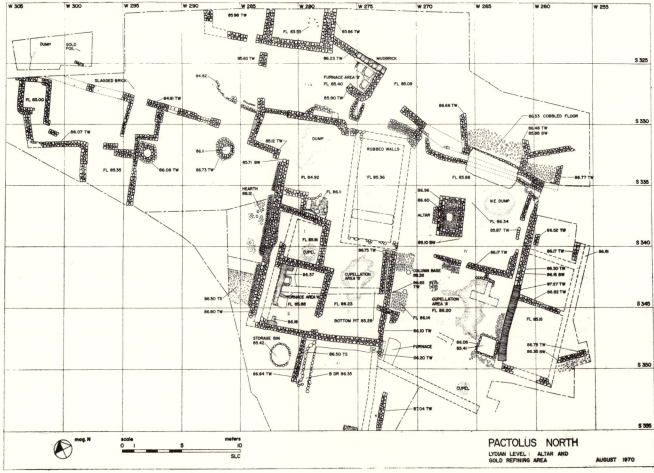

Fig. 13. Sector PN at Sardis, plan

Fig. 14. *Terracotta sima with Pegasus from Sardis*

Fig. 15. *Reconstruction of a sima from Sardis*

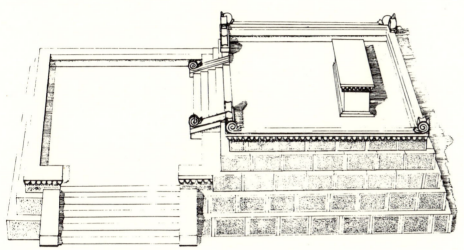

Fig. 16. *Altar of Artemis, Sardis*

Fig. 17. *North slope, Acropolis at Sardis*

Fig. 18. Old Smyrna

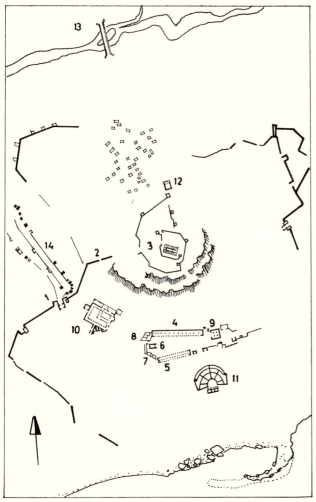

Fig. 19. Plan of Assos

Fig. 20. Ephesus, Archaic Artemision

a

b c

Fig. 21a-c. Fragments of Greek dedicatory inscription of Croesus

Fig. 22. Lydian inscription of Croesus

Fig. 23. Monument to a goddess from Sardis

Fig. 24. Detail of monument (Fig. 23), priestess

Fig. 25. Drawing of back of monument (Fig. 23)

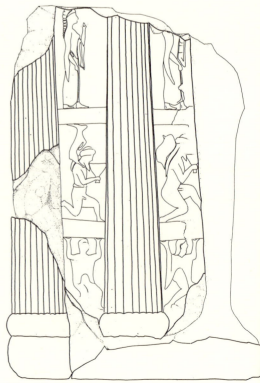

Fig. 26. Monument (Fig. 23), spectator's left side

Fig. 27. Tray with bulls' heads and hand of priestess from Ephesus

Fig. 28. God or hero
with feline skin from Ephesus

Fig. 29. Female head
with crown from Ephesus

Fig. 30. Bearded Lydian
from Sardis

Fig. 31. Limestone lioness from Sardis

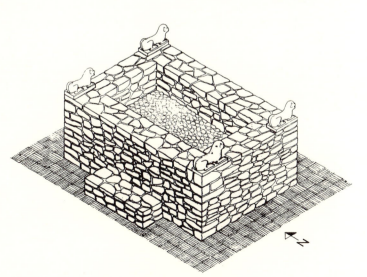

Fig. 32. Altar with lions at corner, Sardis

Fig. 33. *Achilles and Troilus, painting, Tarquinia*

Fig. 34. *Proposed reconstruction of the lion of Croesus*

Fig. 35. *Croesus on the Pyre*

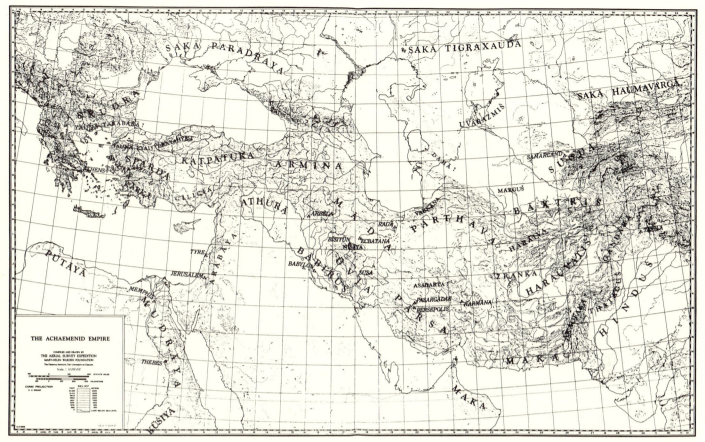

Fig. 36. Map of the Persian Empire

Fig. 37. Pyramid Tomb, Sardis

Fig. 38. The "B" staircase of the Takht, Pasargadae

Fig. 39. Reconstruction of the palace facade, Larisa

Fig. 40. Stele of Elnap from Daskylion

Fig. 41. Stele with funerary meal from Daskylion

Fig. 42. Pediment with funerary meal from Sardis

Fig. 43. Pyramidal seal
with Lydian inscription and griffin

Fig. 44. Pyramidal seal
with Lydian inscription and two royal sphinxes

Fig. 45. Kizilbel Tomb, Pegasus and Chrysaor

Fig. 46. Amazon from Villa of Hadrian

Fig. 47. Wounded Amazon, New York

Fig. 48. Amazon, Capitolino, Rome

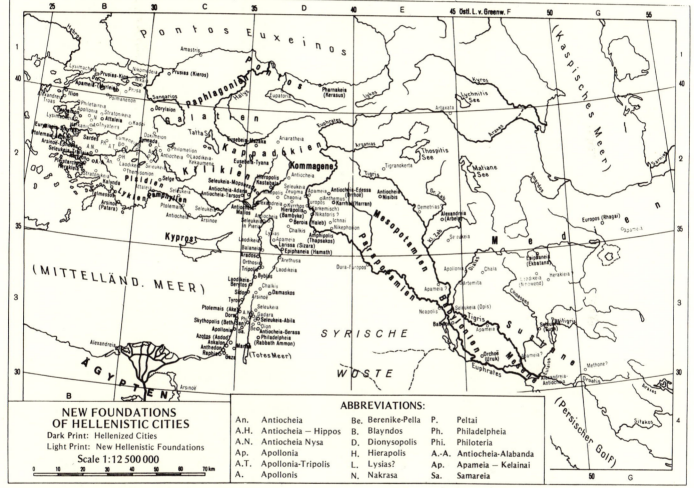

Fig. 49. New foundations of Hellenistic cities

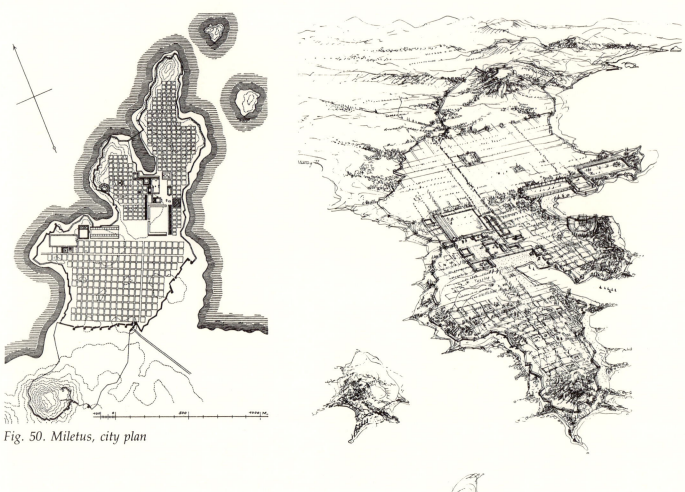

Fig. 50. Miletus, city plan

Fig. 51. Bird's-eye view of Miletus

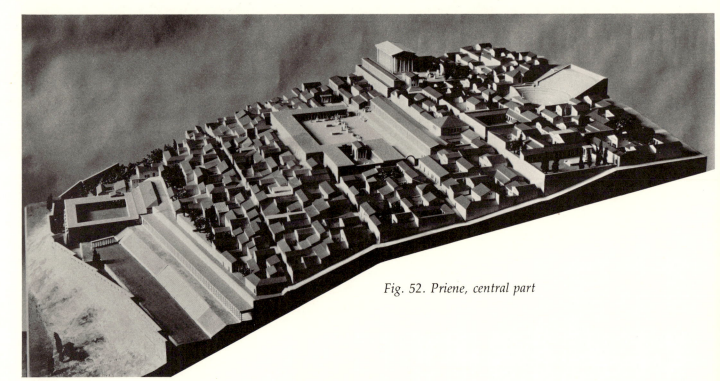

Fig. 52. Priene, central part

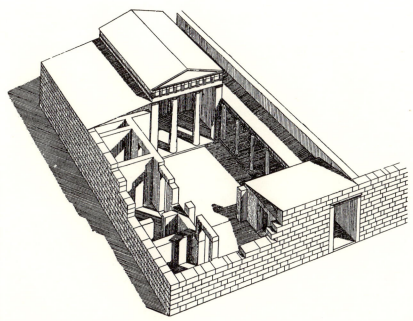

Fig. 53. House XXXIII at Priene

LOCATION OF
MAUSSOLEUM

Fig. 54. Halicarnassus with site of maussoleum

Fig. 55. Halicarnassus from the sea

Fig. 56. Pergamon, upper city

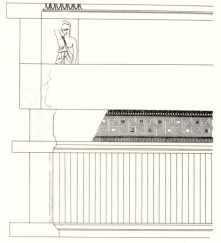

Fig. 57. Altar of Artemis, Ephesus

Fig. 58. View of Altar of Zeus, Pergamon

Fig. 59. Altar of Zeus, Nyx, Giant, Moira

Fig. 60. Sketch map of ancient sites of Lycia

Fig. 61. Silver stater of Perikles of Lycia

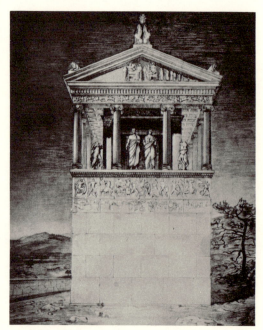

Fig. 62. Nereid monument, Xanthos

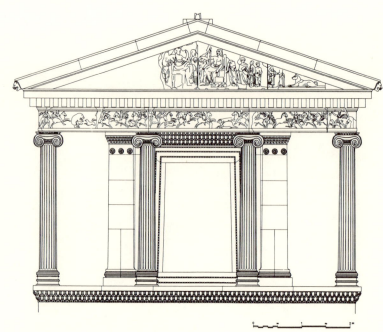

Fig. 63. Nereid monument, Xanthos

Fig. 64. Ruler accepts surrender of a city, Nereid monument

Fig. 65. Assyrian relief, Nineveh, surrender of Lachish to Sennacherib

Fig. 66. Tribute bearers, Nereid monument

Fig. 67. Palace of Darius, Persepolis, servants

Fig. 68. Apadana, eastern stairway, Persepolis, tribute bearers

Fig. 69. Heroon at Limyra

Fig. 70. Caryatid, Limyra

Fig. 71. Frieze of horsemen, Limyra

Fig. 72. Maussoleum of Halicarnassus, Amazon frieze

Fig. 74. Squatting Oriental from Halicarnassus

a

b

Fig. 73 a, b. Statues of Maussolus (a) and Artemisia (b)

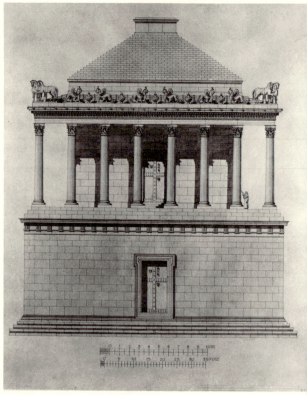

Fig. 75. Maussoleum of Belevi

Fig. 76. Lion-griffins flanking crater, Belevi

Fig. 77. Centauromachy, Belevi

Fig. 78. Centauromachy, Belevi

Fig. 79. Wrestlers and umpire, Belevi

Fig. 80. Ruler reclining on couch, Belevi

Fig. 81. Statue of Oriental servant, Belevi

Fig. 82. Statues in the Agora, Priene

Fig. 84. Great Harbor Monument, Miletus

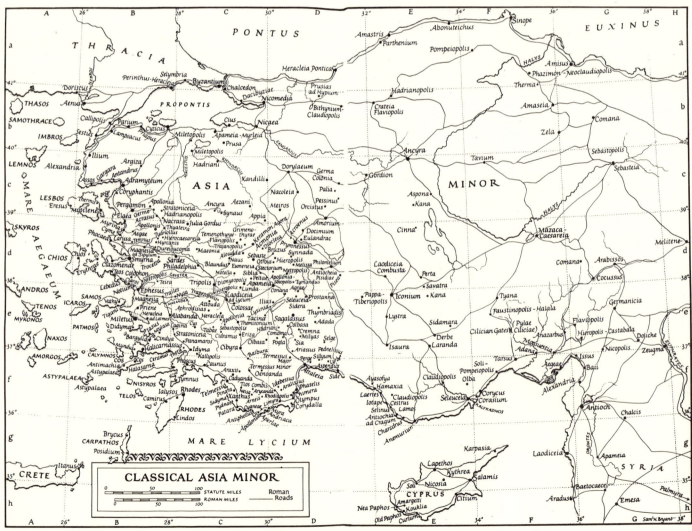

Fig. 83. Map of Roman Asia Minor

Fig. 85. Great Harbor Monument, Triton and dolphins

Fig. 86. Poseidon, Amphitrite, and Marine Thiasus, Munich

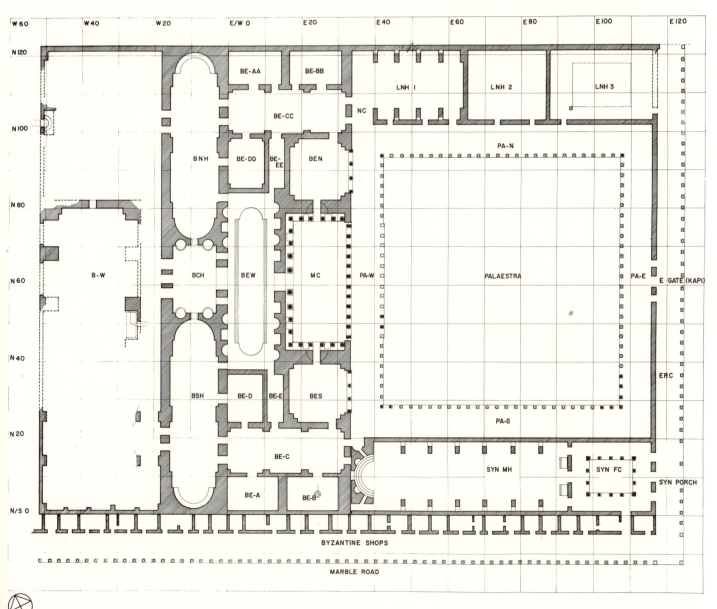

Fig. 87. Plan of Roman gymnasium-bath complex, Sardis

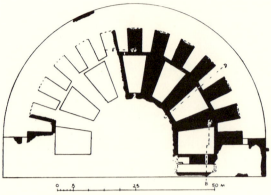

Fig. 88. Theater of Nicaea, plan

Fig. 89. Theater of Nicaea, view of substructures

Fig. 90. Theater of Nicaea, Southeast pier

Fig. 91. Temple of Hadrian at Kyzikos

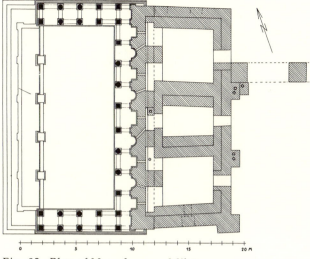

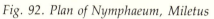

Fig. 92. Plan of Nymphaeum, Miletus

Fig. 93. Reconstruction of Nymphaeum

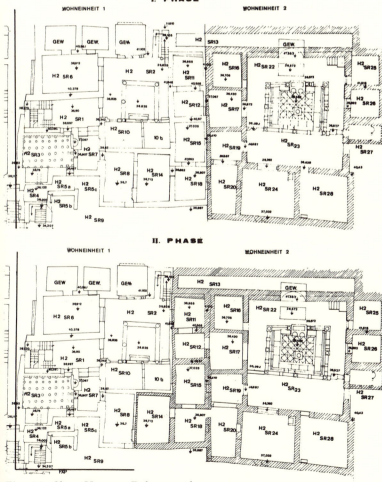

Fig. 94. Slope Houses, Ephesus, plan

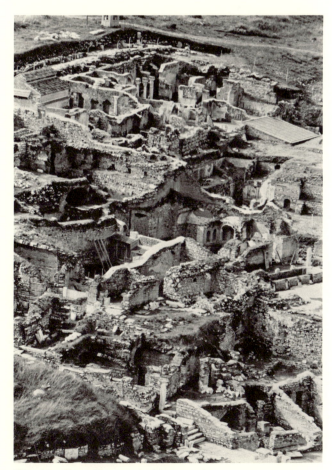

Fig. 95. Slope Houses, looking south

Fig. 96. Slope House, Peristyle

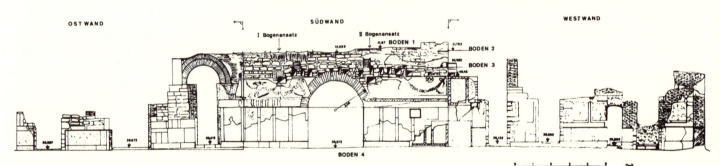

OSTWAND   SÜDWAND   WESTWAND

I Bogenansatz   II Bogenansatz   BODEN 1

BODEN 2

BODEN 3

BODEN 4

Fig. 97. Slope House, Peristyle

Fig. 98. View of Artemis Shrine in situ

Fig. 99. Hellenistic hero relief found in Slope House

Fig. 100. Central unit of gymnasium, Sardis

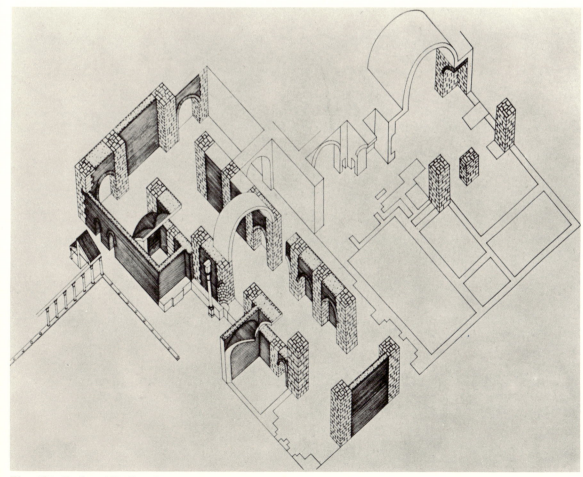

Fig. 101. Baths of Vedius Gymnasium, Ephesus

Fig. 102. *Synagogue main hall with skoutlosis, Sardis*

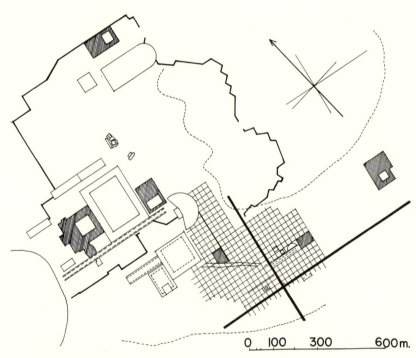

Fig. 103. *Plan showing locations of baths and gymnasia, Ephesus*

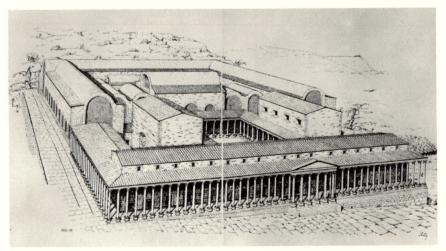

Fig. 104. *Vedius Gymnasium, Ephesus*

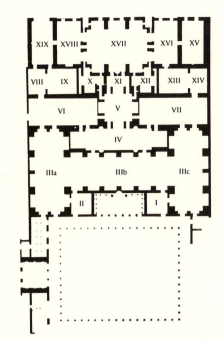

Fig. 105. Vedius Gymnasium, Ephesus, plan

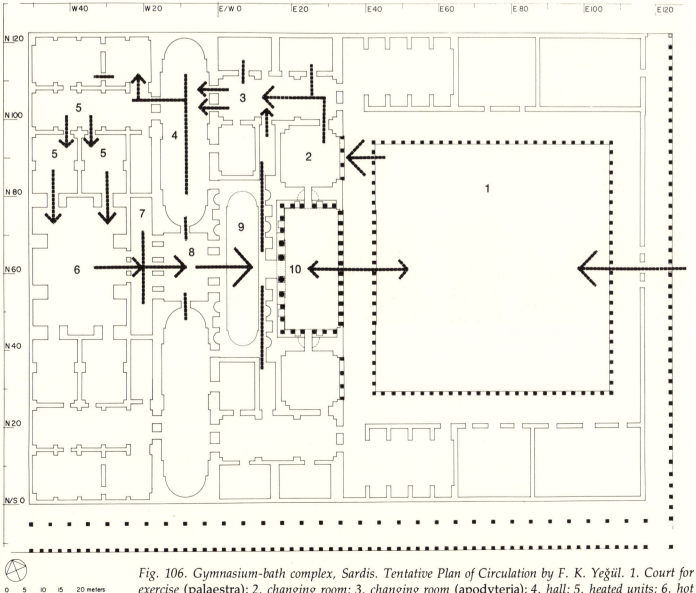

Fig. 106. Gymnasium-bath complex, Sardis. Tentative Plan of Circulation by F. K. Yeğül. 1. Court for exercise (palaestra); 2. changing room; 3. changing room (apodyteria); 4. hall; 5. heated units; 6. hot bath (caldarium); 7. warm bath (tepidarium); 8. central hall; 9. swimming pool (frigidarium, natatio); 10. "Marble Court" (originally Hall of Imperial Cult, then entrance hall).

Fig. 107. Gymnasium, "Marble Court," Sardis

Fig. 108. Gymnasium, head capital from
Marble Court, Sardis

Fig. 109. Gymnasium, north side of
Marble Court, Sardis

Fig. 110. Temple at Aizani, west side

Fig. 111. Model of Sanctuary of Asclepius, Pergamon

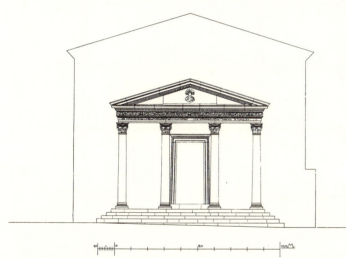

Fig. 112. Temple of Serapis, Miletus

Fig. 113. Temple of Serapis, Miletus, pediment

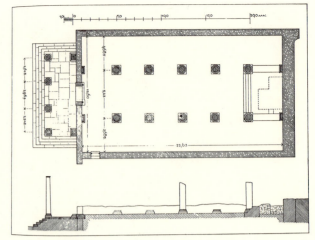

Fig. 115. Plan and section of Temple of Serapis, Miletus

Fig. 114. View of theater, city, and bay, Ephesus

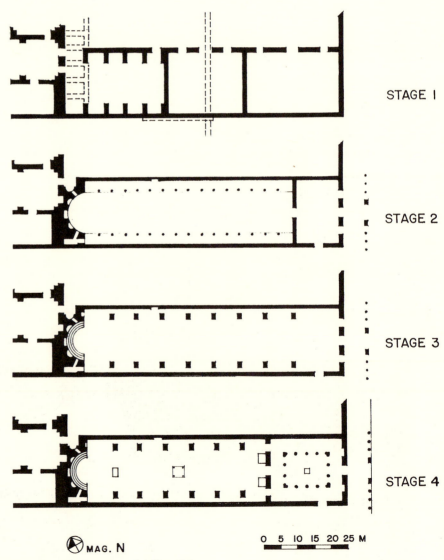

STAGE 1

STAGE 2

STAGE 3

STAGE 4

MAG. N   0 5 10 15 20 25 M

Fig. 116. Synagogue, Sardis, plans

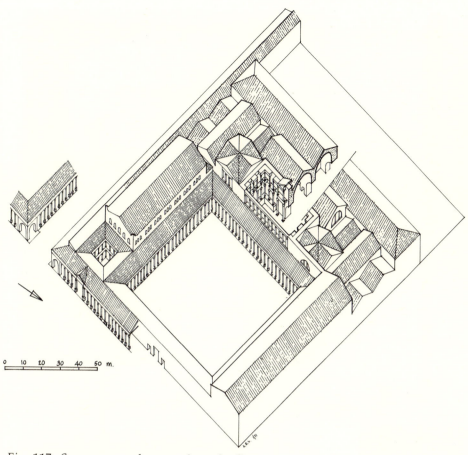

Fig. 117. Synagogue and gymnasium, Sardis

Fig. 120. Door jamb with relief of
Zeus and Kouretes(?), Manisa

Fig. 118. Temple of Hadrian, Ephesus

Fig. 119. Stele of Trophime from Gölde

Fig. 121. Stele of Matis from Sardis

Fig. 122. Stele from Notion

Fig. 123. Horsemen relief, Izmir

Fig. 124. Stele of Marcus Antonius Fronton, Istanbul

Fig. 125. Hero relief, Fitzwilliam Museum

Fig. 126. Relief with funerary meal from Smyrna

Fig. 127. Funerary stele of Theodotos, Istanbul

Fig. 128. Aphrodisias, preliminary drawing of Zoilos frieze

Fig. 129. *Zoilos frieze, Demos and Herm*

Fig. 130. *Zoilos frieze, head of Zoilos with new fragment*

Fig. 131. *Zoilos frieze,* Aion

Fig. 132. *Frieze from Ionic portico, Aphrodisias*

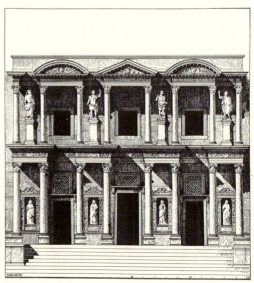

Fig. 133. *Library of Celsus, Ephesus*

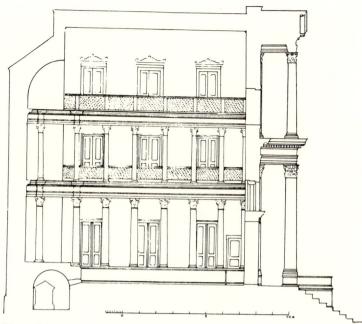

Fig. 134. Library of Celsus, cross section

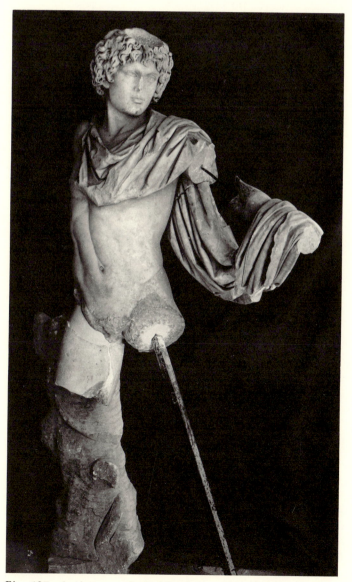

Fig. 135. Antinoos as Androklos from Vedius Gymnasium, Ephesus

Fig. 136. Sappho(?) from Vedius Gymnasium

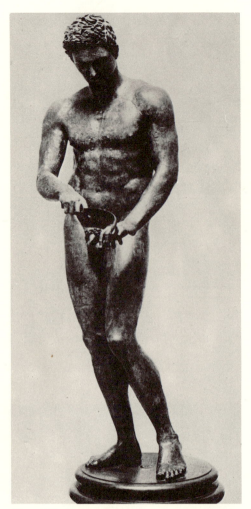

Fig. 137. Bronze athlete
from Harbor Baths, Ephesus

Fig. 138. Rivergod Maeander from Vedius Gymnasium

Fig. 139. Harbor Baths, Hall of Imperial Cult, Ephesus

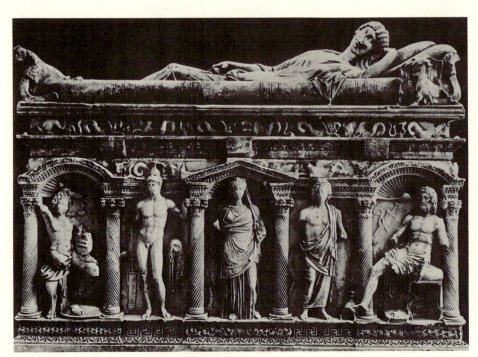

Fig. 140. "Asiatic" sarcophagus, Melfi

Fig. 141. *Sarcophagus, Odysseus and Diomed, Melfi*

Fig. 142. *Sarcophagus, woman and sage, Ankara*

Fig. 143. *Claudia Antonia Sabina and daughter, from Sardis*

Fig. 144. *Claudia Antonia Tatiane and husband, from Ephesus*

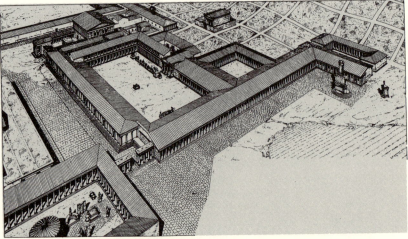

Fig. 145. North Market, Miletus

Fig. 146. Kuretes Street with statue of Alexandros, Ephesus

Fig. 147. Sarcophagus of Marcus Aurelius Diodorus Kallimedes

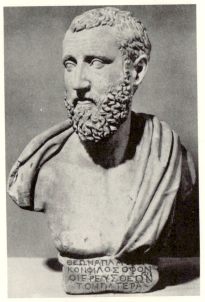

Fig. 148. Theon from Smyrna

Fig. 149. Flavius Damianus from Ephesus

a

b

Fig. 150 a, b. Flavius Damianus

Fig. 151. Bearded man from Sardis

Fig. 152. Aphrodite of Aphrodisias

Fig. 153. Aphrodite from the Zoilos frieze,
Aphrodisias

Fig. 154. Coin of Achaeus

Fig. 155. Fragment of colossal head
of Zeus, Sardis

Fig. 157. Colossal head of Antoninus Pius, Sardis

Fig. 156 a, b. (a) Colossal head of Domitian(?)   (b) Colossal arm of Domitian(?)

Fig. 159. Colossal head of Caracalla, Pergamon

Fig. 158. Colossal head of Faustina from Sardis

Fig. 160. Head of Diocletian from Nicomedia

Fig. 161. Nicaea-Iznik panorama

Fig. 162. Nicaea-Iznik, plan of ancient city

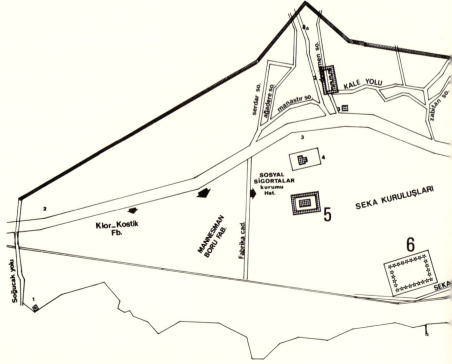

Fig. 165. Nicomedia-Izmit, plan

Fig. 163. Nicomedia-Izmit, view of citadel from the bay

Fig. 164. Nicomedia-Izmit, view from the theater toward eastern part of the bay

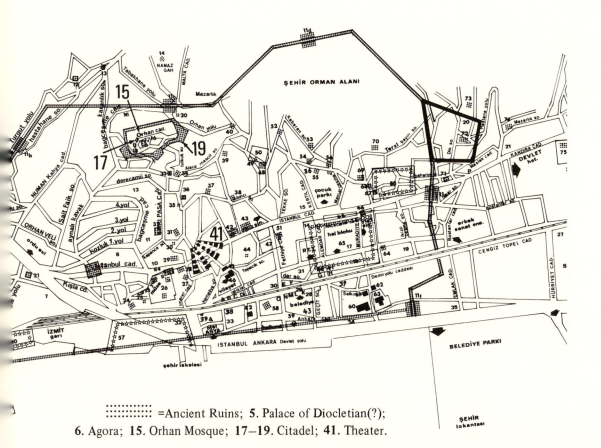

::::::::: =Ancient Ruins; **5.** Palace of Diocletian(?);
6. Agora; **15.** Orhan Mosque; **17–19.** Citadel; **41.** Theater.

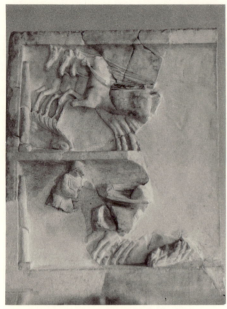

Fig. 166. Circus relief from the Paç region, Izmit

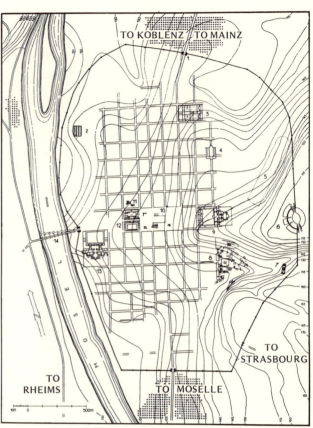

1: Porta Nigra. 2: Horrea. 3: Cathedral. 4: Palace Hall (Basilica). 5: Circus. 6: Amphitheatre. 7: Temple. 8: Temple precinct on the Altbach. 9: Imperial Baths. 10: Forum. 11: Palace of Victorinus. 12: Palace. 13: Barbara Baths.

Fig. 168. Roman Trier, city plan

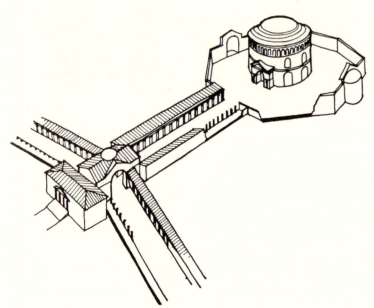

Fig. 167. Maussoleum of Galerius and entrance to palace, Thessalonike

Fig. 169. Trier, restoration of palace hall

Fig. 170. Interior of palace hall

Fig. 171. Trier, aerial view

Fig. 172. Istanbul, aerial view looking across Golden Horn toward Beyoğlu-Galata

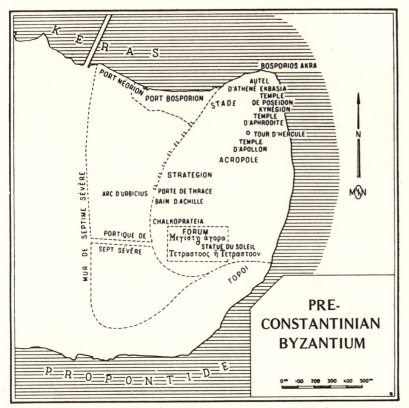

Fig. 173. Plan of pre-Constantinian Byzantium

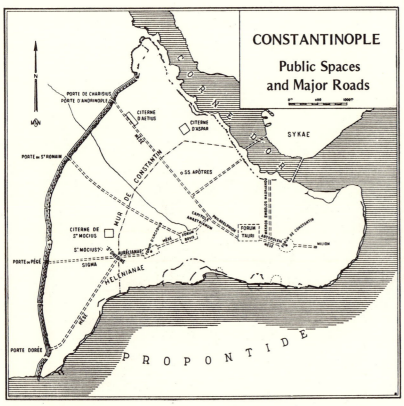

Fig. 174. Constantinople, public spaces and major roads

Fig. 175. Gerasa, oval piazza

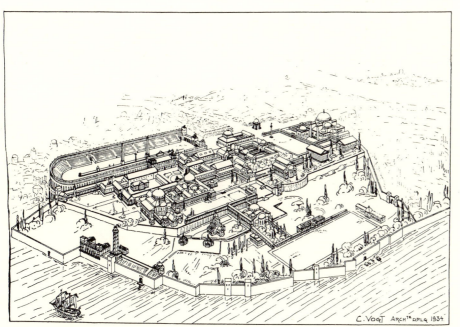

Fig. 176. The Great Palace at Constantinople

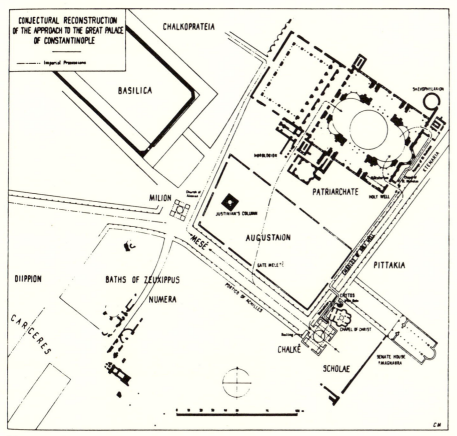

CONJECTURAL RECONSTRUCTION
OF THE APPROACH TO THE GREAT PALACE
OF CONSTANTINOPLE

------- Imperial Processions

CHALKOPRATEIA

BASILICA

SKEVOPHYLAKION

MILION

PATRIARCHATE

HOLY WELL

HOROLOGION

Church of Alexios

JUSTINIAN'S COLUMN

AUGUSTAION

GATE MELETE

MESÉ

PITTAKIA

PORTICO OF THE HOLY WELL

DIIPPION

BATHS OF ZEUXIPPUS

NUMERA

PORTICO OF ACHILLES

CARCERES

CHYTOS

CHAPEL OF CHRIST

CHALKÉ

SENATE HOUSE & MAGNAURA

SCHOLAE

CM

Fig. 177. Great Palace, approach

Fig. 178. The Milion, Constantinople

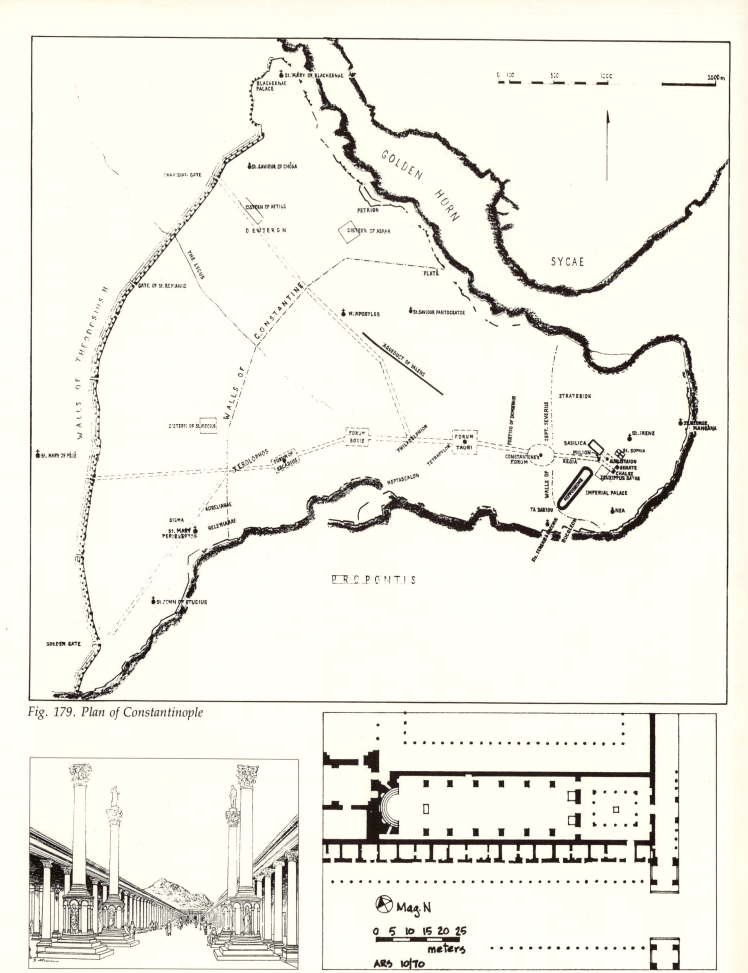

Fig. 179. Plan of Constantinople

Fig. 180. Arkadiane Avenue, Ephesus

Fig. 181. Synagogue and surroundings, Sardis

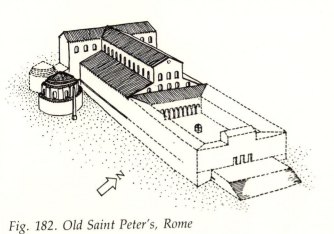

Fig. 182. Old Saint Peter's, Rome

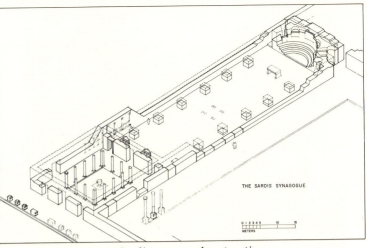

Fig. 183. Synagogue, Sardis, proposed restoration

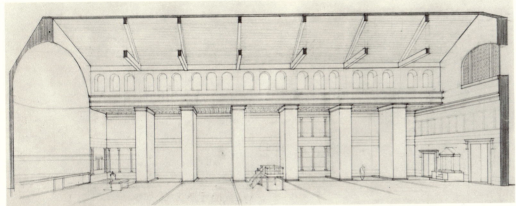

Fig. 184. Synagogue, Sardis, interior of main hall

Fig. 185. Column of
Constantine, Istanbul

Fig. 186. Constantinopolis *from*
Tabula Peutingeriana

Fig. 187. Gold medallion of Constantine

Fig. 188. Gold coin of Constantine

Fig. 189. Gold medallion, Constantine and Sol

Fig. 190. *Horses of San Marco, Venice*

Fig. 191. *Tetrarchs at corner of San Marco, Venice*

Fig. 192. *Frieze from Temple of Hadrian, Ephesus: General sacrificing, Herakles and Amazons*

Fig. 193. *Temple of Hadrian: Dionysus, emperor and gods*

Fig. 194. *Painted ceiling, Trier, woman with veil and crown of pearls*

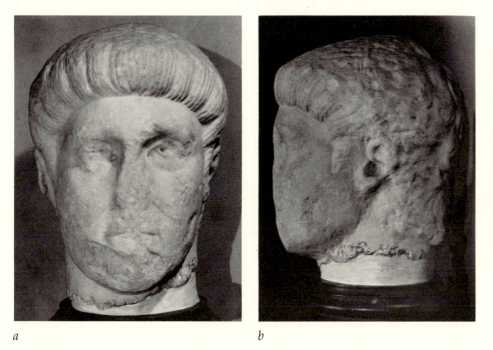

Fig. 196. Head of
Constantius II(?), Izmir

a   b

Fig. 195 a, b. Head of Constantine, front and profile, Istanbul

Fig. 197. Fragment of porphyry sarcophagus of Constantine(?), Istanbul

Fig. 198. Relief from Çapa,
Istanbul

Fig. 199. Jonah relief from Constantinople, Istanbul

Fig. 200. Relief of Flavius Eutyches, Istanbul

Fig. 201. *Relief with seated figure found in church of Aya Sophia, Nicaea*

Fig. 202. *"Prince's Sarcophagus," apostles flanking cross, Istanbul*

Fig. 203. *"Prince's Sarcophagus," angel victories, Istanbul*

Fig. 204. *Kuretes Street, Ephesus*

Fig. 206. *Basilica of Constantine, Rome*

Fig. 205. *Early Byzantine official from Ephesus*

Fig. 207. Head of colossus of Constantine, Conservatori, Rome